Quality of Work Life of Textile Employees-Descriptive Analysis

Dr.R. Kanakarathinam

Published by

Quality of Work Life of Textile Employees-Descriptive Analysis

ISBN 978-93-86638-48-9

Author

Dr.R. Kanakarathinam
Bonfring
309, 2nd Floor, 5th Street Extension, Gandhipuram,
Coimbatore-641 012.
Tamilnadu, India.
E-mail: info@bonfring.org
Website: www.bonfring.org
Phone: 0422 4213231

Chapters	Contents	Page No

CHAPTER 1

Introduction and Design of the Study

1.1.   Introduction

India has a rich and diverse tradition in the field of Textile. It is perhaps the world's oldest Textile tradition. The history of textiles in India dates back to Indus valley civilization and the Vedas. The two ancient Indian epics- Ramayana and Mahabharata also speak of a variety of fabrics of those times. Various sculptures belonging to Mauryan and Gupta age, Buddhist scripts and murals stand evidence to India's magnificent history of textile. Indian textile was reputed all over the world and admired for their excellent quality, beauty, design and texture. Evidently, India was among the forerunners in the textile trade.

Indian textile is embellished, enhanced, decorated and given its character through various modes and techniques, [1]Textile refers to dressing, style, comfort as well as attraction or grooming. Dress serves two purposes: on one hand it is a sign of civilized society and on the other hand it shows the level of aesthetics - science of beauty in art or nature. Dress is a sign of a personality[2].

The Indian Textiles Industry has an overwhelming presence in the economic life of the country. Apart from providing one of the basic necessities of life, the textiles industry also plays a vital role through its contribution to industrial output, employment generation, and the export earnings of the country. The sector contributes about 14 per cent to industrial production, 4 per cent to the gross domestic product (GDP), and 11 per cent to the country's export earnings. It is the second largest provider of employment after agriculture. Thus, the growth and all round development of this industry has a direct bearing on the improvement of the economy of the nation. The Indian textile industry is set for strong growth, buoyed by both strong domestic consumption as well as export demand. Abundant availability of raw materials such as cotton, wool, silk and jute and skilled workforce has made India a major sourcing hub.[3]

In the early 18th century, artisans were inventing ways to become more productive. Silk, wool, fustian, and linen were being eclipsed by cotton, which was becoming the most important textile. The main steps in the production of cloth are producing the fibre, preparing it, converting it to yarn, converting yarn to cloth, and then finishing the cloth. The cloth is then taken to the manufacturer of garments. The preparation of the fibres, it differs the most, depending on the fibre used. Flax requires retting and dressing, while wool requires carding and washing. The spinning and weaving processes are very similar. [4]

1.2.   The Present Global Textile Scenario

According to statistics, the global textile market is currently worth more than $400 billion. In a more liberalized environment, the industry is facing competition as well as opportunities. It was predicted that Global textile production will grow up to 25 % by the year 2010 and 50 % by 2014. The world textile and apparel industry has gone into a phase of transformation since the elimination of quota in the year 2005. Many new competitors as well as consumers have entered the global market with their immense capabilities and the desire to grow[5].

Mills, power-looms, handlooms and garments constitute four independent sectors of the Indian Textiles Industry. The mill sector is organized, mechanized and modernized concentrating in the production of yarn whereas the power-loom and handloom sectors have remained technologically backward and stagnant. Almost all the spun yarn made in India comes from the organized mill sector, reflecting the highly capital intensive nature of yarn spinning. Weaving in the mill sector has been gradually suffering due to the competition from the power-looms and the trend may continue. Most of the India's competitors in textiles in the world market have a much larger number of shuttles-less looms. The hosiery sector caters mainly to the inner garment requirements.[6]

Textile is among the industries identified in the National Manufacturing Policy as a key labour-intensive sector, according to Ajay Shankar, Member Secretary of the National Manufacturing Competitiveness Council (NMCC). This statement by Mr. Shankar was made in his interaction with the textile industry representatives of Tirupur and Coimbatore on 04/04/2012. He told The Hindu that the objective of the interaction was to feel the pulse of the industry. The council has advised the Government on measures needed to make India successful in the manufacturing sector. The NMCC is looking at a partnership process with State Governments, Planning Commission, industries, and the departments concerned to evolve a road map for the growth of the manufacturing sector. The road map is sector-specific and an on-going process that fosters evolution of these sectors.[7]

Tirupur is a textilecity located on the banks of Noyyal River. It is called as small Japan and Dollar city. It is the administrative headquarters of the Tirupur District. It forms a part of the ancient Kongu Nadu region of South India, where its people were the first to establish territorial state. Tirupur is a textile hub and a vast generator of employment for unskilled temporary workers. It is an important trade centre of India. Tirupur has gained universal recognition as the leading source of hosiery, knitted garments, casual wear and sportswear. Tirupur has emerged as the knitwear capital of the country for more than three decades.[8]

1.3.   Features of Tirupur Textile Cluster

The following are the predominant features of Tirupur Textile Cluster:

- Cotton based knitted garments.
- Majority of the units are proprietorship/partnership firm of organization controlled and directed by family management.
- Large number of units is involved in doing cutting, making and trimming knitted fabrics in pieces.
- Limited number of vertically integrated production units and a high degree of subcontracting relationship to knitting, processing and finishing operation[9].

Tirupur leads back to the "Thottams" or well irrigated farms around the town. Though various perception about the farmers lives and work, it has been realized that it was these modest farmers who have innovated in the organization of the industry. There are many ways in which these ex-farmers came to the industry, worked in knitwear firms and got to know the production close at hand and entered as small owners, often in family partnerships. As the industry grew from the old interlock banians to fine banians with an all-India market in the 1970s, the first generation of ex-farmer industrialists created "sister" units, often managed by their relatives, expanding the industries in dispersed units throughout the city. The uniqueness of Tirupur's work culture has made it difficult for the big Indian textile giants to enter and capture a large market share, as the rules and norms governing manufacturing and job working are often informal and personalised[10].

From being the producers of basic garments for lower end of the domestic market, Tirupur cluster has today a diversified production range comprising, T-shirts, polo shirts, sportswear, sweat shirts, ladies dresses, children garment, nightwear, etc. This cluster reflects high degree of specialization in most areas including machinery supply besides every area of the manufacturing operation. Innovative business development services such a pre-production checks, initial checks and production checks, product consultancy, laboratory testing, sourcing assistance are provided by several enthusiastic entrepreneurs who help the industry to improve.[11]

1.4.   Statement of the Problem, Need and Importance of the Study

Tamil Nadu is one of the main states for the development of Textile Industry in India. These units are the back bone of Textile Industry development in Tamil Nadu and they have magnificent impact on the national economy. Tirupur is the largest and fastest growing district in Tamil Nadu. Tirupur provides employment opportunities for millions of people in Tamil

Nadu, Kerala, Orissa, Bihar and North East States. Tirupur cluster comprises of around 5000 units which are involved in one or the other activities of Textile value chain. There are no precise data available as to the exact number of units in the different areas of value chain.

Now-a-days textile industry employees are dissatisfied with the various working conditions of the job. This is evident through many earlier researches on several aspects of human resources in textile industry. Employees of this industry predominantly face two types of problems. They are physical and psychological problems. The physical problems faced by the employees are such as occupational fatigue syndrome and body aches. Psychological problems include work stress and depression. The common causes of these physical and psychological problems are due to daily targets, stringent company rules and regulations, low wages, worst working conditions and fear of job security.

The regular effects of the mentioned causes are fatigue, absenteeism, annoyance, anxiety, reduction in efficiency, changes in pulse rate, blood pressure as well as sleep disorders and low turnover. Occupational fatigue syndrome is due to tiring works leading to exhaustion of energy at the end of the day. Most of the workers in Tirupur are found to work hard and work overtime under hectic schedules with great pressure to meet targets. Body pain is a natural phenomena due to the required body posture and positioning (sitting in a bent position and standing for long hours) during work. These physical sufferings reported are pain in shoulders, arms, and legs. On the other hand, employees invariably suffer from occupational stress due to lot of managerial inconvenience in the working place. Managerial inconveniences are caused due to poor supervision, lack of autonomy, unfair treatment and undue reprimands.

Employees are compelled to work overtime work on weekdays, weekend and public holidays for completion of huge orders in short periods and urgent orders during festive seasons. To cope with such situations firm managements impose strict rules and regulations on arrival time, lunch breaks, and working patterns without any consideration for employees' genuine problems. Fear of job security is another concern and many firms pose a threat of dismissal. Most of the firms have not provided adequate facilities for a conducive work environment during summer where the climate at Tirupur is extremely hot. Poor ventilation and building structures add sour to this.

Generally, in the present era, the textile industry is facing a severe competition all over the world. It is a labour-intensive industry and is largely dependent on skilled, semi-skilled and unskilled workers. But, the industry is presently suffering from scarcity of labourers due to the workers reluctance to take up jobs in firms belonging to textile industry. Labourers from prominent places from where firms use to source them are attracted towards jobs in other industries where the working conditions are lucrative. However, managements of firms have not realized the accurate causes of labour demand. They have also not realized the importance of quality of work life. It is high time for textile industry to take necessary steps to overcome this situation. Managements should know the employees preferences as to working conditions which are not fulfilled by them. The increase in QWL will resolve such human resource problems resulting in increased productivity. Improved QWL leads to improved performance. Performance means not only physical output but also the behavior of the worker in helping his colleague in solving job-related problems, team spirit and accepting temporary unfavorable work conditions without complaint.

So it is time for managements of textile firms to realize and concentrate on factors that influence quality of work life. Attention on QWL factors such as compensation, working conditions, safety, human capabilities and career growth, is essential. QWL also brings balance between work life and personal life improving employee happiness, productivity and longevity in textile industry.

The above issues raised the following questions in the minds of the researcher.

1. How the personal profile of the employees of Textile Industry of Tirupur District support the QWL?
2. To what extent the employees of Textile Industry in Tirupur District are affected by occupational stress?
3. What are the factors that influence the QWL of employees in Textile Industry?
4. What kind of support and facilities are expected by the employees to enhance the QWL in Textile Industry?

These issues have not been addressed adequately in the earlier studies on Tirupur Textile Industry. Hence, the researcher has made an earnest attempt to study the Quality of Work Life prevailing in the Textile Industry of Tirupur.

1.5. Objectives of the Study

The study was undertaken with the following objectives:

- To study the personal and occupational profile of the employees' of Textile Industry in Tirupur district.
- To study the causes of occupational stress among the employees of Textile Industry in Tirupur district.

- To find the impact of personal and occupational profile of employees on the various factors of QWL.
- To study the employees' level of satisfaction with reference to job related aspects in the Textile Industry.
- To provide valuable suggestions to enhance the employees' QWL in the Textile Industry.

1.6. Hypotheses of the Study

The following hypotheses were formulated and have been tested in the study.

- Ho: There is no relationship between unit size and occupational stress.
- Ho: There is no relationship between type of job activity and occupational stress.
- Ho: There is no relationship between work experience and occupational stress.
- Ho: There is no relationship between income (wage) and occupational stress.
- Ho: There is no relationship between work schedule and occupational stress.
- Ho: There is no significant association between employees' opinion towards employer-employee relationship and their personal / occupational profile.
- Ho: There is no significant association between employees' opinion towards incentives and their personal / occupational profile.
- Ho: There is no significant association between employees' opinion towards development and encouragement and their personal / occupational profile.
- Ho: There is no significant association between employees' opinion towards grievance redressal and their personal / occupational profile.
- Ho: There is no significant association between employees' opinion towards stress management and their personal / occupational profile.
- Ho: There is no significant association between employees' opinion towards wage structure and their personal / occupational profile.
- Ho: There is no significant association between employees' opinion towards training and their personal / occupational profile.
- Ho: There is no significant association between employees' opinion towards working conditions and their personal / occupational profile.
- Ho: There is no significant association between employees' opinion towards work life balance and their personal / occupational profile.
- Ho: There is no significant association between employees' opinion towards job satisfaction and their personal / occupational profile.

- Ho: There is no significant association between employees' opinion towards autonomy and their personal / occupational profile.
- Ho: There is no significant association between employee job satisfaction and their personal / occupational profile.

1.7.   Scope of the Study

The present research seeks to analyse the human resource problems related with Quality of Work Life of Textile Industry employees in Tirupur District. This study attempts to provide an insight into the issue of the Quality of Work Life of the Textile Industry employees. QWLis the opportunity for employees at all levels to have substantial influence over their work environments by participating in the decision-making process relating to their work and thereby, enhancing their self-esteem and overall satisfaction from their work. Hence QWL calls for an open style of management, i.e., sharing of information and genuinely encouraging the efforts relating to the improvement of the organization. This, therefore, amply makes it clear that QWL in fact is an important HRD activity and proper HRD intervention can enrich the QWL for employees of an organization"[12]. The Textile Industry in Tirupur would be in a position to take adequate steps to improve the QWL of employees. This study describes the factors determining the Quality of Work Life in the firms located in Tirupur district and this may hold good for all the firms in Textile Manufacturing Industry operating with a similar culture.

1.8.   Research Methodology

The present study is descriptive in nature. The study describes the socio-economic status of the employees in Textile Industry and their Quality of Work Life along the factors contributing to it. The blueprint of data collection, measurement of respondents' opinion and analysis of data are given below.

1.8.1. Source of Data

The study has employed both primary and secondary data. The primary objective of the present piece of research is to examine the Quality of Work Life in Textile Industry. Required primary data were collected from the Textile employees of Tirupur district.

- *Primary Data*

The primary data were collected by using a well structured interview schedule. Data were collected by directly meeting the respondents individually and asking questions which were in the researcher's interview schedule. Doubts were cleared and checked over the answers as most of the respondents had only school level education. They were not able to respond to the questions appropriately. This measure of checking the answers was taken as a result of the pilot study. The pilot study was conducted to identify and check the reliability of the data and evaluate the questions after preparation.

- ***Secondary Data***

Secondary data were collected through already available sources such as publications in international and national journals, newspapers, magazines, books, university libraries, reports, publications of associations like AEPC and TEA, earlier literatures, dissertations and websites.

1.8.2. Sample Design

The sampling unit of the research comprises the employees of textile industry in Tirupur District. The respondents were selected using the non- probability sampling technique, "convenient sampling". 524 employees were conveniently approached with the interview schedule to collect data. 500 filled in interview schedule were found to be complete and fit for further analysis. Hence, the sample size of the study is 500.

1.8.3. Period of Study

The current study was done in Tirupur District, because more than 50 per cent of India's garment exports and local sale are contributed by Tirupur, a town that provides popular brands to world market and local market. Data have been extensively collected through primary source. The major primary source constitutes the textile industry employees. These data were collected during the year 2011 and 2012 and the study was carried for a period of 4 years from 2010 to 2014.

1.8.4. Tools for Analysis

The data collected were organized and classified by coding and transferring the data into a Master table. The data thus collected were analyzed with suitable statistical tools like simple percentage analysis, mean, standard deviation, ANOVA, F-test, t-test, factor analysis, multiple discriminant function, correlation, Chi-square test and multiple regression analysis.

- ***Chi- Square Test***

Chi-square test is used to assess two types of comparison. They are, test of goodness of fit and test of independence. A test of goodness of fit establishes whether or not an observed frequency distribution differs from a theoretical distribution. A test of independence assesses whether paid observation on two variable are independent of each other. The chi-square test is used to test the association of two attributes. It is often applied to judge the significant difference between the observed and expected values. In other words, the test is used to test the significance of one factor over the other. This test is used to find the relationship between the occupational profiles and the stress of textile employees in Tirupur District. The null hypothesis was framed for this purpose assuming that these two variables are unrelated.

- *T-test and ANOVA (F-test)*

T-test is used on 't' distribution and is considered an appropriate test for judging the significance of a sample mean or for judging the significance of difference between the means of two samples. ANOVA technique is applied when three or more number of groups is to be compared on the basis of their mean. It is an extension of 'F-test' is used to test the homogeneity of several means. Using these tests, an attempt to examine the association between the personal and occupational related variables and QWL of employees is made. Further, the association between personal and occupational related variables and employees level of satisfaction is also tested through these tools. T-test and F-test have been applied to find such association by formulating null hypothesis.

- *Factor Analysis*

Factor analysis is usually used in any study on social sciences and management. In this study, the factor analysis is employed using extraction method. The principle component analysis under variance with KMO method is applied for identifying and grouping the different factors of Quality of Work Life.

- *Multiple Discriminant Function Analysis*

The Multiple discriminant function was used to find whether any significant difference exist among the employees of three types of units, Small, Medium and Large in deciding their opinion on Quality of Work Life.

- *Correlation analysis*

Correlation is a statistical measurement of the relationship between two variables. Possible correlations range from +1 to –1. A correlation of –1 indicates a perfect negative correlation, meaning that as one variable goes up, the other goes down. A correlation of +1 indicates a perfect positive correlation, meaning that both the variables move in the same direction together. Correlation is used to study the relationship between different factors of quality of work life and employees level of satisfaction.

- ***Multiple Regression Analysis***

The regression analysis is used to find the statistical relationship between two or more variables. When there are two or more independent variables, the analysis that describes the relationship is multiple regression analysis. This analysis is adopted when there is one dependent variable that is presumed to be a function of two or more independent variables. The effect of various personal and work related variables on overall quality of work life is studied using multiple regression analysis. Overall QWL score was considered as the dependent variable. The personal and occupational variables were considered as independent variables.

1.9. Limitations of the Study

- The outcome of study is confined to the QWL of employees of textile industry firms in Tirupur, Tamil Nadu. It is certain that firms in the study region operate with a similar culture. Hence, generalization of the results may or may not be applicable to firms operating in different cultures and different industries.
- The employees were reluctant to express some of their feeling and this may have response bias.
- The determinant factors of Quality of Work Life used in this study may or may not be applicable to other factories or other states.
- Textile industry was in a recession during this period. The industry was also suffering from problem of improper treatment of effluents (dyeing) and scarcity of electricity during this period. Hence, the outcome of the study carried during this period may considerably vary with times of prosperity.

1.10. Chapter Scheme

Chapter I: This chapter deals with introduction and design of the study. Introduction to the study, the present global textile scenario, features, QWL problems, objectives, hypotheses, methodology, sampling technique used, statistical tools used and the limitations of the study are briefly presented.

Chapter II: This focuses on the brief review of national and international literatures related to Quality of Work Life of employees in different industries.

Chapter III: An overview of QWL, measuring Quality of Work Life, principles of humanization of work, factors influencing the Quality of Work Life, Quality of Work Life and productivity, Quality of Work Life programmes, Textiles committee and profile of Tirupur Textile Industry is given in this chapter.

Chapter IV: An analysis of the primary data and appropriate interpretations of data using various statistical tools to arrive at meaningful findings have been summarised in this chapter. This chapter consists of five sections based on the need of the research on textile industry and they are classified as section I, II, III, IV and V.

Section I: It presents the analysis of data relating to personal and occupational profile of textile employees.

Section II: This section consists of three parts. Part A: It presents the analysis of data relating to occupational stress of employees of textile industry. Part B: It presents the analysis of data relating to stress in association with occupational differences and Part C: It presents the analysis of data relating to factors contributing to stress management.

Section III: This section consists of two parts. Part A: It presents the analysis of data relating to   factors determining Quality of Work Life and Part B: It presents the analysis of data relating to Quality of Work Life in association with personal and occupational differences.

Section IV: It presents the analysis of data relating to job satisfaction in association with personal and occupational difference.

Section V: It presents the analysis of data relating to QWL factors discriminating employees of large, medium and small units.

Chapter V: This chapter recapitulates the key findings and conclusion of the study. Based on these findings, a   few suggestions are given to improve the employees' Quality of Work Life in the Textile Industry.

References

[1] F.M. Khri, "Indian Textile-ethnic and beyond, Super book house", Mumbai-5, Pp. 1-3, 2009.

[2] M. Rastogi, "Textile Forming, Sonoli publications", New Delhi-2, Page No: 2 preface page: 1-2, 2009.

[3] http://www.ibef.org

[4] http://encyclopedia.thefreedictionary.com

[5] http://www.teonline.com

[6] http://www.scribd.com

[7] The Hindu, "Textiles a key manufacturing sector", 04/04/2012,

[8] http://tiruppurinfo.blogspot.in

[9] www.dynamiccity-doc-casestudytirupur-rangarajan.pdf

[10] http://tiruppurinfo.blogspot.in

[11] http://en.wikipedia.org

[12] D. Kumar Bhatacharyya, "Human Resource Management", 2th Edition, Excel Books, New Delhi, Pp. 412-413, 2009.

CHAPTER 2

Review of Literature

This literature review is a body of text that aims to highlight the critical points of current knowledge and methodological approaches on QWL. It has brought the researcher up to date with available literature on QWL and forms the basis for research needed in the area of study. This structured literature review is characterized by a logical flow of ideas, current and relevant references with consistent, appropriate referencing style, proper use of terminology and comprehensive view of the previous research on QWL. This section provides a sketch of related studies arranged logically at international and national levels. The present review of literature has been confined to employee quality of work life in the various industries of different countries and India.

Lupton.T (1975) [1] in his study, "Efficiency and Quality of Work Life: Technology of reconciliation", made an attempt to increase business efficiency and the Quality of Working Life by designing a new manufacturing system. Six alternative production systems were proposed and then job characteristics were measured according to their variety, autonomy, responsibility, interaction and completion of task. The system finally selected and tried was fairly successful to balance automation with worker autonomy. The system's goals included high volume output at low cost, safe and healthy working conditions, job enlargement and enrichment, and greater mechanization. Further, it disclosed that jobs with a low quality of work life were nevertheless necessary.

Dwivedi. R.S (1977)[2] carried out a case study on "Quality of Work Life in Volvo automobile plant located at Sweden". It was visualized by the head of the Volvo that severe turnover and absenteeism problems were symptoms of the employees' values. There were demands by the employees for meaningful work, embracing better pay and securing as well as participation in the decision making process and self-regulation. Autonomous work groups with five to twelve workers were made and asked to select a supervisor. These groups were made responsible to schedule, assign and inspect their own work. 25 groups were established to perform different modules in the manufacture of an automobile. These groups had complete control over their work, including inspection. In addition, a human work climate was evolved. This led to substantial improvements in quality of work life and reduced the turnover and absenteeism. Till date, Volvo continues to innovate in its application of Quality of Work Life activities, discussions on inter-personal relationships, group working and problem solving.

Manga M.L. and Maggu A.(1981)[3] in their study on " Quality of Work Life : A study of public sector in India", the influence of Quality of Work Life on the health of the public sector organizations as such on the members of such organizations were discussed. They have concluded that Quality of Work Life in the public sector is poor and there exists a significant gap between what managers expect and what they have. They also point out the nature of obstructions of Quality of Work Life efforts like too much bureaucratization, rule-orientation and adherence to traditional management styles.

Sayeed O.B. and Sinha (1981)[4] in their study on "Measuring Quality of Work Life relation to job satisfaction and performance in two organizations", examined the relationship between Quality of Work Life, job stress and performance. The results indicate that higher of work life leads to greater job satisfaction.

Singh .P (1983)[5] in his study on "Motivational profile and quality of corporate work life: A case of mismatch", reports on Quality of Work Life experiments in India. The study was conducted on chemical and textile factories to improve the Quality of Work Life by reorganizing the work and introducing participatory management. He also studied managers from the public sector. He found that Quality of Work Life is perceived to be the poorest in the area of demonstration of work culture leading to a stage of mismatch between motivation and the existing Quality of Work Life.

Sangeetha Jain (1986)[6] carried out a study entitled , "Quality of Work Life" with twin objectives i.e., 1) to study the hierarchical effect in viewing Quality of Work Life and 2) to study the effect of Quality of Work Life on group behavior in a large scale private sector in India. The private sector consisted of eight departments with a total number of 644 workers out of which 105 employees were selected 15 percent population from each stratum but not less than 10 employees from each department. The employees groups comprised of the executives, supervisors, skilled workers, semi-skilled workers and unskilled workers according to their position level. The data for this study were collected through a questionnaire, which was developed based on basis factors of Richard Walton(1975), to ascertain the index of internal consistency, bi-serial correlation and inter correlation were adopted and 52 items of questions were selected with 35 as true and 17 were as false keyed. The findings of the study revealed that the higher the status in the organization, the higher the Quality of Work Life factors score and vice versa. It indicated that the individual who enjoyed greater benefits in terms of pay, fringe benefits and promotional opportunities considered the Quality of Work Life as favorable.

Gopi.M.A (1987)[7] in his study explored certain problems faced by Hosiery Industry such as inefficiency due to non-composite units, out dated bleaching and dyeing equipments, non-availability of training facilities to employees, insufficient market information, out molded and insufficient facilities, lack of product research centre, high restrictions for import knitting machines, shortage of Hosiery yarn, labor problems and insufficient working condition.

Keller.R.T (1987)[8] in his study entitled," Cross cultural influence on work and non work contributors to Quality of Life' attempted to investigate the relative contributors of Quality of Work Life-127 Whites, 30 Hispanic, 33 Black Americans and 121 Mexican nationals were randomly selected as sample for this study. The data were collected through a structured questionnaire administered to the samples. Multiple regression analysis and hierarchical regression analysis were used to find out the association between ethical group membership and Quality of Work Life. The findings of the study revealed that there is no significant relationship between ethical group membership and Quality of Work Life. Further it denoted that home life and family network variables accounted for more unique variance in Quality of Work Life than did the work variables of job satisfaction, job stress and job level, self esteem explained the unique variance in Quality of Work Life across the sample.

Gupta.P and Khandelwak.P (1989)[9] conducted a study to find out "Quality of Work Life in relation to role efficacy" with 170 professionals working in Government public sector organizations in India. Data for this study was collected by close ended questionnaire. The findings revealed that there is a significant positive relationship between QWL and the role of efficacy. Apart from that, they also found that supervisory behavior is the most important dimension of QWL, contributing 21 percent of variance in the employee's role efficacy.

Cauvery.R and Sudha Nayak.U.K (1990)[10] made an attempt to measure the Quality of Work Life with reference to female domestic servants in Salem of Tamil Nadu, India, under the title, "Quality of Work Life and gender poverty nexus: A case study of housemaids". The samples of the study comprised of 300 female respondents engaged in domestic servants have entered the job in domestic service below the age of 15. They found that overall shortage of opportunities and lack of bargaining power made them work in this low paid job at an early age. This poverty of domestic servants is strikingly shown by the high percent of young women in the informal sector. Further, this study revealed that lengthy work day, low income and poor working conditions are the main factors for low quality of work life.

Dov Elizur (1990)[11] in his study on "Quality circles and Quality of Work Life", attempts to analyze the relationships between employees' participation in Quality circles, their sense of

Quality of Work Life, perceived job reinforcement capacity and job satisfaction. One hundred and forty-three employees of a large industrial corporation in Israel, half of them regularly participating in quality circles and half not participating, were surveyed. A positive relationship was found between participation in quality circles and various aspects of Quality of Work Life, perceived job reinforcement capacity and job satisfaction. Results are discussed in the context of the arguments concerning the effects of participation in quality circles

Anne Wilcock and Marina Wright (1991)[12] in the study entitled, "Quality of Work Life in knitwear sector of the Canadian Textile Industry" made an attempt to find out the existence of activities of Quality of Work Life in a sample of knitwear companies in South Western Ontario, Canada. Three levels of activities were identified (1) Active companies were largely non-unionized with high annual sales, high levels of technology and an articulated corporate responsibility towards employees, (2) Midrange companies were privately owned, unionized with a medium level of technology and (3) Inactive companies were young privately owned companies with low technology levels and were attempting to establish corporate stability. The sample of the study consists of 275 employees, selected randomly from those who represented various occupational groups. The qualitative data were collected by interviews from the sample employer on the basis of components hypothesized by Walton as being comprehensive of Quality of Work Life concept. One way Analysis of Variance was performed to test the hypotheses. The results of the study revealed that employees of midrange companies were more satisfied with 'working condition', 'social integration', 'constitutionalism' and 'work and life components' than the employees of the active companies.

Adrienne E.Eaton, Michalel E.Gordon and Jeffrey H. Keefe (1992)[13] conducted a study entitled "The impact of Quality of Work Life programs and grievance system effectiveness on Union commitment", based on an analysis of data from a 1987 survey of four different bargaining units within the same local union to assess union members' views who participated in Quality of Work Life programs and non-union members' view of the Quality of Work Life. Participants were members of a private sector, industrial union that had represented both technicians and clerical workers employed by four companies. A sample of 400 employees was randomly selected for this study. The findings of the study revealed that union members who participated in Quality of Work Life programs were less likely than non-participants to view Quality of Work Life as a threat to the union and also more loyal to the union. Further, it found that the perceived effectiveness of the grievance procedure was a much stronger determinant of attitudes towards union than the participation in Quality of Work Life programmes.

Benjamin Christopher.S and Maruthupandian.P (1992)[14] conducted a study of Quality of Work Life with special reference to mill workers in Pollachi Taluk. A sample of 91 mill workers was selected for this study under random sampling method. Data were collected through a questionnaire broadly covering details about six factors :(i) General particulars of the work (ii) working conditions (iii) developmental facilities (iv) participation in management (v) industrial relations and (vi) family life. Based on mean value, the respondents have been divided into three groups low, median and high, to ascertain the level as well as variation in Quality of work life. Chi-square test has also been employed to test, significance of influence of selected factors of Quality of work life. The findings of the study disclosed that middle age and old age group, the family income and years of experience also influence the level of Quality of Work Life. Married workers have high Quality of Work Life than unmarried employees. In addition to that, higher the number of dependents, lesser is the level of Quality of work life. Day shift employees were found to have higher Quality of work life than night shift workers. Working conditions, developmental facilities, participation in management, industrial relations, over time, promotional policy and family life were also found to be significant predictors of Quality of Work Life.

Haque ABMZ (1992) [15] in his study on "Quality of Work Life and job satisfaction of industrial workers in relation to size of the organization" found that Quality of Work Life is positively related to performance and negatively correlated to absenteeism. But found number of relationship between perceived Quality of Work Life and workers age, education and job experience.

Deepak Kumar Battacharya (1993)[16] has conducted a study on "Promotion from within: A positive reinforce for enriching Quality of Work Life for white collar employee", with an aim to identity whether technological advancement, structural changes in the economy and change in the occupational pattern influence the perceptual QWL for Indian workers in general and working company employee in particular working in public sector banks in the city of Calcutta. 390 sample employees have been interviewed in person with the help of structured questionnaire. ANOVA, the Kenderall coefficient of concordance and Chi-square were used to analyze the data. The major findings of the study disclosed that perceived QWL of bank employees remain unchanged even after computerization. High degree of dependence of the sample employees on union tribunals and other legal machinery for redressal of their grievances, monotonous and repetitive jobs, and inter-alia also badly reflect the QWL on the bank employees.

Dhulasi, Brindha, Varadarajan and Ramasubramanian.A (1993) [17] in the study on "A Quality of Work Life in a Cement Industry" , have focused on occupational disease in the cement industry workers and the various safety measures undertaken by the management to control the cement dust pollution in that Industry. For this study, under stratified random sampling method 100 employees were selected as sample respondent from 11 different groups according to the nature of work. It was found that 80 percent of the sample respondents are suffering from occupational disease. The main occupational diseases include tuber culosis (TB), breathing problems and cough. Lack of enforcement of safety measures is the main reason for low level of Quality of Work Life.

Gani.A (1993) [18]carried out a study entitled "Quality of Work Life in a State setting: Findings of an empirical study" to examine the problems related to QWL faced by the employees in Cement and Textile manufacturing industries situated at Jammu and Kashmir States in India. The sample of the study comprised 250 respondents selected through stratified random sampling method. Data required for this study were collected through personal interviews. Average, Chi-square test, and t-test were used to analyze the data. The findings of the study revealed that the current state of QWL in this organization is far from satisfactory level. Wage discontent, deplorable working and living conditions, job insecurity and poor industrial relation climate are the main reasons for low Quality of Work Life.

Namita P. Kumar (1993) [19] carried out a study entitled "Quality of Work Life and gender issues: A study of female secretarial workers in Lucknow city" to measure an important aspect of autonomy in Quality of Work Life in the sense of physical and social environment at the place of work of female employees. The study is based upon a sample survey of 133 female secretarial employees. In total 30 establishments were surveyed and 5 females per establishment were interviewed from three categories of Central Government, State Government and Private Sector. The findings of the study revealed that most of the respondents of private sector face greater amount of harassment due to their gender. Further it revealed that 8 per cent of the respondents felt that they have two works harder to succeed in their career than their counter parts.

Chakraborthy.S.K (1994) [20] compared the Walton's list of eight major conceptual categories in terms of human needs and aspirations for the improvement of working life like fair compensation, safety and healthy working conditions - theory of work mentioned in Bhagavat Geetha an old well known epic of India. He concludes that Indian approach towards the quality of work life and work ethic is founded on the premise that man has a spiritual Meta physical dimension too to his personality, a dimension inherently superior to that of his economic, biological and social dimensions.

Gani.A and Ahmad Royaz (1995) [21]conducted a study on "Correlates of Quality of Work Life: An analytical study", to throw some light on the components and correlates of QWL derivating their basis from theoretical expositions and empirical study. The sample of the study is covered on 150 workers and 50 managerial personnel of Hindustan Machine Tools (HML) in Kashmir State. The study components were categorized into four factors: (i) working environmental factor (ii) relational factor (iii) job factor and (iv) financial factor. The study unfolds a grim story of the economy and living condition of workers. The results drew attention to the fact that adequate financial returns from the job, besides desire for job securing better working conditions and advancement opportunities continue to be the major concerns for better Quality of Work Life.

Karrir .N and Khurana .A. (1996)[22] in their study on "Quality of Work Life managers in Indian Industry", examined the Quality of Work Life of 491 managers from three sectors of Industry. Results have revealed significant correlations of Quality of Work Life of managers with some of the background variables such as educational qualifications, native / migrant status and income level.

Wadud .N (1996)[23] in his study on " Job stress and Quality of Work Life among working women", found that Quality of Work Life was significantly higher among the private sector women employees than their counter parts in the public sector. It also showed that younger group and higher experienced groups had significantly higher perception of Quality of Work Life than the older and low experienced groups.

Yousuf.S.M.A (1996)[24] mentioned that QWL is a generic phrase that covers a person's feeling about every dimension of work including economic rewards, benefits, security working conditions, organizational and interpersonal relations. In his view, it can be said that QWL denotes all organizational inputs which aim at improving the employees' satisfaction and enhancing organizational effectiveness.

Louis and Karen Seashore (1998)[25] in their study on "Effects of teachers' Quality of Work Life in secondary schools on commitment and sense of efficacy" explores how teachers' quality of working life contributes to their commitment to work and sense of efficacy in eight schools. It ties workplace characteristics to important behaviors, attitudes, and psychological characteristics that affect teaching. Classroom observation and survey data suggest that

Quality of Work Life measures are strongly associated with teacher commitment and sense of efficacy.

Ekramul Hoque.M and Alinoor Rahman (1999)[26]conducted a study on "Quality of Working Life and job behavior of workers in Bangladesh: A comparative study of private and public sector" to ascertain whether there is any significant relationship among Quality of Work Life, job behavior i.e. performance, absence and accident and demographic variables namely age, education, experience and income of the workers. Samples for this study consisted of 100 male workers, of whom 50 were taken from a Private sector Textile mill and the rest from Public sector Textile mill. It was selected randomly using systematic random sampling method. The 't' test, Pearson's product moment correlation and descriptive statistical tools were applied to analyze the data. The results of the study revealed that (i) workers of private sector Textile mills perceived significantly higher Quality of Work Life than their counterparts in the public sector, (ii) Quality of Work Life has significant positive correlation with performance and (iii) Quality of Work Life has significant negative correlation with demographic profile of workers. It was suggested that managements of both private and public sector organizations should take necessary measures to improve the Quality of Working Life of the workers, enhance performance, reduce accident and absenteeism among the workers.

Hossain M.D. Mosharraf and Tariqual Islam M.D (1999)[27] in their study on "Quality of Work Life and job satisfaction of nurses in Government hospitals in Bangladesh", investigated the correlation between Quality of Work Life and job satisfaction, Quality of Work Life and job satisfaction and performance. A total number of 63 nurses were selected from three Governments hospitals on a stratified random sampling method. The findings reveal that there was significant positive correlation between Quality of Work Life and job satisfaction. The Quality of Work Life is the highest contributions to performance. Perceptions of Quality of Work Life and job satisfaction were significantly higher among the respondents in small organizations than in larger ones. Night nurses suffer from more security problems than the nurses in other shifts.

May.B.E, Lau .R.S and Johnson S.K (1999)[28] examined 156 American enterprises during five years and found that quite contrary of the layman's opinion, companies that a high Quality of Work Life achieved better profitability and growth than those did not. In their longitudinal study they also found that high QWL companies tend to attract highly talented employees and become competitive. They concluded that financial under pinning of employee satisfaction, innovation, productivity, product quality, customer service and customer satisfaction are measured and improved.

Venkatachalam.J and Velayudham .A (1999)[29] in their study on "Impact of advanced technology of the Quality of Work Life", analyzed whether Advanced Technology has an impact on the Quality of Work Life of employees. 227 executives and 173 non-executives have been selected as sample under stratified random sampling method from Steal Plant Manufacturing Company Hyderabad in India. The data were analyzed with the help of an alpha value which shows higher reliability, inter correlations between the dimensions were also found to be minimal. The finding of the study revealed that the new technology in the steel plant has no significant impact on the employee's perception on their Quality of Work Life values. Meanwhile, work complexity is significantly influenced by the new technology.

Nallasivam (2000)[30] in his study points out the areas where there are problems and shortfalls in Hosiery Industry and he identified those areas of problems are planning, production defects, labor problems, financial problems, export procedures, administrative problems, political and natural calamities.

Richard Winter, Tony Tayor and James Sarros (2000)[31] carried out a study entitled, "Trouble at mill: Quality of Academic Work Life", and analyzed the issues within a comprehensive Australian University with a view to describe Quality of Academic Work Life. Academics responded to the academic work environment survey, a diagnostic instrument designed to assess the relationships between and among academics, demographic characteristics of age, gender, position, discipline, work environment perceptions of role, work attitudes, self-estrangement and organization commitment. Findings of this study revealed the positive Quality of Academic Work Life features and low levels of self-estrangement (alienation). Negative Quality of Academic Work Life features included role overloaded, low levels of job feedback and limited opportunities to influence university decision making.

Bram Steijn. B. (2001)[32], in his study on "Work systems, Quality of Working Life and attitudes of workers: An empirical study towards the effects of team and non-teamwork", has distinguished four different work systems: the traditional Tayloristic system, 'lean' teamwork, 'socio-technical' teamwork, and the professional work system. Using a survey design the association with several employee outcome variables is analyzed. The results show that:1) work system is an important factor for explaining differences in the quality of working life and attitudes of workers; 2) the Tayloristic work system clearly has detrimental effects on the well-being of workers. 3) in a survey design, comparing just team workers and non-team workers is not enough due to the heterogeneity of both categories.

David Efraty, Sirgy, Philip Siegel.M and Dong Jin lee (2001)[33], in their study on "A new measure of Quality of Work Life based on need satisfaction and spill over theories", found that Quality of Work Life conceptualized the need satisfaction stemming from an interaction of workers needs of survival, social needs, ego needs, self-actualization needs and those organization resources relevant for meeting them. It was hypothesized that need satisfaction is positively related to organization identification, job effort and job performance and negative related to personal alienation. It was found that the results were consistent with the hypothesis and managerial implications were also discussed.

Eric. A Good Man, Raymond F. Zammuto and Blair D. Gifford (2001)[34] in their study on "The competing values frame work: Understanding the impact of organizational culture on the Quality of Work Life", used the competing values framework as a tool to investigate the relationship between organizational culture and several important job related variables. The findings indicate that group cultural values are positively related to organizational commitment, job involvement, empowerment and job satisfaction, and negatively related to organizational commitment, job involvement, empowerment and job satisfaction and negatively related to intent to turnover.

Gillian Considine and Ron Callus (2001)[35] carried out a study entitled "The Quality of Work Life of Australian employees: The development of an Index Quality of Work Life introduction and perspectives". The sample of the study comprised 1001 employees. The samples were selected by using the stratified random sampling technique. The sample respondents reflected the national workforce in terms of location (metro and rural) state of residence, gender and age. An Australian Quality of Work Life Index (AQWL) was created to measure the perception on Quality of Work Life of employees. The finding of the study revealed that young workers were a bit less positive in their relationship at work than their counterparts. The results of the study showed that the majority of Australian workers felt that having good relationship at work and having interesting and satisfying work were the most important issues for a high Quality of Work Life.

Mohammad Saeed, Kamal Kishore Jain and Mohd Mahyudi (2001)[36] ,carried out a study entitled, "Quality of Work Life at Texas Instruments Malaysia (TIM)" with a view to measure the employee perception on Quality of Work Life by using R.E.Walton's criteria of eight components. The required data were collected on personal observations and interviews with key executives and employees of the company. The findings of the study revealed that it goes beyond doubt that the TIM has done a good job so far as Quality of Work Life is concerned. The productivity has improved three fold and factory output has more than doubled.

Saipin Narongrit and Supit Thongsri (2001)[37], dealt with the Quality of Work Life and organizational commitment. The objectives of this research were to study the level of the asset management organization, Thaitoyo Denso Company Limited's staffs' Quality of Work Life and organizational commitment, to compare the organizational commitment according to personal factors, and also to analyze the factors affecting organizational commitment. The population consisted of all the two hundred employees in Thaitoyo Denso Company Limited. The statistics used for analyzing the data were percentage, mean, standard deviation test at the 0.05 percentage level of significance, and Pearson product moment correlation coefficients at the 0.01percentage level of significance. It was found that the levels of the staffs' Quality of Work Life were moderate. Personal characteristics like sex, age, status, education, position, staff salary, and line function caused no difference. All factors of quality of work life had positive correlation with organizational commitment.

Gopal Joshi (2002)[38], in his study concluded that for improving productivity through high value addition and high quality, the Garment Industry can be pursued though a combination of various measures such as investment in new technology and equipment, up gradation of skills among the workers, improvement in production organization and processes, carrying out productivity campaigns and emphasis on quality improvement and improvement in job quality.

Lepi.T, Tarmidi and Muliadi widjaja (2002)[39] ,reveal that the Strengths of Indonesian Garment Industry were low wage rate, large quota allotment, punctuality on delivery, quality and Indonesians long existence in the Apparel Industry. The weakness outlined were low labor productivity, the non-supportive Government, the existence of high black quota market prices, the dependence on expatriate supervisor and managers to instill quality and under developed upstream industries.

Majyd Aziz (2002)[40],in his study on Readymade Garment Industry in Pakistan commented that, the elimination of quantitative restriction would compel exporters re-engineer their approach towards international trade as dependence on their quota- profile would no more be an advantage over new competitors whether domestic or foreign. He also states that visionary entrepreneurs, enthusiastic worker's leaders and proactive Government functionaries must join together to develop and promote a holistic strategy to achieve the export objective so that the working environment of industries as well as those who work in them becomes such that an excellent quality is produced and marketed as a result of the ability to compete by achieving better productivity and by enforcing job quality.

Saman Kelegama and Roshen Epaara Chchi (2002)[41], in their study in Garment Industry in Srilanka highlighted that dismantling of the quota regime will compel the industry to compete for its market share in an intensely competitive global market. They suggested formulation of a national strategy for the Garment Industry with the resolve to improve productivity, undertake human resource development, develop product quality, increase investment in technology, develop codes of business conduct, implement the standards on working conditions and develop alliances.

Samar Verma (2002)[42], in his study on export competitiveness of Indian Textile and Garment Industry observed that the most draconian of all Government policies that has scuttled the growth of garment industry is reservation of garment manufacture for small scale industry. It has not only prevented expansion, but also impeded technological up gradation of the garment manufacturing units. As a result, the garment manufacturing units could neither attain optimal economics of scale, nor produce international quality garments.

Waheedakhan, Meena Osmany and Waseem.M (2002)[43], in their study on "Quality of Work Life and job involvement in bank employees", found that individuals have unique set of standards for evaluation of Quality of Work settings. Quality of Work Life inventory on a sample of 120 clerks and officers, randomly drawn from different nationalized banks of U.P and Delhi State. The results indicated that substantial differences exist between bank employees of U.P and Delhi on the Quality of Work Life dimensions of economy benefits, marital state, union management relations, supervisory relationships and general life satisfaction.

Biswajeet Pattanayak(2003)[44], in his study on "Towards building a better HRD climate: A Study on organizational role stress and Quality of Work Life", has asserted that to survive and excel in the new economy, the HRD climate is a matter of serious concern in Indian public sector organizations. The present study followed a 2x2 factorial design of research. The two factors were types of organization (Old/New) and role positions in the organizational hierarchy (executive/non-executive). The sample consists of 800 employees from two public sector organizations. The objectives were to discover the differences, if any, between the sub groups with regard to organizational role stress (ORS) and perception of Quality of Work Life (QWL). It also aimed to ascertain the relative importance of QWL variables in explaining ORS. The findings revealed that there are significant differences between the executives of the old and new public sector organizations on a number of ORS as well as QWL dimensions.

Duncan Gallie (2003)[45] have made a comparison of employees' perceptions of the Quality of Working tasks, the degree of involvement in decision making, career opportunities, and job security to see whether the Scandinavian countries have a distinctive pattern from other European Union countries. It was found that on the aspects of working life that were most central to the reform programmes, the results were consistent with the view that there could be societal.

Rahul Chaudhar (2003)[46] observed that the Indian Garments Industry have been harping on the low cost advantage and there must be a shift from cost advantage to competitive advantage to face the Global competitions.

Rajesh Bheda (2003)[47] has carried out an important research study for NIFT to assess the technological up gradation needs of Readymade Garment Industry among Garment manufacturing for export in 1999, and it reveals that 80 per cent of respondents had high speed machine, where as in the case of manufacturer of domestic market, 57 per cent of respondents have high speed indigenous machines and the remaining 17 per cent has no sewing machines.

Jayanta Bagchi (2004)[48] argues that the importance should be given for technology advancement and value addition in their operations. The use of IT and ITES should be encouraged to attain competitive growth, in order to improve productivity. Man machine ratio has to be improved substantially. Massive Government intervention and support for modernization of the Textile Industry are stated to be the need of the hour.

Nasl Saraji.G and Dargahi. H.(2006)[49] in their study on "A Study of Quality of Work Life (QWL)" have asserted that a high Quality of Work Life (QWL) is essential for organizations to continue to attract and retain employees. QWL is a comprehensive program designated to improve employee satisfaction. This research aimed to provide insights into the positive and negative attitudes of Tehran University of Medical Sciences (TUMS) Hospitals' employees from their Quality of Life. A cross- sectional, descriptive and analytical study was conducted among 908 TUMS hospitals' employees by questionnaire at 15 studied hospitals. A stratified random sampling technique was used to select respondents as nursing, supportive and paramedical groups. The results showed that the majority of employees were dissatisfied with occupational health and safety, intermediate and senior managers , their income, balance between the time they spent working and with family and also indicated that their work was not interesting and satisfying. TUMS hospitals' employees responding to this survey have a poor Quality of Work Life.

Neil Kearney (2006)[50] General Secretary of the International Textile Garment Leather Workers Federation (ITGLWF) commented that workers world over are worse off now than they were a decade ago and intense activity in the name of corporate social responsibility could bring about little improvement in their work place conditions. Further he points out that conditions have worsened in the past 10 years, especially since the advent of trade liberalizations in textiles and clothing. Everywhere the story is similar: long hours of work, low wages, and workers cheated of benefits and denied fundamental rights.

Rishu Roy (2006)[51] in his study entitled "Impact of Quality of Work Life on job performance: A study of print media employees "has understand how the job performance is influenced by the Quality of Work Life factors. The idea is illustrated by doing a survey of 50 employees as sample that was selected from different press media under a random sampling method. The study was carried out with the help of self-developed structure non-disguised questionnaire. It consisted of 20 statements. The required data were collected through close ended questionnaire which administered with the help of personal interview to get a clear idea about respondents' perception. Uni-variate, bi-variate, multivariate and other statistical techniques of Pearsons product momentum correlation and Z-test has been used to study relationships between the dependent variable of job performance and independent variable of Quality of Work Life. The findings of the study revealed that high job satisfaction is possible due to good Quality of Work Life.

Rose, Raduan Che, Beh, LooSee, Uli, Jegak, Idris and Khairuddin(2006)[52] in their study on

"Quality of Work Life: Implications of career dimensions" have empirically predicted QWL in relation to career-related dimensions. The sample consists of 475 managers from the free trade zones in Malaysia for both the Multinational Corporations (MNCs) and the Small-Medium Industries (SMIs). The result indicates that three exogenous variables are significant: career satisfaction, career achievement and career balance, with 63% of the variance in QWL.

Burton J. Cohen, Susan C. Kinnevy, and Melissa E. Dichter (2007)[53] in their study, compared the Quality of Work Life of child protective investigators in two very different organizational settings-a public child welfare agency and a law enforcement agency. Law enforcement agency - an agency responsible for insuring obedience to the laws FBI, Federal Bureau of Investigation - a federal law enforcement agency that is the principal investigative arm of the Department of Justice Legislation passed in Florida in 1988, transferred responsibility for investigations from the Department of Children and Families Discounted Cash Flows (DCF)to the Sheriff's Offices (SO) in four countries. The survey was conducted of investigators in the four experimental countries and in four comparison countries where DCF was still conducting investigations. The finding indicates that while both groups had similar demographic characteristics and perceptions of their role, the investigators who worked for the SO experienced a higher quality of work life than those who worked for the DCF.

Joshi, Rama.J (2007)[54] have conducted a study on "Quality of Work Life of Women Workers: Role of Trade Unions" in the services and manufacturing (public) sectors, more specifically in Banking, Insurance, PSUs and Hospitals. The study findings reveal that the level of satisfaction of women employees with QWL in their respective organizations was quite high in spite of the overall work life conditions as provided by the company/management being only average (as perceived by them). While the wider issues having implications for the entire workforce were taken care of in their negotiations by the existing union of which they were members the women specific issues were generally ignored (except for in hospitals where the dominant gender was female).

Siegrist .J, Wahrendorf. M, Von Dem Knesebeck .O, Jurges .H andBorsch-Supan. A(2007)[55] in their study on "Quality of Work, well-being, and intended early retirement of older employees: baseline results from the SHARE Study" have given the challenge of a high proportion of older employees who retire early from work. They have analyzed associations of indicators of a poor psychosocial quality of work with intended premature departure from work in a large sample of older male and female employees in 10 countries. Baseline data from the 'Survey of Health, Ageing and Retirement in Europe' (SHARE) were obtained from 3523 men and 3318 women in 10 European countries. Data on intended early retirement, four measures of well-being (self-rated health, depressive symptoms, general symptom load, and quality of life), and quality of work (effort-reward imbalance; low control at work) were obtained from structured interviews and questionnaires. Country-specific and total samples are analyzed, using logistic regression analysis. The result of the study is poor quality of work and reduced well-being are independently associated with the intention to retire from work.

Benny M.E. De Waal andRonald Batenburg (2008)[56], in their study on , "Design decisions in Workflow Management and Quality of Work", have described the design and implementation of a workflow management (WFM) system in a large Dutch social insurance organization. The effect of workflow design decisions on the quality of work is explored theoretically and empirically, using the model of Zur Muehlen as a frame of reference. It was found among a total sample of 66 employees that there was no change in the experience of work quality before and after the introduction of the WFM system. There are however, significant differences in the quality of work before and after the WFM adoption if different functions are distinguished.

Christian Korunka, Peter Hoonakker and Pascate Carayon (2008)[57], in their study titled "Quality of Work Life and turnover intention in Information Technology work", find that high turnover has been a major issue in Information Technology organizations. A conceptual model to explain turnover was developed and tested in two national samples of Information Technology and Information Technology manufacturing work. The model postulates that Quality of Work Life mediates the relations between job, organizational characteristics and turnover intention. The American sample consisted of 677 employees from an International 19 production company. A similar questionnaire was used in both studies. Model was tested with path analysis. A core model with main pathways between job demands and supervisory support to emotional exhaustion, and between emotional exhaustion and job satisfaction to turnover intention was confirmed in the national samples and in subsamples of demographics and job types.

Guna Seelan, Rethinam and Maimunah Smail (2008)[58], in their study entitled "Constructs of Quality of Work Life: A perspective of   Information Technology professional ", examine the work environment which is one of many factors to determine the meaning of Quality of Work Life. A group of work forces that is greatly affected in Quality of Work Life as a result of dynamic changes in work environment is Information Technology professionals. They reviews the meaning of Quality of Work Life, analyses constructs of Quality of Work Life based on models and past research from the perspective of Information Technology professionals in many countries and in Malaysia. The result concludes that Quality of Work Life from the perspective of Information Technology professionals is challenging both to the individuals and organizations.

Hanita Sarah Saad, Ainon Jauhariah Abu Samah and Nurita Juhdi(2008)[59], in their study on "Employees' perception on Quality Work Life and job satisfaction in a private higher learning institution", found the employee's perception of their work-life quality in the University. 251 employees in the University were surveyed in this study. Ten variables to measure Quality of Work Life (QWL) are examined namely support from organization, work-family conflict, relationship with peers, self-competence, impact on job, meaningfulness of job, optimism on organizational change, autonomy, access to resources and time control. All these variables were tested for their relationship with job satisfaction. The test indicated that each of the QWL variables on its own is a salient predictor of job satisfaction. However, seven QWL variables are no longer significant predictors for job satisfaction when all the ten QWL variables are entered into the regression equation. Using multiple linear regressions, only three QWL variables like meaningfulness of job, optimism on organizational change and autonomy were found significantly related to job satisfaction.

Juhani Ukko andJarkko Tenhunen, (2008)[60] in their study on "The impacts of performance measurement on the Quality of Working Life", focuses on the impact of performance measurement on the Quality of the Working Life (QWL) of employees, for example, their work motivation, learning opportunities, job satisfaction, participation in decision making and reward system. Furthermore, they present how the perceptions of management and employees differ from each other and what the key elements in the implementation process are as regards the accomplishment of positive impacts of performance measurement on the quality of working life. This study concludes with the underlying factors behind the positive impact of performance measurement on the Quality of Working Life.

Salam Zadeh.Y, Mansoori.H and Farid.D (2008)[61] in their study on ,"Study of the relation between Quality of Work Life and productivity of human resources in health care Institutes - a case study among nurses in Shahid Sadughi Hospital in Yazd", have found that improving quality of Work Life in nurses causes an increase in productivity and promotes patients received health care. They examined the relation between quality of work life and productivity in nurses, one of the most important personnel's in a hospital. The study sample was drawn from the total number of nurses in Shahid Sadughi Hospital which amounted to 53. Sampling was done by a random method. We used Brook's questionnaire to examine the quality of work life in nurses, of course after we examined is reliability. This study found that the relation between Quality of Work Life and productivity in nurses were in a little less than its average. The study also found that there is a significant and positive relation between Quality of Work Life and productivity in nurses.

Kongkiti Phusavat, Pornthep Anussornnitisarn, Bordin Rassameethes andPekka Kess(2009)[62] in their study on "Productivity improvement: Impacts from Quality of Work", examined the impact of Quality of Work Life (QWL) on productivity. This study took place at one manufacturing unit, the Bangkok Inter-food company limited (BIF) in Thailand. Primary techniques used for this study include the Multi-Criteria Performance/Productivity Measurement Technique (MCPMT), and statistical and mathematical models. The MCPMT helps combine information from all ratios into one dimension less scale of the overall levels of both QWL and productivity. Then, the liner and quadratic models were applied to gain insights on how QWL influences productivity. The results illustrate positive impact of QWL on productivity.

Rajib Lochan Dha (2009)[63] conducted a study on "Quality of work life: A study of municipal corporation bus drivers". The work of professional bus drivers is considered as extremely stressful. It is an environment over which they have no control whatsoever and is an atmosphere that wrecks their schedules, disrupts their home life, makes social activities and regular breaks very hard to plan and supplies constant hassle. The study deals with the Quality of Work Life of the bus drivers and the factors that lead to an imbalance, causing high probability of road accident. A qualitative study was conducted with the help of 15 bus drivers from 4 different Pune municipal corporation bus depots, India. In-depth interviews were conducted and through naturalistic observation method, data were collected. Analysis of the data was done through coding process. Some suggestions were also made for the improvement of quality of work life of the drivers.

Dev Raj Adhikari and Dhruba Kumar Gautam (2010)[64]conducted a study on "Labour legislations for improving Quality of Work Life in Nepal". This study aims to review how far Nepalese firms are complying Quality of Work Life (QWL) provisions of the Labour laws and to assess expectations of union leaders on different dimensions of QWL. To answer the research, three different labour laws are reviewed. In order to understand expectation of union leaders, a questionnaire survey is administered. In Nepalese workplaces, the QWL situation is deteriorating and thus commitment of the part of the Government, employers, and union leaders is required to work on QWL initiatives and to create a sound and harmonious industrial relations environment.

Kala S. Retna andUsha Varatharaju(2010)[65] conducted a study on "Effectiveness of Quality Work Life Balance programmes: Employees' perceptions" The concept of work-life quality is increasingly relevant in enabling positive employee engagement with the demands of work and family. This study explores employees' perception of the effectiveness of work-life quality programmes in a healthcare organization in Singapore. The findings provide useful insight into the tensions and dilemmas experienced by the users of the work-life quality programmes. The study argues that the implementation of work-life quality programmes contribute constructively to the overall quality management movement in organizations

Mohammad Rastegari, Ali Khani, Parvin Ghalriz and Jalil Eslamian(2010)[66] in their study on "Evaluation of Quality of Working Life and its association with job performance of the nurses" have found that nurses often complain about overwork and underpay. It seems that the association between "Quality of Working Life" (QWL) and the degree of nurses' involvement in their carrier is the critical factor in achieving a higher level of quality of care. This was a descriptive-correlation study. Target population included all the nurses who were employed in hospitals affiliated to Isfahan University of Medical Sciences. Sample size was 120 of the mentioned nurses. Sampling method was stratified random and data collection tool was a questionnaire. Finding of the study showed that the most common kind of Quality of Working Life in the nurses was moderate one. The most frequent nurses' task performance was also related to the moderate performance. There was a direct and significant relationship between job performance and Quality of Working Life in all the aspects.

Normala and Daud (2010)[67] in their study on "Investigating the relationship between Quality of Work Life and organizational commitment amongst Employees in Malaysian firms" have strongly said that determining the Quality of Work Life (QWL) of employees is an important consideration for employers interested in improving employees' job satisfaction and commitment. The purpose of this study was to investigate the relationship between Quality of Work Life and organizational commitment among a sample of employees in Malaysia. Seven QWL variables were examined namely growth and development, participation, physical environment, supervision, pay and benefits and social relevance were examined to determine their relationship with organizational commitment. The results showed that there is a relationship between QWL and organizational commitment. The study provides insights on how Malaysian firms could improve upon their employees' commitment

Samsinar Md-Sidin, Murali Sambasivan and Izhairi Ismail (2010)[68] conducted a study on "Relationship between work-family conflict and Quality of Life: An investigation into the role of social support". It seeks to address three different roles of social support that have theoretical and empirical support and the mediating roles of Quality of Work Life and quality of non-work life. The SEM-based approach has been used to study supervisor and spouse supports as moderators between work-family conflict and Quality of Life; independent variables of work-family conflict; independent variables of Quality of Life. The study has been carried out in Malaysia. The main findings are: Work-Family conflict has relationship with Quality of Life; Quality of Work Life and non-work life are "partial" mediators between Work-Family conflict and Quality of Life and among the various roles of social support, its role as an independent variable of Quality of Life gives the best results.

Wolfgang Hoeschele(2010)[69]in his study on "Measuring abundance: The case of Cittaslow's attempts to support better Quality of Life", says that true economic advances promote abundance – the condition when all people feel that they have enough and are enabled to live life as art, meaning self-expression to others. How can we assess whether particular projects are creating greater abundance? This question is addressed by reference to an actual attempt to improve quality of life: the Cittaslow network of cities, which began in Italy but now has member cities in a number of different countries. Are cities that belong to this network creating the conditions for greater abundance? Applying a list of criteria based on the concept of abundance to Cittaslow's charter and list of standards shows that issues of equity receive little attention, while issues of environmental quality and the stimulation of local economic development are addressed comprehensively. The analysis also shows that a list of criteria based on the concept of abundance can be used to pinpoint important policy gaps

Annelies E.M. Van Vianen, Irene E. De Pater, Myriam N. Bechtoldt and Arne Evers (2011)[70] conducted a study on "The strength and quality of climate perceptions". The purpose of this study was to investigate whether and how climate strength and quality are related to employee commitment above and beyond individual climate perceptions. Data were collected from 48 work units in organizations from different branches of Industry. A total of 419 employees completed a questionnaire. Climate quality was related to commitment above and beyond individual climate perceptions. However, this concerned the climate dimensions of cooperation and innovation, but not reward. Climate strength moderated the relationship between individual cooperation and innovation perceptions, and commitment.

Franz Josef Gellert and Rene Schalk (2011)[71] conducted a study on "The influence of age on perceptions of relationship quality and performance in care service work teams". This study examines age-related perceptions of the quality of relationships at work and performance in mentally and physically demanding care service work settings. The study was conducted in six residential homes for the elderly in Germany. Data of 150 respondents were analyzed using multiple hierarchical regression and mediation tests. The mediating role of relationship quality in the relationship between age and employee performance was examined. It was found that older employees experienced better exchange relationships with their supervisors, and that this mediated the relationship between age and job satisfaction.

Martin Lofgren, Lars Witell and Anders Gustafsson (2011)[72]conducted a study on "Theory of attractive quality and life cycles of quality attributes" The purpose of this study was to shed further light on the dynamics of quality attributes, as suggested by the Theory of attractive quality. The study aims to investigate the existence of the life cycle for successful quality attributes and to identify alternative life cycles of quality attributes. The research is based on two surveys in which a total of 1,456 customers participated in the classification of quality attributes. The study identified three life cycles of quality attributes: successful quality attributes, flavor-of-the-month quality attributes, and stable quality attributes. The research also extends the Theory of attractive quality by identifying the reverse movement of certain quality attributes; that is, a quality attribute can take a step backwards in the life cycle of successful quality attributes through, for instance, a change in design.

Mattias Elg, Jesper Stenberg, Peter Kammerlind, Sofia Tullberg and Jesper Olsson (2011)[73] conducted a study on "Swedish healthcare management practices and quality improvement work: Development trends". The purpose of this study was to empirically examine developmental trends in healthcare organization management practice and improvement work. A theoretical framework based on organizational inner context, organizational outer context, external environment and outcomes form the analytical base. Comparisons were made using independent two-sample t-tests. A general aspect, identified empirically, is the tendency toward increased external pressure on leaders in their improvement work. Higher management decisions, patient pressure and decisions made by policymakers increasingly influence and shape the choices made by healthcare managers about where to focus improvement efforts. Three different trends are empirically identified and elaborated: take-control logic, practice-based improvement and patient-centeredness.

Norshahi Nasrin and Samiei Hossein (2011)[74] in their study on, "Examining the Quality of Work Life among Public Universities faculty members in Iran and presenting strategies for its improvement", have used a descriptive and analytical survey method and have used a questionnaire to gather data. Findings illustrate three areas of activities including teaching,scientific research and administrative services. In addition analysis revealed that Quality of Work Life among faculty members was not in a good condition. Faculty level of utilization in development and professional growth opportunities was assessed low to average. Amount of interaction, communication and collaborative activities among faculty members were considered average by most of the correspondents. According to majority of respondents, misbehaviors and lack of observing ethics in scientific and professional lives was below average. Among a set of potential factors, motivational, professional challenges and organizational culture were identified as factors influencing the faculty Quality of Work Life.

Vagharseyyedin. S. A, Vanaki. Z and Mohammadi. E (2011)[75] in their study on "Quality of Work Life: Experiences of Iranian nurses", describes the experiences of Iranian nurses concerning their Quality of Work Life. A purposive sample of nurses was recruited from two University Hospitals. The data were collected through unstructured interviews and were analyzed by using qualitative content analysis. The results indicated that the participants discerned their Quality of Work Life by assessing how favorable were their working conditions, the level of fulfillment of their personal needs and the impact of their working conditions on their private life and their social life. Three main themes were identified: quality of work life, as experienced from a personal perspective; quality of work life, as experienced from a socio-cultural perspective and quality of work life, as experienced from an organizational–professional perspective.

The above studies have concentrated on the various dimensions of quality of work life. The detailed reviews have been conducted to know the factors contributing to quality of work life in different industries. Some of the studies are relevant to the textile industry. These reviews have significantly contributed to the researcher in studying the Quality of Work Life in the textile industry of Tirupur District.

References

[1] T. Lupton, "Efficiency and the Quality of Work Life: Technology of Reconciliation", *Group and Organization studies*, Vol.12, No. 3, Pp. 304-318, 1975.

[2] R.S. Dwivedi, "Human Relation and Organization Behaviour: A global perspective", New Delhi, Willey Eastern, 1977.

[3] M.L. Manga and A. Maggu, "Quality of Work Life: A study of Public Sector in India", ASCI *Journals of Management,* Vol . 8, No. 2, 1981.

[4] O.B. Sayeed and Sinha, "Measuring Quality of Work Life relation to job satisfaction and performance in two organizations", *Managerial Psychology*, Vol. 2, Pp. 15-30, 1981.

[5] P. Singh, "Motivational Profile and Quality of Corporate Work Life: A case of mismatch", *Indian Management,* Vol. 18, No. 4, Pp. 13-20, 1983.

[6] S. Jain, "Quality of Work Life", New Delhi, Deep & Deep Publications, Pp. 25 – 55, 1986.

[7] M.A. Gopi, "A study on the financial performance of Hosiery Units at Tirupur", 1987.

[8] R.T. Keller, "Cross cultural influence on work and non-work contributors to quality of life", *group and organization studies*, Vol. 12, No. 3, Pp. 304-318, 1987.

[9] P Gupta and P Khandelwak, "Quality of Work Life in relation to role efficacy", *Psychological studies*, Vol. 33, No. 1, Pp. 33-38, 1989.

[10] R. Cauvery and U.K. Sudha Nayak, "Quality of Work Life and Gender poverty Nexus: A case study of Housemaids", *Indian Journal of Labour Economics*, Vol. 36, No. 4, Pp. 857-864, 1990.

[11] D. Elizur, "Quality Circles and Quality of Work Life", *International Journal of Manpower*, Vol. 11, Pp. 3 – 7, 1990.

[12] A. Wilcock and M. Wright, "Quality of Work Life in Knitwear sector of the Canadian Textile Industry" , *Public Personnel Management,* Vol. 20, No. 4, Pp. 457-468, 1991.

[13] A.E. Eaton, M.E. Gordon and J.H. Keefe, "The Impact of Quality of Work Life programs and grievance system effectiveness on Union Commitment", *Industrial and Labour Review*, Vol. 45, No. 3, Pp. 591-604, 1992.

[14] S. Benjamin Christopher and P. Maruthupandian, "A study of Quality of Work Life with special reference to Mill workers in Pollachi Taluk", Indian Journal of Labour Economics, Vol. 36, No. 4, Pp. 882-884, 1992.

[15] H. ABMZ, "Quality of Work Life and Job satisfaction of Industrial workers in relation to size of the Organization", *Bangaladesh Journal of Psychological studies*, Vol. 2, No. 1, Pp. 43-45, 1992.

[16] D. Kumar Battacharya, "Promotion from within: A positive reinforce for enriching Quality of Work Life for White Collar Employee", *Indian Journal of Labour Economics*, Vol. 36, No. 4, Pp. 829-839, 1993.

[17] D. Brindha Varadarajan and A. Ramasubramanian, "A Quality of Work Life in a Cement Industry", *Indian Journal of Labour Economics*, Vol. 36, No. 4, Pp. 849-85, 1993.

[18] A. Gani, "Quality of Work Life in a State setting: Findings of an Empirical study", *Indian Journal of Labour Economics,* Vol. 36, No. 4, Pp. 817-823, 1993.

[19] N.P. Kumar, "Quality of Work Life and Gender Issues: A study of Female Secretarial workers in Lucknow City", *The Indian Journal of Labour Economics*, Vol. 36, No. 4, Pp. 865-872, 1993.

[20] S.K. Chakraborthy, "Managerial Effectives and the QWL Indian insights", New Delhi, 1st Edition, Tata Mc Graw Hill Publishing Co., 1994.

[21] A. Gani and A. Royaz, "Correlates of Quality of Work Life: An Analytical study", *Indian Journal of Industrial Relation*, Vol. 31, No. 1, 1995.

[22] N. Karrir and A. Khurana, "Quality of Work Life Managers in Indian Industry", *Journal of the Indian Academy of Applied Psychology*, Vol. 22, No. 1-2, Pp. 19 –26, 1996.

[23] N. Wadud, "Job Stress and Quality of Work Life among Working Women", *Bangaladesh Psychological studies,* Vol. 6, Pp. 31-37, 1996.

[24] S.M.A. Yousuf, "Evaluating the Quality of Working Life", *Management and Labour studies*, Vol. 21, No. 1, 1996.

[25] Louis and Karen Seashore, "Effects of Teacher Quality Work Life in Secondary Schools on Commitment and Sense of Efficacy", *School Effectiveness and School Improvement*, Vol. 9, No. 1, Pp. 1-27, 1998.

[26] M. Ekramul Hoque and A. Rahman, "Quality of Working Life and Job behavior of workers in Bangalasesh: A Comparative study of Private and Public sector", *Indian Journal of Industrial Relations*, Vol. 35, Vol. 2, Pp. 175-184, 1999.

[27] M.D. Hossain, Mosharraf and M.D. Tariqual Islam, "Quality of Work Life and Job Satisfaction of Nurses in Government Hospitals in Bangaladesh", *Indian Journals of Industrial relations*, Vol. 34, No. 3, Pp. 33–40, 1999.

[28] B.E. May, R.S. Lau and S.K. Johnson, "A Longitudinal Study of QWL and Review Business Performance", *South Dakota Business Review*, Vol. 58, No. 2, Pp. 1-4, 1999.

[29] J. Venkatachalam and A. Velayudham, "Impact of Advanced Technology of Quality of Work Life", *A survey of Management and Labour Studies*, Vol. 24, No. 4, Pp. 251 -254, 1999.

[30] Nallasivam, "A study on Knitted Fabrics Garments in Tirupur", South India Textile Research Association (SITRA), 2000.

[31] R. Winter, T. Tayor and J. Sarros, "Trouble at Mill: Quality of Academic Work Life", *Routledge*, Vol. 25, No. 3, Pp. 279-294, 2000.

[32] B. BramSteijn, "Work systems, Quality of Working Life and Attitudes of Workers: An Empirical Study towards the effects of Team and non-Teamwork", *New Technology, Work and Employment*, Vol. 6, No. 3, Pp. 191-203, 2001.

[33] D. Efraty and M. Sirgy Philip Siegel and D. Jin lee, "A new measure of Quality of Work Life based on need satisfaction and spill over theories", *Social Indicators Research*, Vol. 55, Pp. 241 – 302, 2001.

[34] E.A Good Man, R.F. Zammuto and B.D. Gifford, "The competing values Frame work: Understanding the impact of organizational culture on the Quality of Work Life", *Organizational Development Journal*, Vol. 19, No. 3, Pp. 58 – 68, 2001.

[35] G. Considine and R. Callus, "The Quality of Work Life of Australian Employees: The development of an Index- Quality of Work Life-Introduction and perspectives", *ICFAI University Press, Hyderabad*, Pp. 145-167, 2001.

[36] M. Saeed, K. Kishore Jain and M. Mahyudi, "Quality of Work Life at Texas Instruments Malaysia (TIM)", *Human Capital*, Vol. 2, No. 1, Pp. 24-28, 2001.

[37] S. Narongrit and S. Thongsri, "A research report published by Thaitoyo Denso Company Limited", Thailand, 2001.

[38] G. Joshi, "Garment Industry in South India: Rags or Riches?", ILO, New Delhi, 2002.

[39] T. Lepi Tarmidi and M. Widjaja, "A study on Strengths and Weakness of Indonesian Garment Industry", 2002.

[40] M. Aziz, "Readymade Garment Industry", *Economic Review*, Pp. 27-28, 2002.

[41] S. Kelegama and R. Epaara Chchi, "Garment Industry in South Asia: Rags or Riches?", ILO, 2002.

[42] S. Verma, "Export Competitiveness of Indian Textile and Garment Industry, working paper", *Indian Council for research on International Economic Relations* (ICRIER), New Delhi, No. 94, 2002.

[43] Waheedakhan, M. Osmany and M. Waseem, "Quality of Work Life and Job involvement in Bank Employees", *Journal of the Indian Academy of Applied Psychology*, Vol. 28, No. 1-2, Pp. 63-68, 2002.

[44] B. Pattanayak, "Towards building a better HRD climate: A Study on Organisational role stress and Quality of Work Life", *International Journal of Human Resources Development and Management*, Vol. 3, No. 4 Pp. 371 - 378, 2003.

[45] D. Gallie, "The Quality of working life: Is Scandinavia Different?", *Oxford Journal*, Vol. 19, Pp. 61-79, 2003.

[46] R. Chaudhar, "Indian Garments Industry: what is real competitive edge?", *Clothesline*, Pp. 43-45, 2003.

[47] R. Bheda, "Managing productivity in the Apparel Industry", First Edition, New Delhi, CBS Publishers and Distributors, Pp. 36-37, 2003.

[48] J. Bagchi, "Indian Textile Industry Liberalization and world market", Sanskrit Publications, First Edition, Pp. 267-291, 2004.

[49] G. Nasl Saraji and H. Dargahi, "A Study of Quality of Work Life (QWL)", *Iranian Journal Publ Health*, Vol. 35, No. 4, Pp. 8-14, 2006.

[50] N. Kearney, "General Secretary, ITGLWF, Garment workers worse off now than a decade age", ed., G.Gurumurthy, *Business line*, 2006.

[51] R. Roy, "Impact of Quality of Work life on Job performance; A study of Print Media Employees", *The ICFAI Journal of Organizational Behavior*, Vol. 1, Pp. 26 – 31, 2006.

[52] R. Raduan Che, B. LooSee, U. Jegak Idris and Khairuddin, "Quality of Work Life: Implications of Career Dimensions", *Journal of Social Sciences*, 2006.

[52] J. Burton Cohen, S.C. Kinnevy and M.E. Dichter, "The Quality of Work Life of Child Protective Investigators: A comparison of two work environments", Child and Youth Services Review, Vol. 29, Pp. 474-89, 2007.

[53] B.J. Cohen, S.C. Kinnevy and M.E. Dichter, "The Quality of Work Life of Child Protective Investigators: A comparison of two work environments", Child and Youth Services Review, Vol. 29, Pp. 474-89, 2007.

[54] J. Rama, "Quality of Work Life of Women Workers: Role of Trade Unions", *Indian Journal of Industrial Relations*, 2007.

[55] J. Siegrist, M. Wahrendorf, O. Von Dem Knesebeck, H. Jurges and A. Borsch-Supan, "Quality of Work, well-being, and intended early retirement of older employees: baseline results from the SHARE Study", *European Journal of Public Health,* Vol.17, No. 1, Pp. 62-68, 2007.

[56] B.M.E. De Waal and R. Batenburg, "Design decisions in Workflow Management and Quality of Work", *International Journal of Information Systems and Change Management*, Vol.3, No. 4, pp. 359-374, 2008.

[57] C. Korunka, P. Hoonakker and P. Carayon, "Quality of Work Life and Turnover intention in Information Technology work", *Human factors and Ergonomics in Manufacturing and Service Industries,* Vol.18, No. 4, Pp. 409-423, 2008.

[58] G. Seelan Rethinam and M. Smail, "Constructs of Quality of Work Life: A perspective of Information Technology professional", *European Journal of Social Sciences*, Vol. 7, No. 1, 2008.

[59] H. Sarah Saad, A. Jauhariah Abu Samah and N. Juhdi, "Employees' Perception on Quality Work Life and Job Satisfaction in a Private Higher Learning Institution", *International Review of Business Research Papers,* Vol. 4, No. 3, Pp. 23-34, 2008.

[60] J. Ukko and J. Tenhunen, "The impacts of performance measurement on the Quality of Working Life", *International Journal of Business Performance Management,* Vol. 10, No. 1, Pp. 86 - 98, 2008.

[61] Y. Salam Zadeh, H. Mansoori and D. Farid, "Study of the relation between Quality of Work Life and Productivity of Human Resources in Health Care Institutes - A Case Study among Nurses in Sahid Sadughi Hospital in Yazd" , *Journal of Urmia Nursing and Midwifery faculty*, Vol. 6, No. 2, 2008.

[62] K. Phusavat, P. Anussornnitisarn, B. Rassameethes and P. Kess, "Productivity Improvement: Impacts from Quality of Work", *International Journal of Management and Enterprise Development*, Vol. 6, No. 4 Pp. 465 - 478, 2009.

[63] R. Lochan Dha, "Quality of Work Life: A Study of Municipal Corporation Bus Drivers", *International Journal of Indian Culture and Business Management*, Vol. 2, No. 6, Pp. 638 - 653, 2009.

[64] D. Raj Adhikari and D. Kumar Gautam, "Labour legislations for improving Quality of Work Life in Nepal", *International Journal of Law and Management*, Vol. 52, No. 1, 2010.

[65] K.S. Retna and U. Varatharaju, "Effectiveness of Quality Work Life Balance Programmes: Employees' Perceptions", *International Journal of Quality and Innovation*, Vol. 1, No. 2, Pp. 97 - 111, 2010.

[66] M. Rastegari, A. Khani, P. Ghalriz and J. Eslamian, "Evaluation of Quality of Working Life and its association with Job Performance of the Nurses", *The Isfahan University of Medical Sciences*, Vol. 15, No. 4, Pp. 224-228, 2010.

[67] Normala and Daud, "Investigating the Relationship between Quality of Work Life and Organizational Commitment amongst Employees in Malaysian Firms", *International Journal of Business and Management*, Vol. 5, No. 10, 2010.

[68] S. Md-Sidin, M. Sambasivan and I. Ismail, "Relationship between Work-Family conflict and Quality of Life: An investigation into the Role of Social Support", *Journal of Managerial Psychology*, Vol. 25, No. 1, 2010.

[69] W. Hoeschele, "Measuring Abundance: The case of Cittaslow's attempts to support better Quality of Life", *International Journal of Green Economics*, Vol. 4, No. 1, pp. 63-81, 2010.

[70] A.E.M. Van Vianen, I.E. De Pater, M.N. Bechtoldt and A. Evers, "The Strength and Quality of Climate Perceptions", *Journal of Managerial Psychology*, Vol. 26, No. 1, 2011.

[71] F. Josef Gellert and R. Schalk, "The influence of age on perceptions of relationship Quality and Performance in Care Service Work Teams", *Employee Relations*, Vol. 34, No. 1, 2011.

[72] M. Lofgren, L. Witell and A. Gustafsson, "Theory of Attractive Quality and Life Cycles of Quality Attributes", *The TQM Journal*, Vo. 23, No. 2, 2011.

[73] M. Elg, J. Stenberg, P. Kammerlind, S. Tullberg and J. Olsson, "Swedish Healthcare Management Practices and Quality Improvement Work: Development Trends", *International Journal of Health Care Quality Assurance*, Vol. 24, No. 2, 2011.

[74] N. Nasrin and S. Hossein, "Examining the Quality of Work Life among Public Universities Faculty Members in Iran and Presenting Strategies for its Improvement", *Quarterly journal of Research and Planning in Higher Education*, Vol. 17, No. 1, Pp. 91-114, 2011.

[75] S.A. Vagharseyyedin, Z. Vanaki and E. Mohammadi, "Quality of Work Life: Experiences of Iranian Nurses", *Nursing and Health Sciences*, Vol. 13, No. 1, Pp. 65–75, 2011.

CHAPTER 3

Quality of Work Life and Textile Industry in Tirupur District

3.1.   Quality of Work Life - Introduction

The changes taking place in the operating environment are enormous. We have been transformed to a great extent from an agricultural society, which we primarily were, to becoming an information savvy society with nuclear power. Technology has taken hold of the lives of all industrialized nations, electronic commerce has taken over business, and India is no exception. India has not only attained self-sufficiency in food but, we even export it to other countries by the use of technology that works for us. One cannot help but notice several changes currently occurring at the workplace. Chief among these is a diverse workforce, global organizations, changing customer and employee expectations, organizational ethics. [1]

During the 1970s, much of the interest in work satisfaction and performance focused on the quality of working life. In his 1971 Labor Day address, President Nixon said, "In our quest for a better environment, we must always remember that the most important part of the quality of life is the quality of work, and the new need for job satisfaction is the key to the quality of work" (O"Toole, 1974, p. 712). This concern was heightened by changing attitudes toward work and a challenging of traditional work roles and career patterns, and by an influx of young people into the work force. [2]

Quality of work life is gaining increasing interest and importance in both industrialized as well as developing countries of the world. In India, its scope seems to be broader than the labor legislation enacted to protect the workers. It is more than a sheer work organization movement which focuses on job security and economic growth to the employees.[3]

3.1.1.   *Definition of Quality of Work Life (QWL)*

The Quality of Working Life represents a consensus regarding the adequacy of such factors in an actual work situation.

A more formal definition says that Quality of Work Life is "the degree to which members of a work organization are able to satisfy important personal needs through their experiences in an organization" (Walton, 1974).)[4]

QWL is widely used to refer to "a philosophy of management that enhances the dignity of all workers, introduces changes in an organization's culture and improves the physical and emotional well-being of employees (e.g., providing opportunities for growth and development". Indicators of quality of work life include accident rates, sick leave usage, employee turnover, and number of grievances field.[5]

3.1.2. *Need for Quality of Work Life (QWL)*

Work is an integral part of a person's everyday life and it is a person's livelihood or career or business. An average person spends around twelve hours daily in the work place. One third of a person's entire life is spent in the workplace and it influences the overall quality of the person's entire life. It should yield job satisfaction, give peace of mind, a fulfillment of having done a task as it is expected, without any flaw and having spent the time fruitfully, constructively and purposefully. Even if it is a small step towards a person's lifetime goal, at the end of the day it gives satisfaction and eagerness to look forward to the next day.[6]

Indian organizations are going for innovative practices to keep their employees happy. Even a business solution providing company promotes ROWE (Results Only Work Environment) culture within the organization. Some organizations have initiatives to provide timely assistance to the employees in a crisis situation rising out of financial or personal problems.[7]

Quality of Work Life is specifically related to the level of happiness a person derives for his career. Each person has different needs when it comes to their careers, the quality level of their work life is determined by whether those needs are being met. While some people might be content with a simple minimum wage job as long as it helps pay the bills, others would find such a job to be too tedious or involve too much physical labour and would find such a position to be highly unsatisfactory. Thus, requirements for having a high" Quality of Work Life" vary from person to person. Regardless of their standards, those with a high Quality of Work Life generally make enough to live comfortably, find their work to be interesting or engaging and achieve a level of personal satisfaction or fulfillment from the jobs that they do. In other words, employees who are generally happy with their work are said to have a high Quality of Work Life, and those who are unhappy or unfulfilled by their work are said to have a low Quality of Work Life.[8]

Unfortunately, despite their best efforts, some people find themselves with a low Quality of Work Life. They may be forced to take a job they do not enjoy because of personal or financial circumstances such as a lack of options or education or qualifications. For those with a low Quality of Work Life who are unable or unwilling to change jobs, it is important to cope effectively with the situation. Unhappy employees can attempt to improve their Quality of Work Life by choosing to focus on the positive components of their jobs. A shift in mindset to focus on the benefits, even if those benefits are minimal, can improve the Quality of Work Life. Unhappy employees can also explore opportunities to speak to coworkers and management to remove factors that reduce the Quality of their Work Life, if possible depending on the job situation.

Better Quality of Work Life leads to increased employee morale. It minimizes attrition and checks labour turnover and absenteeism. There will be better communication and understanding among all employees leading to cordial relations. It enhances the brand image for the company as that, in turn, encourages entry of new talent into the company[9].

3.1.3. *Criteria of measuring QWL*

The improvements in work conditions are leading to better Quality of Life, while others feel a fair compensation and job security should be emphasized. Walton (1975) proposes eight conceptual categories that together make up the Quality of Work Life. These are presented below.

- **Adequate and Fair Compensation**

This refers to a just and fair balance between effort and reward. It includes such things as a fair job evaluation, training to perform the job reasonably, ability of the organization to pay, demand and supply of talent and skills and profit sharing. In summary, it should respond to whether the compensation helps in "maintaining a socially desirable standard of life" (adequate) and whether compensation "bears an appropriate relationship to the pay received for other work" (fair). It may be useful to point out here that in India such labour legislations as payment of Wages Act.1936 and Minimum Wages Act, 1948 ensure adequate and fair compensation to the employees.

- **Safe and Healthy Working Conditions**

In order to improve QWL, the work environment should be free from hazards or other factors detrimental to health and safety of the employees. Walton (1975) specifically refers to reasonable hours of work, zero risk, physical conditions of work and age restrictions on both lower and upper side. Once again, concern for safety in the work place in India is enshrined in the Factories Act, 1948 which lays down minimum standards of protection from machine and other hazards (noise, pollution, fume, gases) at the place of work.

- **Immediate Opportunity to use and Develop Human Capacities**

The work today has become repetitive and fragmented. The average worker often responds mechanically to the demands of machine without much control on them. QWL can be improved if the job allows sufficient autonomy and control, uses a wider range of skills and abilities, provides immediate feedback to workers to take corrective action, is seen as a total activity and provides opportunity to plan and implement by himself.

- **Opportunity for Continued Growth and Security**

Opportunities for promotions are limited in case of all categories of employees either due to educational barriers or due to limited openings at the higher level. QWL provides future opportunity for continued growth and security by expanding one's capabilities, knowledge and qualifications.

- **Social Integration in the Work Organization**

One of the objectives of QWL is to generate satisfying identity with the organization and develop a feeling of self-esteem. The variables that inculcate these are absence of hierarchical status, opportunity for upward mobility, openness and trust, a sense of community feeling on the job, and freedom from prejudice based on sex, caste, race, creed and religion. Once again Article 16 of the Indian Constitution guarantees equal opportunity of employment irrespective of race, creed, caste, religion and sex.

- **Constitutionalisation in the Work Organization**

Enhanced QWL should also ensure zero violation of the constitutional guarantee by executive organizational decisions. Such guarantees as right to personal privacy free speech, equitable treatment and governance by the "Rule of Law" are necessary to improve QWL.

- **Work and the Total Life Space**

The demands of the work, like late hours, frequent travel, and quick transfers are psychologically and socially very costly to the employee and his family. Such phenomena occurring on a regular basis necessarily depress the QWL.

- **The Social Relevance of Work Life**

The organization's lack of concern for social causes, like waste disposal, low quality product, over aggressive marketing and employment practices make workers depreciate the value of their work and career which, in turn effects their self esteem. The social responsibility of the organization is an important determinant of QWL.

The eight criteria indicated above constitute the broad realm of Quality of Work Life. It is possible that all of them may not be relevant to all group of employees but irrespective of the criteria the underlying assumption which define the QWL is the individuals own experience of satisfaction and dissatisfaction. According to Takezawa (1976) "what constitute a 'high' Quality of Work Life may vary in relation to both the workers aspirations and the objective reality of the work and society. It is ultimately defined by the worker himself[10].

The basic concept underlying the QWL is what has come to be known as "humanization of work". It involves basically the development of an environment of work that stimulates the creative abilities of the workers, generates cooperation and interest in self-growth.

3.1.4. Principles of Humanization of Work

Herrick and Maccoby (1975) have identified four basic principles which summaries the humanization of work. These principles are briefly discussed below.

- **The Principle of Security**

Humanization of work implies freedom from anxiety, fear and the loss of future employment. The working conditions should be safe and there should be no fear of economic want. These preconditions will guarantee utmost development of skills and ideas.

- **The Principle of Equity**

Hostility is generated if there are substantial differences between efforts and rewards. The equity principle requires that there is a just way of evaluating the conditions of an employee. Another aspect of equity refers to paying for knowledge and skill to carry out the task and not for the task alone. If work has to be humanized, equity would also require sharing in the profits of the organization according to the individual or group contribution.

- **The Principle of Individuation**

Individuation refers to the work environment in which employees are encouraged to develop themselves to their utmost competence, a system of work that facilitated blossoming of individual potential. A basic precondition for this is the availability of freedom and autonomy in deciding person's own pace of activity and design of operations.

- **The Principle of Democracy**

Akin to the principle of individuation, this also implies greater authority and responsibility vested into the work force. Interesting controls, close supervision and a general institutionalization inhibit humanization of work. Meaningful participation in decision-making also guarantees the "right of citizenship".

Quality of Work Life is a complex and multi-faced concept implying a concern for the member of an organization irrespective of the level they belong to. It includes job factors like wage and hours of work and also the nature of work itself[11]".

3.1.5. *Measurement of QWL*

There are few recognized measures of quality of working life and of those that exist, few have evidence of validity and reliability, that is, there is a very limited literature based on peer reviewed evaluations of available assessments. A recent statistical analysis of new measure are the Work-Related Quality of Life scale (WRQoL), The Job and Career Satisfaction (JCS) scale, The General well-being (GWB) scale, The WRQoL Stress at Work sub-scale (SAW), The Control at Work (CAW),The WRQoL Home-Work Interface scale (HWI) and The Working Conditions scale of the WRQoL. They are as follows

- **The Work-Related Quality of Life Scale (WRQoL)**

It indicates that this assessment device should prove to be a useful instrument, although further evaluation would be useful. The WRQoL measure uses six core factors to explain most of the variation in an individual's quality of working life: Job and career satisfaction, working conditions, general well-being, home-work interface, stress at work and control at work.

- **The Job and Career Satisfaction (JCS) Scale**

The scale of the Work-Related Quality of Life scale (WRQoL) is said to reflect an employee's feelings about, or evaluation of, their satisfaction or contentment with their job and career and the training they receive to do it. Within the WRQoL measure, JCS is reflected by questions asking how satisfied people feel about their work. It has been proposed that this positive job satisfaction factor is influenced by various issues   including clarity of goals and role ambiguity, appraisal, recognition and reward, personal development, career benefits and enhancement and training needs.

- **The General Well-Being (GWB) Scale**

The scale of the Work-Related Quality of Life scale (WRQoL) aims to assess the extent to which an individual feels good or content in themselves, in a way which may be independent of their work situation. It is suggested that general well-being influences and is influenced by work. Mental health problems, predominantly depression and anxiety disorders, are common, and may have a major impact on the general well- being of the population. The WRQoL GWB factor assesses issues of mood, depression, anxiety, life satisfaction, general quality of life, optimism and happiness.

- **The WRQoL Stress at Work sub-scale (SAW)**

It reflects the extent to which an individual perceives they have excessive pressures and feel stressed at work. The WRQoL SAW factor is assessed through items dealing with demand and perception of stress and actual demand overload. Whilst it is possible to be pressured at work and not be stressed at work, in general, high stress is associated with high pressure.

- **The Control at Work (CAW)**

This subscale of the WRQoL scale addresses how much employees feel they can control their work through the freedom to express their opinions and being involved in decisions at work. Perceived control at work as measured by the Work-Related Quality of Life scale (WRQoL) is recognized as a central concept in the understanding of relationships between stressful experiences, behaviour and health. Control at work, within the theoretical model under pinning the WRQoL, is influenced by issues of communication at work, decision making and decision control.

- **The WRQoL Home-Work Interface Scale (HWI)**

It measures the extent to which an employer is perceived to support the family and home life of employees. This factor explores the interrelationship between home and work life domains. Issues that appear to influence employee HWI include adequate facilities at work, flexible working hours and the understanding of managers.

- **The Working Conditions Scale of the WRQoL**

It assesses the extent to which the employee is satisfied with the fundamental resources, working conditions and security necessary to do their job effectively. Physical working conditions influence employee health and safety and thus employee Quality of Working Life. This scale also taps into satisfaction with the resources provided to help people do their jobs.[12]

3.1.6.   *Factors influencing the Quality of Work Life*

There are many factors which can contribute to Quality of Work Life. It covers all aspects of worker's life with special reference to his interaction with his work and his working environment. These factors influencing the quality of work life of employees as follows

- **Attitude**

The person who is entrusted with a particular job needs to have sufficient knowledge, required skill and expertise, enough experience, enthusiasm, energy level, willingness to learn new things, dynamism, sense of belongingness in the organization, involvement in the job, inter personnel relations, adaptability to changes in the situation, openness for innovative ideas, competitiveness, zeal, ability to work under pressure, leadership qualities and team-spirit.

- **Environment**

The job may involve dealing with customers who have varied tolerance level, preferences, behavioral pattern, level of understanding; or it may involve working with dangerous machines like drilling pipes, cranes, lathe machines, welding and soldering machines, or even with animals where maximum safety precautions have to be observed which needs lot of concentration, alertness, presence of mind, quick with involuntary actions, synchronization of eyes, hands and body, sometimes high level of patience, tactfulness, empathy , compassion and control over emotions.

- **Opportunities**

Some jobs offer opportunities for learning, research, discovery, self-development, enhancement of skills, room for innovation, public recognition, exploration, celebrity-status and loads of fame. Others are monotonous, repetitive, dull, routine, no room for improvement and in every sense boring. Naturally the former ones are interesting and very much rewarding also.

- **Nature of Job**

A driller in the oil drilling unit, a diver, a fire-fighter, traffic policeman, train engine driver, construction labourers, welder, miner, lathe mechanic have to do dangerous jobs and have to be more alert in order to avoid any loss of limb, or loss of life which is irreparable; whereas a pilot, doctor, judge, journalist have to be more prudent and tactful in handling the situation; a CEO, a professor, a teacher have more responsibility and accountability but safe working environment; a cashier or a security guard cannot afford to be careless in his job as it involves loss of money, property and wealth; a politician or a public figure cannot afford to be careless, for his reputation and goodwill is at stake. Some jobs need soft skills, leadership qualities, intelligence, decision making abilities, abilities to train and extract work from others; other jobs need forethought, vision and yet other jobs need motor skills, perfection and extreme carefulness.

- **People**

Everyone has to deal with three set of people in the work place. Those are namely boss, co-workers in the same level and subordinates. Apart from this, some professions need interaction with people like patients, media persons, public, customers, thieves, robbers, physically disabled people, mentally challenged, children, foreign delegates, gangsters, politicians, public figures and celebrities. These situations demand high level of prudence, cool temper, tactfulness, humor, kindness, diplomacy and sensitiveness.

- **Stress level**

All these above mentioned factors are inter-related and inter-dependant. Stress level need not be directly proportional to the compensation. Stress is of different types – mental stress/physical stress and psychological or emotional stress. A managing director of an organization will have mental stress, a labourer will have physical stress, and a psychiatrist will have emotional stress. Mental stress and emotional stress cause more damage than physical stress.

- **Career Prospects**

Every job should offer career development. That is an important factor which decides the Quality of Work Life. Status improvement, more recognition from the management and appreciations are the motivating factors for anyone to take keen interest in the job. The work atmosphere should be conducive to achieve organizational goals as well as individual development. It is a win-win situation for both the parties; an employee should be rewarded appropriately for his good work, extra efforts, sincerity and at the same time a lethargic and careless employee should be penalized suitably; this will motivate the former to work with more zeal and deter the latter from being so, and strive for better performance.

- **Challenges**

The job should offer some challenges at least to make it interesting; That enables an employee to upgrade his knowledge and skill and capabilities; whereas the monotony of the job makes a person dull, non-enthusiastic, dissatisfied, frustrating, complacent, initiative – less and uninteresting. Challenge is the fire that keeps the innovation and thrill alive. A well-accomplished challenging job yields greater satisfaction than a monetary perk; it boosts the self-confidence also.

- **Growth and Development**

If an organization does not give chance for growth and personal development, it is very difficult to retain the talented personnel and also to find new talent with experience and skill.[13]

QWL in an organization is high when the benefits accrue to the individuals and to the organization.QWL form the perspectives of job design and the patterns of work scheduling.

Obviously, if people differ in their needs, personality characteristics and expectations at the work place, there can hardly be "one best way "of designing jobs that would offer a high QWL to all employees. This is where the fit between the individual and job becomes important. First an examination of the different kinds of jobs that can be designed and then examination of the job-person fit is essential.[14]

3.1.7. *Quality of Work Life and Productivity*

"Quality of Work Life" encompasses aspects of good experiences and advantages for employees, the organization and the society at large. Among the various indices of the Quality of Work Life are such factors as job involvement, job satisfaction, sense of competence, job performance, productivity, organizational vitality, clean air with minimal pollution and product safety.

Job involvement indicates the extent of people's identification with, or ego investment in, the job. The more central the job to the individual's life, the more he or she gets involved in it and therefore spends more time and energy at work. Job involved people are interested in turning high quality of work and are motivated to put forth their best efforts on the job. Research has shown that challenging jobs that require skill variety influence employees to get involved in their jobs (sekaran.1989). Correlates of job involvement are such personality characteristics as an achievement and high work ethic values (Rabinowitz and Hall, 1977; Sekaran, 1977).

Job satisfaction indicates the positive affective responses of employees to their job environment. More specifically, job satisfaction indicates employees' satisfaction with (1) the nature of the work they do (2) the quality of supervision they receive (3) the co-workers (4) pay and (5) opportunities for promotion. Job satisfaction is correlated to job characteristics (skill variety, autonomy) and job involvement. That is, when people are involved in their jobs, they are also satisfied with them and when they experience more job satisfaction, they are also satisfied with them and when they experience more job satisfaction (Sekaran, 1985), they could emanate from role ambiguity, role conflict, and role overload or role difficulty.

Sense of competence denotes the feeling of confidence in one's own competence. By engaging in work that calls for a variety of skills, abilities and talents, individuals gain mastery over their work environment. As workers engage themselves more and more in work activities, they acquire a greater sense of competence and experience higher levels of job involvement, because the more competence they feel, the more motivated they are to interact with the job, and hence become more involved in it. The greater the involvement, the greater is their sense of competence. Thus, job involvement and a sense of competence mutually reinforce each other. When both, sense of competence and involvement, are high, employees' level of satisfaction increases naturally as well (Sekaran, 1986). The following exhibit depicts the relationships between job characteristics, motivation, sense of competence and job satisfaction.

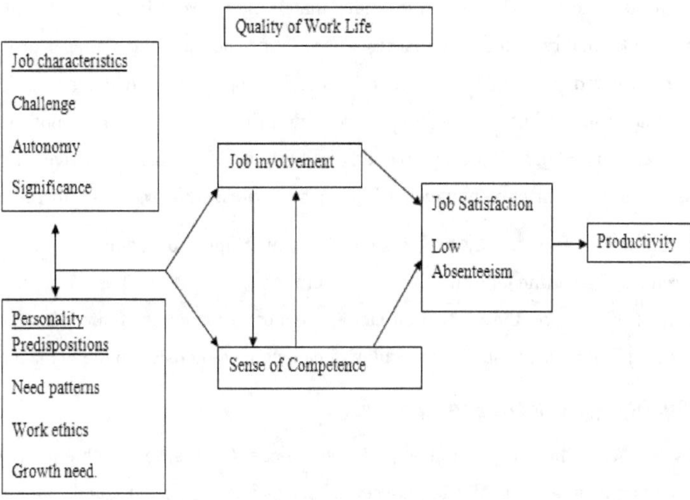

Exhibit 3.1: Fit between Job Characteristics, Personality Predispositions and Quality of Work Life Outcomes.

Job performance would also continue to improve as people's level of involvement, competence and satisfaction increase. In essence, all the four factors are significantly correlated. Though it may be controversial as to whether performance causes satisfaction or satisfaction leads to better performance, one can safely state that when job involvement, sense of competence and job satisfaction are all present , as a natural corollary, job performance is likely to be high.

Productivity ensues when there is a fit among the predispositions of workers and the type of jobs they are assigned. Since job involvement, motivation, sense of competence and job satisfaction ensues due to congruence between the worker and the job, a high level of job performance manifests itself and increases the quality and quantity of output. When the same number of workers turns a larger quantum of output in the same period of time, productivity increases for the organization as well. When high quality, safe products and services are the outcomes, society itself benefits.

Good job designing results in a high quality of work life for individuals, the organization and the society. It therefore becomes important that managers pay attention to job design. If the skills, abilities, experience, training and personality dimensions such as tolerance for ambiguity, need patterns and work ethic values match the types of jobs that individuals are placed in, a good quality of life will ensure. Whereas enriched jobs may appeal to the more achievement-oriented individuals, repetitive jobs might appeal to individuals who have low level skills and training but have a high work ethic orientation. So, it may not always be beneficial to enrich all kinds of jobs. Moreover, certain types of routine, repetitive jobs that do not lend themselves to enrichment have perforce to be performed in organizations.

While robotics may be a way to get around manning dull jobs, some individuals might actually prefer to do routine jobs and earn whatever money they fetch. Thus it is wise to take a contingency of the job and the contextual factors. In a country such as India where labour is plentiful in supply, job design adds a particularly challenging dimension to the manager's job.[15]

3.1.8.   *Quality of Work Life Programmes*

Quality of Work Life Programmes generally focus on the environment within the organization and include basic physical concerns such as heating and air conditioning, lighting and safety precautions; additional physical amenities such as food and beverage facilities, recreation, and aesthetics; and psychological and motivational factors such as flexible work hours, freedom to suggest changes or improvements, challenging work, and varying degrees of autonomy.[16]

QWL program is to change and improve the work climate so that the interface of people, technology, and the organization makes for a more favorable work experience and desired outcomes.[17]

QWL is ensuring when members of an organization are able to satisfy their important personal needs through their experiences in the organization[18].

Indian Organizations are setting up policies for maintaining a QWL. They are going in for innovative methods to keep their employees happy and satisfied, as it makes office a better place to work and also positively impacts productivity.

Human Resource Departments are involved with efforts to improve productivity through changes in employee relations. QWL means having good supervision, good working conditions, good pay and benefits and an interesting, challenging and rewarding job. High QWL is sought through an employee relations philosophy that encourages the use of QWL efforts, which are systematic attempts by an organization to give workers greater opportunities to affect their jobs and their contributions to the organization's overall effectiveness. That is, a proactive human resource department finds ways to empower employees so that they draw on their "brains and wits," usually by getting the employees more involved in the decision-making process.

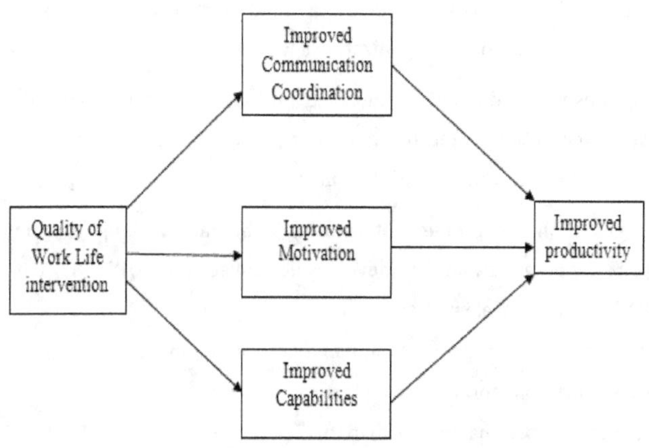

Exhibit 3.2: QWL and Productivity

Source: E. Lawler III and G. Ledford, "Productivity and the Quality of Work Life", National Productivity Review 2 (Winter 1981-1982), Pp. 29.

Vigorous domestic and International competition drives organizations to be more productive. Proactive managers and human resource departments respond to this challenge by finding new ways to improve productivity. Some strategies rely heavily upon new capital investment and technology[19]

Quality of Work Life programs typically includes a combination of different organizational-development technique and no two programs are ever quite the same. However, all QWL programs share the organizational development focus on improving the quality and effectiveness of employee interactions, on the assumption that improved organizational outcomes such as increased productivity will no doubt follow.

QWL programs are examples of broader scope organizational development programs. QWL programs are best characterized as system wide attempts to simultaneously enhance organizational effectiveness (usually defined in terms of productivity) and employee well-being through a commitment to participative organizational decision making.

QWL programs aim to enhance the work experience of the individual worker. They typically have a strong flavor of worker rights and industrial democracy, and many QWL programs have been designed as cooperative ventures between unions and firm management. The typical objectives of a QWL program would include fair compensation, a conductive work environment, development of individual capacities, social integration of the work force, protection of the dignity and rights of each individual worker, and social relevance of the organization and its activities for the organization's work force.

All QWL programs may additionally include a team-building or survey-guided development component. QWL intervention is improving such organizational processes as communication, coordination, motivation and personal development"[20]

QWL focuses on the problem of creating a human working environment where employees work cooperatively and achieve results collectively. QWL, as it is understood today, includes four essential elements:

- The programme seeks to promote human dignity and growth.
- Employees work collaboratively.
- They determine work changes participatively
- The programmes assume compatibility of people and organizational goals.[21]

3.2.   Textile Industry in Tirupur District

The history of textile is almost as old as that of human civilization and as time moves on, the history of textile has further enriched itself. In the 6th and 7th century BC, the oldest recorded indication of using fibre comes with the invention of flax and wool fabric at the excavation of Swiss lake inhabitants. In India the culture of silk was introduced in 400AD. While spinning or cotton traces are back to 3000 BC. The discovery of machines and their widespread application in processing natural fibres was a direct outcome of the industrial revolution of the 18th and 19th centuries. The discoveries of various synthetic fibres like nylon created a wider market for textile products and gradually led to the invention of new and improved sources of natural fibre. The development of transportation and communication facilities facilitated the path of transaction of localized skills and textiles among various countries.[22]

A textile is a flexible material consisting of a network of natural or artificial fibres often referred to as thread or yarn. Yarn is produced by spinning raw wool fibres, linen, cotton, or the material on a spinning wheel to produce long strands known as yarn. Textiles are formed by weaving, knitting, crocheting, knotting, or pressing fibres together. [23]

Textile industry is one of the main pillars holding the Indian Economy. It constitutes about 14 percent of industrial production, 20 percent of total export earnings, 4 percent of GDP and provides direct employment to an estimated 35 million people. In spite of these, India's entire share in the world textiles trade is still maintained at around 3 percent.[24]

Tirupur is the "knitwear capital" of India. It has spurred up the textile industry in India for the past three decades. Its economic boom boosts the morale of Indian industrialists." It contributes to a huge amount of foreign exchange in India. As of 2005, when Tirupur was a part of Coimbatore district, Coimbatore was the highest revenue earning district in Tamil Nadu, but when Tirupur grew more, the city increased its status as a District, thus separating it from Coimbatore. Tirupur was constituted as Municipality during the year 1947. It was upgraded as Special Grade Municipality during 1983 and upgrades as Corporation from 2008.[25]

The first export of knitted garments was made to US and Ghana by Mohan Knits through a Bombay Merchant Exporter in 1972. However, it could not be sustained. In the later years, the entrepreneurial spirit and heavy competition for the domestic market forced the manufacturers to look beyond national boundaries. Thus, in 1980s a few units made sustained efforts to exports and succeeded. In 1987 the exports revenue of Tirupur was Rs.75 crores. Since then, it has not looked back and the exports during the year 2004 touched a figure of more than Rs. 5000 crores contributing almost 80 percent of country's exports in this sector. [25]Some 90 percent of India's total knitwear exports originate from here. The Indian Export Import Policy of 2002-2007 includes a special tribute to Tirupur and calls it a "Town of Export Excellence."[26]

The first banyan factory in Tirupur was started in 1925. With the advent of electricity in 1931 more knitting and weaving factories came into existence. Initially, all the knitting machines were imported from Germany, Japan and New York. By 1942, there were 34 hosiery factories in all. [27]. By 1968 this increased to 250 and today sophisticated machines are being imported from Germany, Japan, Italy, U.S.A., Korea, Taiwan and many other countries. Though there are more than 6000 units operating within the limits of Tirupur, almost 50 percent of them are unregistered units and they take up only job works. As documented by the Tirupur Exporters Association, the composition of the knitwear industry in Tirupur today is as follows

Knitting and/or stitching units: 4500

Dyeing and/or bleaching units: 750

Printing units: 300

Embroidery units: 100

Other (Compacting, Raising, Calendaring): 200 [28]

Tirupur also has large people working for textile industrial units who hire people mostly from various southern districts of Tamil Nadu viz., Madurai, Tiruchirappalli, Dindigul, Ramanathapuram, Sivagangai, Tirunelveli, Virudhunagar, Thoothukudi and Nagercoil. Also there are plenty of workers from Northern districts of Tamilnadu viz., Vellore, Thiruvannamalai, Dharmapuri, Krishnagiri, Villupuram, Cuddalore, Ariyalur, Perambalur, Thiruvallur, Kanchipuram and Chennai. They are usually unskilled labours but still get a decent pay compared to other places in South India. Large numbers of people are also from other South Indian states like Kerala, Karnataka and Andhra Pradesh. Since there is always a demand for workers in Tirupur, there are no unemployment problems. Nowadays there are also people coming from the Indian states of Orissa and Bihar to work in the garment processing factories in and around Tirupur.[29]

Some of the world's largest retailers including C&A, Switcher SA, Walmart, Primark, Oviesse, Switcher, Polo Ralph Lauren, Diesel, ARMY, Tommy Hilfiger, M&S, FILA, Respect, H&M, HTHP, Whale, Reebok import many textile items and clothing from Tirupur. Recently in 2010, PGC Industries (export wing as PremDurai Exports) acquired controlling interest in Switcher Holding SA (Switzerland) which is the top T-Shirt brand of Switzerland.[30]

3.2.1. Role of Associations in Tirupur Textile Industry

3.2.1.1. Textiles Committee

The Parliament in its 14th year of the Republic enacted the Textiles Committee Act, 1963. The Committee is under the administrative control of the Ministry of Textiles, Government of India. Its main objective is to ensure the quality of textiles and textile machinery both for internal consumption and export purposes. As corollary objectives, the Textiles Committee has been entrusted with the following functions, under Section 4 of the Act:

- To undertake, assist and encourage, scientific, technological and economic research.
- To establish standard specifications for textiles, textile machinery and the packing materials.
- To establish laboratories for the testing of textiles and textile machinery.
- To provide training in the techniques of quality control.

- To provide for the inspection and examination of textiles and textile machinery.
- To promote export of textiles.
- To collect statistics and
- To advise the Central Government on all matters relating to textiles and textile machinery.

The Textiles Committee is managed by a committee comprising of 29 members as laid down under Section 3(3) of the Act and Rule 3 of the Textiles Committee Rules, 1965. It comprises of a Chairman (a member from the Industry), a Vice-chairman (Textile Commissioner from the Govt. ex-officio), and a Member Secretary, who is the Chief Executive of the organization. There are 12 ex-officio members representing various Textile Federations, Export Promotion Councils and 14 other members representing almost all interests of the textile sector. The committee has powers to constitute Standing Committees and Ad hoc Committees.[31]

3.2.1.2. *Apparel Export Promotion Council (AEPC)*

Apparel Export Promotion Council (AEPC), a nodal agency under the aegis of the Ministry of Textiles, Government of India, has been entrusted with the task of working towards projecting India's image and introducing Indian Apparel Exporters to the International market. All exporters of apparel in India are members of the AEPC, helping its over 40,000 registered members of both woven and knitted items develop long-term relationship with leading fashion houses overseas and offers them wide range of export promotion services. [32&33]

3.2.1.3. *List of Supportive Associations*

- Apparel Export Promotion Council (AEPC).
- Banian Cloth Manufacturers Association.
- Computer Embroidery Association.
- Coimbatore District Powerloom cloth Dealer Association.
- Indian Hosiery Yarn Mill Association.
- South India Hosiery Manufacturers Association.
- Tirupur Bleachers Association.
- Tirupur Collar Stitching Section Association.
- Tirupur Cotton Merchants Association.
- Tirupur Dyers Association.
- Tirupur Exporters Association.
- Tirupur Export Knitwear Industrial Complex Association.

- Tirupur Export Knitwear Manufacturers Association.
- Tirupur Hosiery Yarn Merchants Association.
- Tirupur Kaja Button Owners Association.
- Tirupur Power Table Owners Association.
- Tirupur Powerloom Association.
- Tirupur Screen Printing Association.
- Tirupur Steam Calendering Association[34]

3.2.1.4. *South India Hosiery Manufacturers Association (SIHMA)*

SIHMA is one of the oldest association established in 1951 with 60 export members and 1200 domestic members assisting the manufactures to get financial assistance from the banks and financial institutions. On the procedural front, assistance is also provided in getting the registration certificate to small-scale units, RBI Code, export import licence. It also files legal suits in courts and represents on behalf of their members. SIHMA offers various HRD training programmes in the following areas:

- Women entrepreneurship training through SISI.
- CAD course for exporters.
- Skill upgradation courses for merchandisers in pattern making and quality control.
- Facilitating ISOP certification through BDI providers [35&36]

3.2.1.5. *Tirupur Exporters Association (TEA)*

TEA was established in the year 1990. It is an Association exclusively for the cotton knitwear having production facilities in Tirupur. TEA has a membership of 532 life members and 154 associate members. The members have resolved to develop their organization focusing on:

- Multilateral growth of knitwear industry and export.
- Development of infrastructural needs for Tirupur.
- Implementation of scheme for the benefit of the society and for the public.
- Promotion of constructive cooperation with workers with fair division of reward.
- General upliftment of quality of life of Tirupur [37]

Even though Tirupur is very prosperous, the infrastructure is very minimal. Tirupur grew very quickly due to the high demand for manufacturing popular clothing brands mostly in the United States and Europe. The lack of infrastructure facilities comparatively for the foreign exchange which the city brings is a big negative point to be noticed. The Tirupur Exporters and

Manufacturers Association (TEAMA) and other associations are taking actions directly to get some sort of facilities done. The association formed by the Exporters of Tirupur (TEA) called TEAMA is one of the most successful associations in India trying hard and been successful in helping the trade in Tirupur. [38]

3.2.2. *Technology Up gradation Fund (TUF)*

Technology Upgradation Fund Scheme(TUFS) is one of the flagship schemes of the Ministry of Textiles and has helped the industry to garner investments of Rs. 2.43 thousand crore. The scheme was launched in 1999 and has been instrumental in helping India achieve new heights in the development of the textile sector and particularly in the spinning segment.

The Finance Minister in his Budget Speech of February, 2013, had announced continuation of TUFS in the 12th Plan with a major focus on modernization of the powerloom sector. Higher subsidies for weaving / powerloom sector have accordingly been planned in the continued TUFS. The Cabinet Committee on Economic Affairs today gave its approval for continuing the Technology Upgradation Fund Scheme (TUFS) during the 12th Plan period with a major focus on powerlooms in accordance with the Budget announcement for the financial year 2013-14.The total budget outlay for continuation of the scheme will be about Rs.11, 900crores, out of which Rs. 2,400 crores have been allocated for the financial year 2013-14.[39]

3.2.3. *Major Problems of Textile Industry in Tirupur*

3.2.3.1. *Scarcity and Spur in Cotton Price*

At the end of the year 2009 the city suffered as the cotton prices increased. Big billionaire's in India started to do a new business of stocking cotton in big quantity, which can make a demand for the cotton in the local market and when the demand reaches its peak the billionaire's sell the cotton for higher prices. This began to trouble the domestic markets where the garments cannot be sold for higher prices. Many domestic companies suffered heavy losses and many people lost their jobs. The export companies also suffered from this problem. The cotton price increased by 50%.[40]

Tirupur Exporters and Manufacturers Association (TEAMA) conducted a huge strike, with more than 3000 people participating in it, on 10 June 2010, insisting the Central Government to ban export of raw cotton and cotton yarn which was backed by all major industry associations in Tirupur.[41]TEAMA also called for 2 days closure of all shops and establishments across Textile towns of Tamil Nadu. Major Associations in Textile towns of Erode, Kumarapalayam, Karur, Salem, Palladam and Rajapalayam participated in this 2 day closure and insisted the Govt. to immediately intervene and curb the export of Cotton and Cotton yarn.[42, 43&44]

3.2.3.2. Poor Effluent Treatment in Dyeing Units

Tirupur suffered a lot from dyeing problems. Since dyeing is an important activity of the industry strikes in the dyeing units lead to the decrease in production of the garment items. In pursuance of the orders of Madras High Court, water and power supply to 18 CETPs with 754 dyeing and bleaching units and 68 IETPs was disconnected as they did not fulfill zero liquid discharge conditions for effluent treatment.

Tirupur Exporters And Manufacturers Association (TEAMA) had represented to the High Court of Madras, insisting that the CETPs to be run by the State Government and the Central Pollution Board jointly, so that the Pollution issue can be resolved ensuring the smooth run of industry and also agriculture. The High Court has directed the State Government, Central Ministry of Environment and Forests, CPCB and 4 others to consider the plea of the Association. This is one and only judgment awarded in favor of the plea, where in the Misc. petition of all the other associations and Labour unions were turned down by the High Court. Tirupur Exporters Association has represented to Government that export revenues of ₹11 billion were lost and about 100,000 labours lost their job, due to closure of Dyeing units in Tirupur[45, 46&47]

In the year 2011, the political party which came to power took steps to improve the infrastructure and help the dyeing units. It was stated that the units must clean the effluents up to 2500 TDS (15% of the impurity) before disposing it to the river. The Government announced a total sum of Rs 200 crores for CETPs as a non interest borrowing. These measures of the Government have only partially solved the problems in dyeing unit.[48]

3.2.4. Employees Quality of Work Life (QWL) in Textile Industry

In this competitive era, the Textile industry finds difficult to produce world class quality, on par with the developed nations. It is now rare for a person to stay with a single company throughout their entire working life because employees are often willing to leave a company for better opportunities. Companies need to find better ways not only to hire qualified people, but also to retain them.

Quality of Work Life is gaining attention especially in the wake of very competitive business environment. Quality of Work Life is nothing but the Quality of life that an employee experiences at his or her work place. Due to changes in technology and to meet various demands of the employees and to withstand the place in the Global market, the company has to focus on employees satisfaction on major areas like job security, job satisfaction, medical facilities, canteen facilities, rewards, ESI.[49]

In addition to that, Textile industries has undergone rapid changes towards globalization and liberalization and have been facing problems due to Global Competition, dyeing units, shortage of cotton and power scarcity. These pose a threat to the textile industry. In addition to these threats, extended working hours, compulsory overtime, committed deliveries by the firms, shorter manufacturing cycles and other related issues detoriate the Quality of Work life in Tirupur textile firms posing a big threat to its productivity and human resource management. Employees stress at their job lead to job dissatisfaction which ultimately end up with high rate of labor turnover and absenteeism.

References

[1] U. Sekaran, "Organisational Behaviour Text and Cases", 2nd Edition, Tata McGraw Hill Education Pvt Ltd, New Delhi, 2009.

[2] J.W. Walker, "Human Resource Planning, Grolier Incorporated", Pp. 202-203, 1980.

[3] M.S. Saiyadain, "Human Resource Management", 3rd Edition, Tata McGraw Hill Publishing Co., Ltd, New Delhi, 2005.

[4] J. W. Walker, "Human Resource Planning", Grolier Incorporated, 1980.

[5] J.M. Ivancevich, R. Konopaske and M.T. Matteson, "Organizational Behavior and Management", 7th edition, Tata McGraw Hill education Pvt Ltd, New Delhi, 2006.

[6] http://ejournal.srmuniv.ac.in

[7] http://www.articlesbase.com

[8] http://www.ehow.com

[9] http://www.scribd.com

[10] M.S. Saiyadain, "Human Resource Management", 3rd Edition, Tata McGraw Hill Publishing Co., Ltd, New Delhi, Pp. 360-361, 2005.

[11] ibid

[12] http://en.wikipedia.org/

[13] D. Kumar Bhatacharyya, "Human Resource Management", 2th Edition, Excel Books, New Delhi, 2009

[14] U. Sekaran, "Organisational Behaviour Text and Cases", 2nd Edition, Tata McGraw Hill Education Pvt Ltd, New Delhi, Pp. 237-238, 2009.

[15] U. Sekaran, "Organisational Behaviour Text and Cases", 2nd Edition, Tata McGraw Hill Education Pvt Ltd, New Delhi, Pp. 245-246, 2009.

[16] T.V. Rav, "Readings in Human Resource Development", Oxford and IBH Publishing Co., Pvt Ltd- New Delhi, 2001.

[17] F. Luthans, "Organisational Behavior", 10th edition, McGraw Hills International Edition, New York, 2005.

[18] K. Aswathappa, "Human Resource Management Text and Caess", 6th Edition, Tata McGraw Hill Education Pvt Ltd, New Delhi, 2010.

[19] E. Lawler III and G. Ledford, "Productivity and the Quality of Work Life", National Productivity Review (Winter 1981-1982).

[20] O.B. Gregory B. Northcraft and Margaret A. Neale, "The Dryden Press, Tokyo", Pp. 741-742, 1990.

[21] V.S.P. Rao, "Human Resource Management Text and Cases- 2nd Edition", Excel Books, New Delhi, 2004.

[22] http://www.fibre2fashion.com

[23] http://www.china-qualityinspection.com

[24] http://www.screenprinttekpa.com

[25] http://xklsv.org

[26] indiatirupurnew-developmentsfwfcountrystudy.pff

[27] http://jobwork.ne/

[28] indiatirupurnew-developmentsfwfcountrystudy.pff

[29] http://xklsv.org

[30] https://www.facebook.com

[31] http://www.indiantextilejournal.com

[32] http://tiruppur.tn.nic.in

[33] www://indiaknitfair.com

[34] http://www.tiruppur.com

[35] http://www.thehindu.com

[36] http://mytirupur.biz.

[37] ibid

[38] http://www.kadavapatidar.com

[39] http://pib.nic.in

[40] 40. http://www.hindu.com.

[41] ibid

[42] ibid

[43] ibid

[44] http://pd.cpim.org.

[45] www.fibre2fashion.

[46] http://www.thehindubusinessline.com

[47] http://www.hindu.com.

[48] http://xklsv.org

[49] www.iosrjournals.org

CHAPTER 4

DATA ANALYSIS AND INTERPRETATION

4.1. Introduction

For the purpose of the study, structured interview schedule were prepared to study the Quality of Work Life of Textile employees in Tirupur District. Accordingly, the data were collected from the respondents and these data were analyzed systematically and are presented in this chapter. This chapter consists of five sections based on the study viz., Section I, II, III IV and V.

Section I: It presents the analysis of data relating to personal and occupational profile of textile employees.

Section II: This section consists of three parts. Part A: It presents the analysis of data relating to occupational stress of employees in textile industry. Part B: It presents the analysis of data relating to stress in association with occupational difference and Part C: It presents the analysis of data relating to factors contributing to stress management.

Section III: This section consists of two parts. Part A: It presents the analysis of data relating to   factor determining Quality of Work Life and Part B: It presents the analysis of data relating to Quality of Work Life in association with personal and occupational differences.

Section IV: It presents the analysis of data relating to employee job satisfaction in association with personal and occupational differences.

Section V: It presents the analysis of data relating to QWL factors discriminating employees of large, medium and small units.

Section I

Personal and Occupational Profile of Employees

4.1.1. Introduction

Managing non-human resources such as materials and machinery is relatively simple, managing human resources is more complex.

When an employee joins an organization, there is a "psychological contract" that is established between that individual and the organization.

That is, there are certain mutual expectations tacitly set between the two. For instance, the organization expects the employee to put forth his best effort, have organizational loyalty and work towards the goals of the organization, similarly, the employee who joins the organization also has certain expectations of the organization-that it will care for his well-being, be fair in its dealings, reward adequately and offer opportunities to develop and advance in the system[1].

Proper assessment of employees will be helpful to know the Quality of Work Life of employees.

Therefore, the first objective of this study aims to know about the personal and occupational profile of the employees that may possibly influence their Quality of Work Life. This section has been devoted to understand the personal and occupational profile of the employees.

The personal and occupational profile of the respondents have been described with the help of simple percentage analysis.

The simple percentage analysis is one of the most common graphical tools used to describe the distribution of the respondents in demographics and other categories.

As it is expressed in percentage, it facilitates comparison. Suitable exhibits are also drawn for tables to improve the understanding.

4.1.2. Profile of the Respondents

In this study, totally 500 employees have been taken as sample respondents. The socio-economic profile of the respondents is classified in to two broad categories, viz.

1. Personal profile.
2. Occupational profile.

1. Personal Profile of the Respondents

Personal profile of the respondents is taken into consideration to assess whether it influences the Quality of Work Life of Textile employee.

The personal profile depicts the profile of the respondents in terms of age, gender, marital status, educational qualification, status of residence, family members, nature of family, family income and family debt. The personal profile of the respondents is given in table.4.1.1.

Table 4.1.1: Distribution of Respondents Based on Personal Profile

S.No	Personal profile		No. of respondents	Percentage
A	Age	18 - 25 yrs	113	22.6
		25 - 35 yrs	**179**	**35.8**
		35 - 45 yrs	95	19.0
		45 - 55 yrs	76	15.2
		Above 55 yrs	37	7.4
		Total	**500**	**100.0**
B	Gender	Male	**289**	**57.8**
		Female	211	42.2
		Total	**500**	**100.0**
C	Marital Status	Unmarried	124	24.8
		Married	**248**	**49.6**
		Divorced	85	17.0
		Widowed	43	8.6
		Total	**500**	**100.0**
D	Educational Qualifications	Illiterate	58	11.6
		Primary	**283**	**56.6**
		Higher Secondary	137	27.4
		Graduate	15	3.0
		Diploma	7	1.4
		Total	**500**	**100.0**
E	Status of Residence	Own house	157	31.4
		Rented	**208**	**41.6**
		Accommodation provided by employer	135	27.0
		Total	**500**	**100.0**
F	Family Members	1 – 3	120	24.0
		4- 6	**315**	**63.0**
		Above 6	65	13.0
		Total	**500**	**100.0**
G	Nature of Family	Nuclear	**287**	**57.4**
		Joint	213	42.6
		Total	**500**	**100.0**
H	Family Income	Rs.5001 - Rs.10000	33	6.6
		Rs.10001 - Rs.15000	71	14.2
		Rs.15001 - Rs.20000	**222**	**44.4**
		Above Rs.20000	174	34.8
		Total	**500**	**100.0**
I	Family Debt	No	88	17.6
		Yes	**412**	**82.4**
		Total	**500**	**100.0**

Source: Primary Data

A. Age

It is found that, 35.8 percent of the respondents belong to the age group of 25-35 years. Another 22.6 percent of them belong to the age group of 18-25 years. 19 percent of the respondents fall in the age group of 35-45 years. 15.2 percent of the respondents belong to the age group of 45-55 years. Only 7.4 percent of them belong to the age group of above 55 years.

Thus, from the above analysis it can be concluded that a majority of the sample respondents belong to the age group of 25-35 years.

B. Gender

As it could be seen in the Table 4.1.1, among the 500 sample respondents, 57.8 percent of the respondents are male and 42.2 percent are female.

Thus, from the analysis it can be concluded that a majority of the sample respondents are male.

C. Marital Status

The study reveals that 49.6 percent of the respondents are married. However, 24.8 percent of the respondents are unmarried.

Another 17 percent of the respondents are divorced and 8.6 percent respondents are widows.

Thus from the analysis, it can be concluded that a majority of the sample respondents are married.

D. Educational Qualifications

Out of the total sample of 500 respondents surveyed, 56.6 percent of the respondents are educated up to primary level. 27.4 percent of the sample respondents are educated up to higher secondary level. 11.6 percent of them are illiterate. 3 percent of them are educated up to graduate level and the remaining 1.4 percent of them is educated up to diploma level.

Thus from the above table, it can be concluded that a majority of the sample respondents are educated up to primary level.

E. Status of Residence

It is clearly indicated that, among the sample respondents, 41.6 percent lives in rented house. Another 31.4 percent lives in own house. 27 percent of the sample respondents are provided accommodation by the employers.

Thus from the above table, it can be concluded that a majority of the sample respondents are living in rented houses.

F. Family Members

The study clearly shows that, out of 500 respondents, 63 percent of the respondents family comprises 4-6 members. 24 percent of the respondents family comprises 1-3 members and 13 percent of the respondents family consists more than 6 members.

Thus from the above table, it can be concluded that a majority of the respondents family size is of 4 to 6 members.

G. Nature of Family

The study portrays that majority of the respondents (57.4 percent) are belonging to nuclear family whereas rest of the respondents (42.6 percent) follow joint family system.

Thus from the above table, it can be concluded that a majority of the sample respondents are belonging to nuclear family.

H. Family Income

The study highlights that 44.4 percent of the respondents family income lies between Rs.15001 and Rs.20000. 34.8 percent respondents family income lies above Rs.20000. 14.2 percent of respondents family income ranges between Rs.10001 and Rs.15000 and 6.6 percent respondents family income lies between Rs.5001 and Rs.10000.

Thus from the above table, it could be concluded that a majority of the sample respondents family income lies between Rs.15001and Rs.20000.

I. Family Debt

Among the 500 respondents, 82.4 percent of the respondents have family debt. 17.6 percent of them do not have family debt.

Thus from the above table, it can be concluded that a majority of the respondents are having debt in the family.

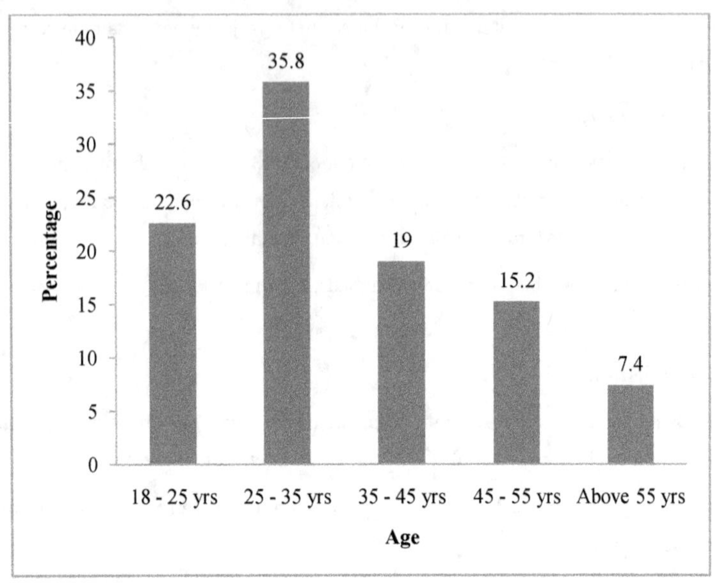

Exhibit 4.1.1: Exhibit Showing the Distribution of Respondents Based on Age

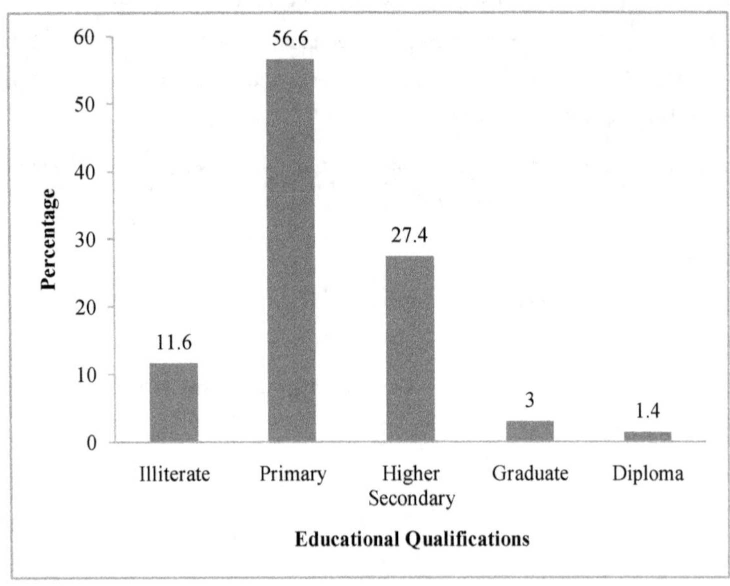

Exhibit 4.1.2: Exhibit Showing the Distribution of Respondents based on Educational Qualifications

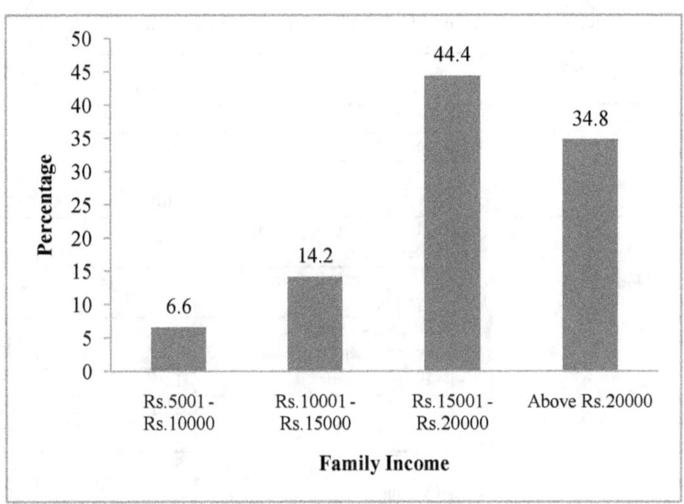

Exhibit 4.1.3: Exhibit Showing the Distribution of Respondents based on Family Income

2. *Occupational Profile of the Respondents*

Occupational profile of the respondents is taken into consideration to assess whether it influences the Quality of Work Life of Textile employee. The work related profile expresses their spread in terms of unit size, type of job activity, working section, employment status, total experience in Textile Industry, wage and work schedule. The distribution of the employees based on this occupational profile is given in table.4.1.2

A. *Size of Unit*

Among 500 respondents, 40 percent of the respondents are working in small and medium size units and the remaining 20 percent of the respondents are working in large size units. Thus from the above table, it can be concluded that majority of the respondents are working in small and medium size units.

B. *Type of Job Activity*

41 percent of the respondents are working in cutting, sewing, embroidering and packing unit. Another 27.4 percent of them work in composite unit. 21.2 percent of them work in fabrication, compacting and calendaring unit and the remaining 10.4 percent of the respondents are working in dyeing, bleaching and printing unit.

Thus from the above table, it can be concluded that a majority of the respondents are working in cutting, sewing, embroidering and packing units.

Table 4.1.2: Distribution of Respondents based on Occupational Profile

S.No	Occupational profile		No. of respondents	Percentage
A	Size of Unit	Small	200	40.0
		Medium	200	40.0
		Large	100	20.0
		Total	500	100.0
B	Type of Job Activity	Fabrication, Compacting and Calendaring	106	21.2
		Dyeing, Bleaching and Printing	52	10.4
		Cutting, Sewing, Embroidering and packing	205	41.0
		Composite unit	137	27.4
		Total	500	100.0
C	Working Section	Fabrication	128	25.6
		Dyeing	54	10.8
		Cutting	5	1.0
		Stitching	155	31.0
		Checking	40	8.0
		Ironing	60	12.0
		Packing	58	11.6
		Total	500	100.0
D	Employment Status	Temporary	472	94.4
		Permanent	28	5.6
		Total	500	100.0
E	Total Experience in Textile Industry (in year)	Less than 5	59	11.8
		5 – 10	250	50.0
		10 – 15	122	24.4
		15 – 20	15	3.0
		Above 20	54	10.8
		Total	500	100.0
F	Wage (p.m)	Below Rs.3000	10	2.0
		Rs.3001 -Rs. 6000	49	9.8
		Rs.6001 -Rs. 9000	107	21.4
		Rs. 9001 -Rs. 12000	155	31.0
		Above Rs.12000	179	35.8
		Total	500	100.0
G	Work Schedule	Day shift	165	33.0
		Afternoon shift	29	5.8
		Night shift	9	1.8
		Irregular shift on cal	93	18.6
		Rotating shift	204	40.8
		Total	500	100.0

Source: Primary Data

C. *Working Section*

From the table 4.1.2 it is understood that 31 percent of the respondents are working in stitching section. Another 25.6 percent work in fabrication section, 12 percent work in ironing section, 11.6 percent work in packing section, 10.8 percent work in dyeing section, 8 percent work in checking section and only 1 percent of the respondents are working in cutting section.

Thus from the above table, it can be concluded that a majority of the respondents are working in stitching section.

D. *Employment Status*

The study reveals that 94.4 percent of the respondents are temporary employees and remaining 5.6 percent of the respondents are permanent employees.

Thus from the above table, it can be concluded that a majority of the respondents are temporary employees.

E. *Total Experience in Textile Industry*

It is clear that 50 percent of the respondents have 5 to 10 years' experience, 24.4 percent of them have 10 to 15 years' experience and 11.8 percent of the respondents have less than 5 years' experience. Another 10.8 percent of them are in their job for a period of above 20 years and rest of the respondents (3 percent) have experience ranging between 15 and 20 years.

Thus from the above table, it can be concluded that a majority of the respondents have 5 to 10 years of experience.

F. *Wage*

35.8 percent of the respondents who earn wage above Rs.12000, 31 percent earn between Rs.9001 and Rs.12000 and 21.4 percent receive wage between Rs.6001 and Rs.9000. Another 9.8 percent earn between Rs.3001 and Rs.6000 and 2 percent of the respondent wage is below Rs.3000.

Thus from the above table, it can be concluded that majority of the respondents are earning above Rs.12000.

G. *Work Schedule*

Most of the respondents (40.8 percent) are working in rotating shift, 33 percent of the respondents are working in day shift, 18.6 percent are working in irregular shift , 5.8 percent are working in afternoon shift and remaining 1.8 percent are working in night shift.

Thus from the above table it can be concluded that a majority of the respondents are working in rotating shift.

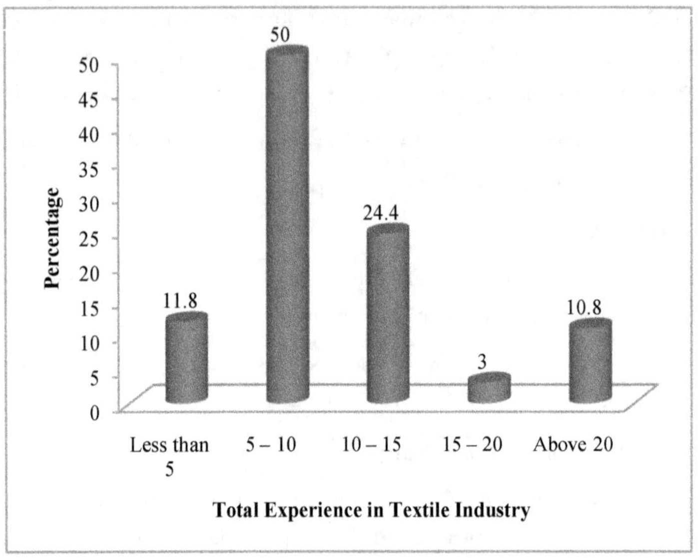

Exhibit 4.1.4: Exhibit Showing the Distribution of Respondents based on Experience in Textile Industry

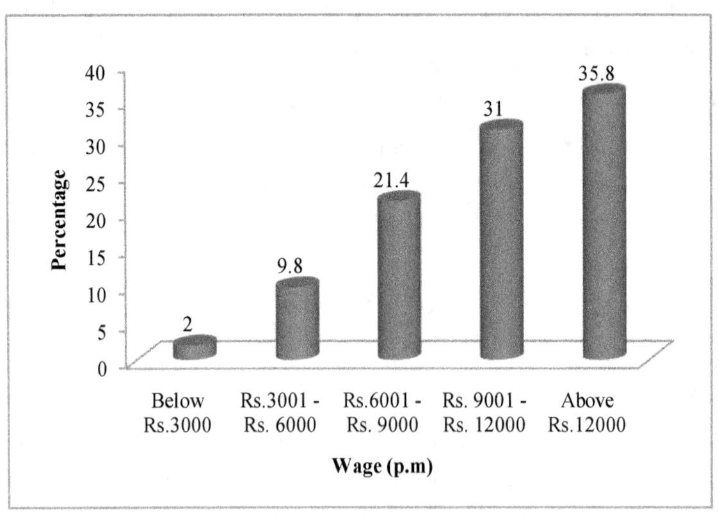

Exhibit 4.1.5: Exhibit Showing the Distribution of Respondents based on Wage (p.m)

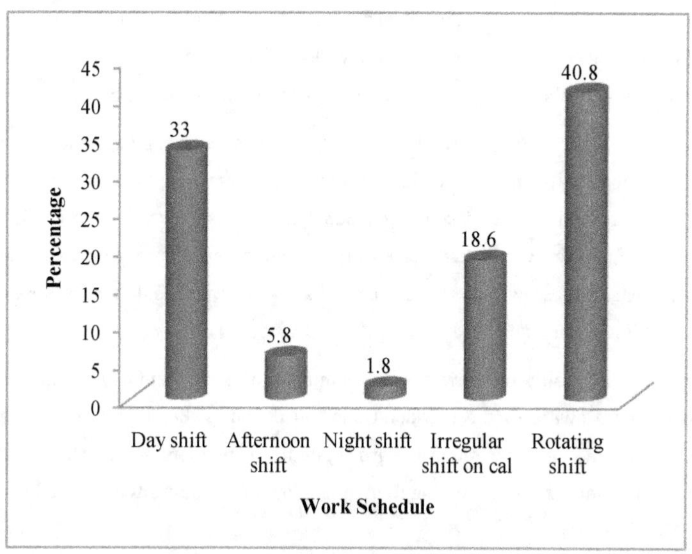

Exhibit 4.1.6: Exhibit Showing the Distribution of Respondents based on Work Schedule

Section II

Occupational Stress in Textile Industry

4.2.1. Introduction

More and more companies are starting to realize that a happy employee is a productive employee and they have started to look for ways to improve the work environment. Many have implemented various work-life programs to help employees, including alternate work arrangements, on-site childcare, exercise facilities, relaxed dress codes, and more. Quality-of-work-life programs go beyond work/life programs by focusing attention less on employee needs outside of work and realizing that job stress and the quality of life at work bears more directly on worker satisfaction. Open communications, mentoring programs and fostering more amicable relationships among workers are some of the ways to improve the quality of work life.

Workplace stress has increased in intensity and societal concern over the past three decades. Beginning in the 1990s, mental health professionals began noting the disturbing rise of work-related stress. Even with the unprecedented prosperity of the late 1990s, work-related stress rose continuously during that decade and continued to increase in the twenty-first century. In 2007, the American Psychological Association (APA) reported that one-third of Americans are living with extreme stress, with work cited as the most common source of stress (74%). Employees are also calling in "sick" in increasing numbers, largely because of stress.

The increasing incidence of work-related stress has wide-ranging effects, including absenteeism, impaired teamwork, workplace violence, decreased efficiency, and burnout. A 2005 survey (reported in the *Silicon Valley/San Jose Business Journal*) found that only 38 percent of the employees who called in sick were actually suffering from a physical illness. The other 62 percent of these workers who failed to show up were dealing with stress, family issues, morale issues, and motivational issues[2].

To improve the quality of work life and eliminate job stress, employers can also make efforts to be more aware of the workload and job demands. Employers need to examine employee training, communication, reward systems, coworker relationships and work environment. Employees often are able to give employers the best advice on reducing work stress.

This section consists of three parts. Part A: It presents the analysis of data relating to occupational stress of employees of textile industry. Part B: It presents the analysis of data relating to stress in association with occupational difference and Part C: It presents the analysis of data relating to factors contributing to stress management.

Proper assessment of employees will be helpful to know the causes of occupational stress of employees in textile industry. Therefore, the second objective of this study aims to know the causes of occupational stress of employees and their quality of work life. This section has been devoted to understand the occupational profile along with the causes of occupational stress. The size of respondents suffering from occupational stress has been described with the help of simple percentage. The occupational stress of the respondents depends mainly on the occupational related factors such as size of unit, type of job activity, total experience in Textile Industry, wage and work schedule. Descriptive statistics have been applied to assess the cause and frequency of occupational stress and factors in overcoming occupational stress.

To evaluate the relationship between occupational stress and occupational difference, Chi-square test has been used. The Chi-square has been used to test the association of the two variables. It is often applied to judge the significant difference between the observed and expected values. In other words, it is used to test the significance of one factor over the other.

Part A: Occupational Stress of the Employees

4.2.2. Occupational Stress of the Employees

The respondents were surveyed to know about the occupational stress. The size of respondents suffering from occupational stress has been described with the help of simple percentage analysis.

Table 4.2.1: Distribution of Respondents based on Occupational Stress

S.No	Occupational stress	No. of respondents	Percentage
	No	110	22.0
	Yes	**390**	**78.0**
	Total	**500**	**100.0**

Source: Primary Data

From the above table it is clearly understood that, 78 percent of the respondents are suffering from occupational stress and remaining 22 percent of the respondents are not suffering from occupational stress.

Thus from the above table, it can be concluded that a majority of the respondents are suffering from occupational stress.

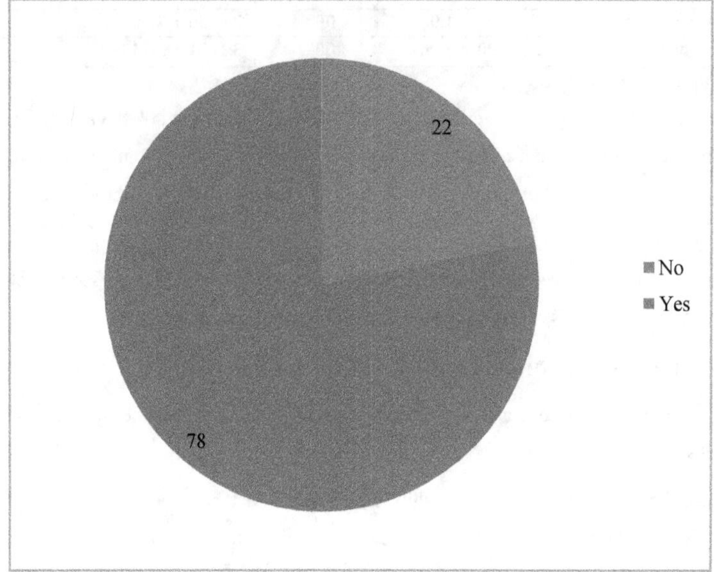

Exhibit 4.2.1: Exhibit Showing the Distribution of Respondents based on Occupational Stress

Part B: Stress in Association with Occupational Difference

4.2.3. *The Cause and Frequency of Occupational Stress*

The respondents were asked to give their opinion on various items relating to causes of occupational stress.

Based on the severity of the occupational stress, the respondents were asked to rate their opinion in four point scale ranging from often (4) to never (1). Higher the rating indicates higher causes of the item towards occupational stress.

Descriptive statistics with minimum, maximum, mean and standard deviation of stress frequency were found for each cause and the table is given below.

Table 4.2.2: Discrete Factors Contributing to Cause and Frequency of Occupational Stress

Cause and frequency	N	Minimum	Maximum	Mean	Standard Deviation
Volume of work	390	1.00	4.00	3.4872	.6639
New duties	390	1.00	4.00	2.1641	.8354
Complexities of work	390	1.00	4.00	2.5231	.9978
Documentation	390	1.00	4.00	1.7051	.9661
Covering for others work	390	1.00	4.00	2.7949	.9398
Changes in policy	390	1.00	4.00	2.2231	.9904
Job demands	390	1.00	4.00	2.9436	.7900
Family demands	390	1.00	4.00	3.1051	.8249

Source: Primary Data

From the above table, it is seen that the causes of occupational stress varied between a minimum of 1 to a maximum of 4. The highest mean was found for volume of work (3.4872) followed by demands for their family (3.1051). The lowest mean was found for documentation (1.7051).

Hence, it can be inferred that, among the various causes of occupational stress, volume of work and family demands contribute more towards occupational stress.

4.2.4. *Relationship between Unit Size and Occupational Stress*

It is assumed that there is a close affinity between the unit size and occupational stress of employees.

To test the significance of relationship, a chi-square test has been performed. The null hypothesis framed for this purpose to test the relationship is stated below.

H_0: There is no relationship between unit size and occupational stress

Table 4.2.3: Distribution of Respondents based on the Relationship between Unit Size and Occupational Stress

Size of Unit	Occupational stress				TOTAL	
	No		Yes		No.	%
	No.	%	No.	%		
Small	42	21.0	158	79.0	200	100.0
Medium	47	23.5	153	76.5	200	100.0
Large	21	21.0	79	79.0	100	100.0
TOTAL	110	22.0	390	78.0	500	100.0

Source: Primary Data

Chi-Square Test

Chi-Square	Value	Table value	df	Sig.	Hypothesis
	.437	5.991	2	Ns	Accepted

Table 4.2.3 shows that 23.5 percent of the respondents do not suffer from occupational stress in medium size units and 21 percent of the respondents do not suffer from occupational stress in small and large units.79 percent of the respondents suffer from occupational stress in small and large unit and 76.5 percent of the respondents suffer from occupational stress in medium size units.

This highlights the fact that majority of the respondents suffer from occupational stress irrespective of the size of units in which the employees of Textile industry are placed.

Chi –square test was applied to find the relationship between unit size and occupational stress. The calculated value of observed frequencies provided in table is 0.437. The table value for 2 degrees of freedom at 5 percent level of significance is 5.991. A comparison of the calculated value with that of the table value indicates, the calculated value is less than the table value and hence the null hypothesis is accepted. This indicates that relationship does not exist between unit size and occupational stress.

Thus from the analysis, it can be concluded that there is no significant relationship between the unit size and occupational stress of employees.

4.2.5. *Relationship between Type of Job Activity and Occupational Stress*

It is assumed that there is a close affinity between the type of job activity and occupational stress of employees. To test the significance of this relationship, a chi-square test has been performed. The null hypothesis framed for this purpose to test this relationship is stated below.

H_0: **There is no relationship between type of job activity and occupational stress.**

Table 4.2.4: Distribution of Respondents based on the Relationship between Type of Job Activity and Occupational Stress

Type of job activity	Occupational stress				TOTAL	
	No		Yes		No.	%
	No.	%	No.	%		
Fabrication, Compacting and Calendaring	20	18.9	86	81.1	106	100.0
Dyeing, Bleaching and Printing	14	26.9	38	73.1	52	100.0
Cutting, Sewing, Embroidering and packing	52	25.4	153	74.6	205	100.0
Composite unit	24	17.5	113	82.5	137	100.0
TOTAL	110	22.0	390	78.0	500	100.0

Source: Primary Data

Chi-Square Test

Chi-Square	Value	Table value	df	Sig.	Hypothesis
	4.297	7.815	3	Ns	Accepted

Table 4.2.4 exhibiting the relationship between type of job activity and occupational stress reveals that 26.9 percent of dyeing, bleaching and printing unit employees do not suffer from occupational stress and 82.5 percent of composite unit respondents suffer from occupational stress. Majority of the respondents suffer from occupational stress irrespective of the type of job activity they are involved.

Chi–square test was applied to find the relationship between the type of job activity and occupational stress. The calculated value of observed frequencies provided in the table is 4.297.

The table value for 3 degrees of freedom at 5 percent level of significance is 7.815. A comparison of the calculated value with that of the table value indicates that the calculated value is less than the table value and hence the null hypothesis is accepted. So, there is no relationship between the type of job activity and occupational stress.

Thus from the analysis, it can be concluded that there is no significant relationship between the type of job activity and occupational stress of employees.

4.2.6. Relationship between Work Experience and Occupational Stress

It is assumed that there is a close affinity between the total experience in textile industry and occupational stress of employees.

To test the significance relationship, a chi-square test has been performed. The null hypothesis framed for this purpose to test the relationship is given below.

H_0: **There is no relationship between work experience and occupational stress.**

Table 4.2.5: Distribution of Respondents based on the Relationship between Work Experience in Textile Industry and Occupational Stress

Work experience	Occupational stress				TOTAL	
	No		Yes		No.	%
	No.	%	No.	%		
Less than 5 years	13	22.0	46	78.0	59	100.0
5 – 10 years	58	23.2	192	76.8	250	100.0
10 – 15 years	24	19.7	98	80.3	122	100.0
15 – 20 years	3	20.0	12	80.0	15	100.0
Above 20 years	12	22.2	42	77.8	54	100.0
TOTAL	110	22.0	390	78.0	500	100.0

Source: Primary Data

Chi-Square Test

Chi-Square	Value	Table value	df	Sig.	Hypothesis
	.632	9.488	4	Ns	Accepted

Table 4.2.5 exhibiting the relationship between work experience in textile industry and occupational stress specifies that 23.2 percent of the respondents between 5 and 10 years experience in textile industry were not suffering from occupational stress and 80.3 percent of the respondents between10 and 15 years experience in textile industry were suffering from occupational stress. Majority of the respondents are suffering from occupational stress irrespective of the work experience in textile industry.

Chi –square test was applied to find the relationship between work experiences in textile industry and occupational stress. The calculated value of observed frequencies provided in table is 0.632. The table value for 4 degrees of freedom at 5 percent level of significance is 9.488. A comparison of the calculated value with that of the table value indicates that the calculated value is less than the table value and hence the null hypothesis is accepted. So, there is no relationship between work experience in textile industry and occupational stress of employees.

Thus from the analysis, it can be concluded that there is no significant relationship between the work experience in textile industry and occupational stress of employees.

4.2.7.   Relationship between Income and Occupational Stress

It is assumed that there is a close affinity between income and occupational stress on work of employees. To test the significance of this relationship, a chi-square test has been performed. The null hypothesis framed for this purpose to test the relationship is given below.

H_0: **There is no relationship between income (wage) and occupational stress.**

Table 4.2.6: Distribution of Respondents based on the Relationship between Income (Wage) and Occupational Stress

Wage (p.m)	Occupational stress				TOTAL	
	No		Yes		No.	%
	No.	%	No.	%		
Below Rs.3000	4	40.0	6	60.0	10	100.0
Rs.3001 -Rs. 6000	19	38.8	30	61.2	49	100.0
Rs.6001 -Rs. 9000	25	23.4	82	76.6	107	100.0
Rs. 9001 -Rs. 12000	39	25.2	116	74.8	155	100.0
Above Rs.12000	23	12.8	156	87.2	179	100.0
TOTAL	110	22.0	390	78.0	500	100.0

Source: Primary Data

Chi-Square Test

Chi-Square	Value	Table value	df	Sig.	Hypothesis
	19.678	13.277	4	**	Rejected

Table 4.2.6 exhibiting the relationship between income and occupational stress portray that 40 percent of the respondents who earn wage below Rs.3000 were not suffering from occupational stress and 87.2 percent of them earning above Rs.12000 were suffering from occupational stress.

Majority of the respondents were suffering from occupational stress irrespective of their earnings.

Chi –square test was applied to find the relationship between income and occupational stress. The calculated value of observed frequencies provided in table is 19.678. The table value for 4 degrees of freedom at 1 percent level of significance is 13.277.

A comparison of the calculated value with that of the table value indicates that the calculated value is higher than the table value and hence the null hypothesis is rejected. So, there is a relationship between income and occupational stress of employees.

Thus from the analysis, it can be concluded that there is a significant relationship between income and occupational stress of employees.

4.2.8. *Relationship between Work Schedule and Occupational Stress*

It is assumed that there is a close affinity between work schedule and occupational stress of employees. To test the significance of this relationship, a chi-square test has been performed. The null hypothesis framed for this purpose to test the relationship is given below.

H_0: There is no relationship between work schedule and occupational stress.

Table 4.2.7: Distribution of Respondents based on the Relationship between Work Schedule and Occupational Stress

Work Schedule	Occupational stress				TOTAL	
	No		Yes		No.	%
	No.	%	No.	%		
Day shift	50	30.3	115	69.7	165	100.0
Afternoon shift	10	34.5	19	65.5	29	100.0
Night shift	5	55.6	4	44.4	9	100.0
Irregular shift on cal	11	11.8	82	88.2	93	100.0
Rotating shift	34	16.7	170	83.3	204	100.0
TOTAL	110	22.0	390	78.0	500	100.0

Source: Primary Data

Chi-Square Test

Chi-Square	Value	Table value	df	Sig.	Hypothesis
	24.157	13.277	4	**	Rejected

Table 4.2.7 exhibiting the relationship between work schedule and occupational stress highlights that 55.6 percent of night shift employees are not suffering from occupational stress and 88.2 percent who are working in irregular shift were suffering from stress. Majority of the respondents are suffering from occupational stress irrespective of work schedule in textile industry.

Chi –square test was applied to find the relationship between work schedules and occupational stress.

The calculated value of observed frequencies provided in table is 24.157. The table value for 4 degrees of freedom at 1 percent level of significance is 13.277. A comparison of the calculated value with that of the table value indicates that the calculated value is higher than the table value and hence the null hypothesis is rejected.

So, there is a relationship between work schedule and occupational stress of employees.

Thus from the analysis, it can be concluded that there is a significant relationship between work Schedule and occupational stress of employees.

Part C: Factors Contributing to Stress Management

4.2.9. Factors Contributing to Overcome the Occupational Stress

The respondents were asked to give their opinion on various items relating to the factors contributing to overcome the occupational stress. Respondents were asked to give their opinion on certain factors overcome stress and were asked to rate those factors on a four point scale ranging from often (4) to never (1). Higher the rating of an item indicates larger contribution to overcome occupational stress by that factor. Descriptive statistics with minimum, maximum, mean and standard deviation of the frequency were found out for each item and the table is given below.

Table 4.2.8: Discrete Factors Contributing to Overcome Occupational Stress

Factor in overcome stress	N	Minimum	Maximum	Mean	S.D
Flexible hours	500	1.00	4.00	2.8140	1.0944
Unpaid leave (at least)	500	1.00	4.00	2.9680	.8925
Supportive Supervisor/ Manager	500	1.00	4.00	2.7980	.8802
Personal calls at work (if emergency)	500	1.00	4.00	2.7340	.9257
Promotional opportunities	500	1.00	4.00	2.2260	.9904
Relationship with other department and superiors	500	1.00	4.00	2.8480	.8755
No discrimination	500	1.00	4.00	2.5140	1.0771
Employee's personal health and family peace	500	1.00	4.00	2.8900	.9228

Source: Primary Data

From the above table, it is seen that the frequency of factors contributing to overcome occupational stress, varied between a minimum of 1 (never) to maximum of 4(often). The highest mean was found for unpaid leave (2.9680) followed by employees' personal health and family (2.8900). The lowest mean was found for promotional opportunities (2.2260). Hence, it can be concluded that, among the various factors in overcoming occupational stress, unpaid leave, employee's personal health and family peace contributes more towards reducing occupational stress.

Section-III

Factors Contributing to Quality of Work Life and their Association with Personal and Occupational Differences of Employees

4.3.1. Introduction

Companies are making noteworthy changes in working conditions. Experiments to improve the "Quality of Work Life" have pointed the way toward flexible job design, flexible working hours, flexible benefits and compensation, more open communications open posting/bidding for job assignments, and other innovations. Many companies are working to build rewards into the design of jobs, and to make compensation incentives more meaningful to employees.

Overall, practices in managing performance are changing significantly as companies feel pressures to improve their productivity through improved management of people. Such traditional practices as performance appraisal and job description are being reexamined and given new vitality through new approaches. As an important management concern, human resource planning focuses on improving performance[3].

QWL is a prescriptive concept, it attempts to design work environments so as to maximize concern for human welfare. It is a goal, as well as a process. The goal is the creation of more involving, satisfying and effective jobs and work environment for people at all levels of the organization. As a process, QWL involves effective efforts to realize this goal through active participation. The whole essence of QWL may be stated thus: "The QWL is cooperative rather than authoritarian: evolutionary and open rather than static and rigid; informal rather than rule-bound; impersonal rather than mechanistic; mutual respect and trust rather than hatred against each other"[4].

This section consists of two parts. Part A: It presents the analysis of data relating to factors determining Quality of Work Life and Part B: It presents the analysis of data relating to Quality of Work Life in association with personal and occupational differences.

4.3.2. *Measurement of Quality of Work Life*

Proper assessment of employees will be helpful to know about the Quality of Work Life of the employees. Therefore, one of the objectives of this study aims to know the various factors of Quality of Work Life based on the personal and occupational profile of employees in the Textile Industry. The personal and occupational profile of the employees have been described with the help of descriptive statistics to assess the factors of Quality of Work Life. The priority of QWL factors have been determined through ranks assigned by the respondents against each factor and the mean scores arrived through the percentages of ranks obtained. Ranking was used to rank the preference of the respondents on different aspects of QWL. By using Factor analysis, 11 major factors were identified within the various factors which influence the Quality of work life of employees in the Textile industry units at Tirupur District. F-test and t-test have been used to find the association between personal and occupational profile of the respondents with the major QWL factors.

T-test is used in the 't' distribution and is considered an appropriate test for judging the significance of a sample mean or for judging the significant difference between the means of two samples of personal and occupational profile of employees and factors of Quality of Work Life. ANOVA technique is applied when three or more number of groups is to be compared on the basis of their means. It is an extension of "T-test" used to test the homogeneity of several means. In this study, ANOVA is used to compare the different personal and occupational profile factors with the factors of Quality of Work Life. The results are presented with suitable hypothesis and relevant interpretations.

Regression is a statistical measure that attempts to determine the strength of the relationship between one dependent variable (usually denoted by Y) and a series of other changing variables (known as independent variables). Here the variable on which the overall factor of Quality of Work Life depends are discussed by applying multiple regression analysis. This is indicated through the coefficient of determination (r^2).

Part A: Factors Determining Quality of Work Life

4.3.3. *Discrete Factors Contributing to Quality of Work Life*

The respondents opinion on forty four factors of Quality of Work Life which determination the employer-employee relationship, incentives, development and encouragement, grievance redressal, stress management, wage structure, training, working conditions, work life balance, job satisfaction and autonomy have been studied individually to find the most favourable and the least favourable factor of QWL.

Five point Likert's scale has been applied to record the score of respondents against each factor of QWL among textile employees in Tirupur District. The scale ranges from 1 to 5.

The scores have been allotted as follows. The respondents were asked to give their opinion on various items determining the Quality of Work Life.

A score of 5 is allotted when the respondents strongly agree with the statement, a score of 4 is allotted when the respondents agree with the statement, a score of 3 is allotted when the respondent takes a neutral statement, a score of 2 is allotted when the respondents disagree and a score of 1 is allotted when respondents strongly disagreed with the statement.

Descriptive statistics with minimum, maximum, mean and standard deviation of respondents agreement were found for each item and the table is given below.

Table 4.3.1: Discrete factors contributing to Quality of Work Life

S.No	Quality of Work Life factors	N	Min.	Max.	Mean	S.D
1	The employees are satisfied with the spirit of team work	500	1.00	5.00	4.0860	.7667
2	The job requires me to work very fast and keep learning	500	2.00	5.00	3.9740	.7941
3	The company provides attractive bonus	500	2.00	5.00	4.1780	.7533
4	Shift mechanism affects the maintenance of family relationship	500	1.00	5.00	3.8440	.8468
5	The employees are invited and encouraged to offer suggestions	500	2.00	5.00	3.7260	.8535
6	Hard work and achievements are recognized appropriately	500	1.00	5.00	3.8700	.9690
7	The company encourages the employees for their self-development	500	1.00	5.00	3.9120	.9066
8	The company provides fair and adequate wage	500	1.00	5.00	4.0080	1.1656
9	The company provides variety of fringe benefits	500	1.00	5.00	2.5820	1.2972
10	The company provides equal wage to the same cadre	500	1.00	5.00	4.1060	.9447
11	The wage plan is consistent with the other companies	500	1.00	5.00	4.3320	.7791
12	The organization is providing enough instruction, high quality tools and techniques	500	1.00	5.00	3.3300	.9502
13	The company provides adequate incentives	500	1.00	5.00	2.3620	1.1721
14	The company provides special incentive for prompt work	500	1.00	5.00	2.0560	1.2570
15	Regular training and development programmes are conducted	500	1.00	5.00	3.4720	1.2777
16	The training helped in improving the quality of work	500	1.00	5.00	3.3900	1.1750
17	The management attempt to understand stresses, its causes	500	1.00	5.00	3.6720	.9952
18	The management arrange periodical workshops for control and reduction of stress	500	1.00	5.00	3.6660	1.0811
19	I trust the management at the place where I work	500	1.00	5.00	3.2200	1.1163
20	The employees are listened to and their views are taken into consideration	500	1.00	5.00	3.8980	.8130
21	The management is really keen to redress the grievances	500	1.00	5.00	3.1340	1.1343
22	The employees have sense of community and inter personal openness	500	1.00	5.00	3.5380	.8521
23	I feel comfortable, secured and satisfied with my job	500	1.00	5.00	3.9000	.7970
24	The employees have a sense of fair chance to ventilate their grievance	500	1.00	5.00	3.7980	.8430
25	The company provides scope for appeal against redressal of grievance	500	1.00	5.00	3.5940	.9915
26	The employees are listened to and their views are taken into consideration	500	1.00	5.00	3.5160	.9652
27	No discrimination based upon race, color, sex, sexual orientation	500	1.00	5.00	2.5140	1.3732
28	The work schedule provide leisure time	500	1.00	5.00	3.4920	1.0431
29	The management takes efforts to reduce monotonous and disinteresting job	500	1.00	5.00	3.5820	1.0889
30	The company promotes mutual trust and community of interests	500	1.00	5.00	3.3120	1.0568
31	The company properly promotes and maintains human relations	500	1.00	5.00	3.4140	1.2254
32	Hours of work interferes with family relationships	500	1.00	5.00	3.5940	1.0542
33	The working conditions provide no risk to the employees	500	1.00	5.00	3.7660	1.0244
34	The company provides adequate safety measures to the employees	500	1.00	5.00	3.8260	.8609
35	The work schedule and timings are followed as per the Government regulations	500	1.00	5.00	3.8660	1.0090
36	I am treated with respect in the work place	500	1.00	5.00	3.7440	1.1546
37	The physical environment of the company is comfortable	500	1.00	5.00	3.9400	.8329
38	The superior is concerned about the welfare activities of the Employees	500	1.00	5.00	3.9380	.7996
39	The management provides greater autonomy to the subordinates	500	1.00	5.00	3.9480	.8041
40	On the job, I know exactly what is expected of me	500	1.00	5.00	3.7800	.9172
41	There is cordial and close relation between management and employees	500	1.00	5.00	2.8740	1.3747
42	Having competency is the basis for promotion	500	1.00	5.00	2.9920	1.3295
43	The company provides large amount of part time work	500	1.00	5.00	2.0980	1.1274
44	Flexible reporting / leaving schedule and lunch timings are allowed	500	1.00	5.00	2.3120	1.0867

From the above table, it is seen that the quality of work life varied between a minimum of 1 to maximum of 5. The highest mean was found for the wage plan that is consistent with other companies (4.3320) followed by the company's attractive bonus (4.1780). The lowest mean was found for the statement company provides special incentive for prompt work (2.0560). Hence, it can be influenced that among the various factors of the quality of work life, consistent wage plan and attractive bonus contributes more towards the quality of work life.

4.3.4. *Priority of Quality of Work Life Factors*

The respondents were asked to rank the item as to which factor contributes more towards the quality of work life. The ranks were assigned based on the importance given to each items. The ranks ranged between 1 and 9 with 1 as the most essential factor and 9 as the least essential. The means of such ranks assigned is given in the table below.

Table 4.3.2: Priority of QWL Factors

Factors	Mean	Rank
State of physical health	5.2200	6
State of pursuits	5.6580	9
State of fulfillment	4.6300	3
Standard of living	4.3640	1
State of relationships	4.5700	2
State of mental outlook	5.3880	8
Capacity to give	4.6520	4
State of job security	5.2040	5
State of job satisfaction	5.2960	7

The mean ranks were found out for each item and they were further arranged from 1 to 9 by assigning 1 for the least mean value and 9 for the maximum mean value. Hence, it can be inferred that standard of living (4.36) ranks at the top as the most essential item followed by the state of relationships (4.57). The least important item is found to be the state of pursuit (5.65).

Part B: Quality of Work Life in Association with Personal and Occupational Differences

4.3.5. *Quality of Work Life and Its Association with Employees' Personal and Occupational Differences*

Factor 1: Employer-Employee Relationship

In this section, an attempt has been made to examine the association between the employees opinion towards employer-employee relationship with their personal and occupational profile. T-test and F-test have been applied to find the association by formulating the null hypothesis.

Ho: There is no significant association between employees' opinion towards employer-employee relationship and their personal / occupational profile.

1. Personal Profile and Employer-Employee Relationship

Table 4.3.3 portrays the mean values of employees' opinion towards employer-employee relationship for all independent variables that determine the personal profile such as age, gender, marital status, educational qualifications, family size, family income and family debt.

Table 4.3.3: Distribution of Respondents based on the Association between Personal Profile and their Opinion Towards Employer-Employee Relationships

S.No	Variables	Group	Mean	SD	No.	F test	T Test	df.	Table Value	Sig.
1	Age	18 - 25 yrs	32.06	2.24	113	152.242		499	4.684	**
		25 - 35 yrs	28.20	2.80	179					
		35 - 45 yrs	22.28	5.21	95					
		45 - 55 yrs	22.46	4.50	76					
		Above 55 yrs	21.16	3.62	37					
2	Gender	Male	26.72	5.54	289		0.821	498	1.968	Ns
		Female	26.32	5.18	211					
3	Marital Status	Unmarried	30.10	3.59	124	30.545		499	3.821	**
		Married	25.75	5.47	248					
		Divorced	25.27	5.10	85					
		Widowed	23.49	5.01	43					
4	Educational Qualifications	Illiterate	23.28	4.51	58	13.343		499	3.357	**
		Primary	26.13	5.57	283					
		Higher Secondary	28.76	4.45	137					
		Graduate	28.13	4.52	15					
		Diploma	24.43	5.77	7					
5	Family Members	1 - 3	25.49	5.44	120	5.658		499	4.648	**
		4- 6	26.61	5.48	315					
		Above 6	28.25	4.34	65					
6	Family Income	Rs.5001 - Rs.10000	26.79	4.39	33	1.828		499	2.623	Ns
		Rs.10001 - Rs.15000	26.51	5.08	71					
		Rs.15001 - Rs.20000	25.99	5.65	222					
		Above Rs.20000	27.25	5.30	174					
7	Family debt	No	26.41	4.96	88		0.278	498	1.968	Ns
		Yes	26.58	5.48	412					

Source: Primary Data

NS-Non Significant,   * - 5 % level of Significance,   ** - 1 % Level of Significance

T-test and F-test results shows that the calculated value is lower than the table value in the case of gender, family income and family debt at 1 percent significance level. The hypothesis is accepted and therefore, there is no association found between these personal variables and the employer- employee relationships. Eventually, *the* calculated *value is higher than the table value at 1 percent significance level in the case of personal variables such as age, marital status, educational qualifications and family members. Therefore, the null hypothesis is rejected* in these cases. The influence of these variables on employer-employee relationships has been discussed as under:

- **Age**

The mean score for opinion towards employer-employee relationship is high for employees aged between 18 and 25 years (32.06) and low for the respondents above 55 years of age (21.16). Young employees are found to agree more on employer-employee relationship compared to old aged employees.

- **Gender**

The mean score for opinion towards employer-employee relationship is high for male employees (26.72) and low for female employees (26.32). Male employees are found to agree more on employer-employee relationships compared to female employees.

- **Marital Status**

The mean score for opinion towards employer-employee relationship is high for unmarried employees (30.10) and low for widow employees (23.49).Unmarried respondent groups are found to agree more on employer-employee relationship compared to widow employees.

- **Educational Qualifications**

The mean score for opinion towards employer-employee relationship is high for the respondent who are educated up to higher secondary level (28.76) and low for illiterate group (23.28). Higher secondary level respondent groups are found to agree more on employer-employee relationship compared to illiterate groups.

- **Family Size**

The mean score for opinion towards employer-employee relationship is high for the respondents whose family has above 6 members (28.25) and low for the respondents whose family members are between 1 and 3 (25.49). That is, respondents whose family has above 6 members are found to agree more on employer- employee relationship compared to the respondents whose family members are between 1 and 3.

- **Family Income**

The mean score for opinion towards employer-employee relationship is high for the respondents whose family income is above Rs.20000 per month (27.25) and low for the respondents family whose income is between Rs.15001 and Rs.20000 per month (25.99).

Respondents whose family income is above Rs.20000 are found to agree more on employer-employee relationship compared to the respondents whose family income lies between Rs.15001 and Rs.20000 per month.

- **Family Debt**

The mean score for opinion towards employer-employee relationship is high for the respondents who have family debt (26.58) and low for the respondents who do not have family debt (26.41). Respondents who have debt in their family are found to agree more on employer-employee relationship compared to the respondents who does not have family debt .

2. Occupational Profile and Employer-Employee Relationship

Table 4.3.4 portrays the mean values of employees' opinion towards employer-employee relationship for all independent variables that determine the occupational profile such as unit size, type of job activity, work experience, wage and work schedule.

Table 4.3.4: Distribution of Respondents based on the Association between Occupational Profile and their Opinion Towards Employer-Employee Relationship

S.No	Variables	Group	Mean	SD	No.	F test	T Test	df.	Table Value	Sig.
1	Size of Unit	Small	22.93	4.45	200	128.669		499	4.648	**
		Medium	28.00	4.56	200					
		Large	30.91	3.85	100					
2	Type of Job Activity	Fabrication, Compacting and Calendaring	27.54	4.92	106	2.294		499	2.623	Ns
		Dyeing, Bleaching and Printing	27.25	4.30	52					
		Cutting, Sewing, Embroidering and packing	25.99	5.49	205					
		Composite unit	26.38	5.85	137					
3	Total Experience in Textile Industry	Less than 5	31.75	2.50	59	106.084		499	3.357	**
		5 - 10	28.57	3.82	250					
		10 - 15	20.95	4.96	122					
		15 - 20	23.67	5.04	15					
		Above 20	25.02	3.01	54					
4	Wage (p.m)	Below Rs.3000	28.70	4.97	10	2.665		499	2.390	*
		Rs.3001 -Rs. 6000	27.47	4.71	49					
		Rs.6001 -Rs. 9000	27.62	5.02	107					
		Rs. 9001 -Rs. 12000	26.05	5.95	155					
		Above Rs.12000	25.98	5.18	179					
5	Work Schedule	Day shift	26.36	5.09	165	1.164		499	2.390	Ns
		Afternoon shift	25.48	5.02	29					
		Night shift	26.67	3.35	9					
		Irregular shift on cal	25.98	6.83	93					
		Rotating shift	27.12	4.97	204					

Source: Primary Data

NS-Non Significant, * - 5 % level of Significance, ** - 1 % Level of Significance.

F-test results shows that the calculated value is lower than the table value in the case of type of job activity and work schedule at either 5 percent or 1 percent significance level. The hypothesis is accepted and therefore, there is no association found between these occupational variables and the employer- employee relationship. At the same time, *the calculated value is higher than the table value at either 5 percent or 1 percent significance level in the case of occupational variables such as unit size, work experience and wage. Therefore, the null hypothesis is rejected* in these cases. The influence of these variables on employer-employee relationship has been discussed as under:

- **Size of Unit**

The mean score for opinion towards employer-employee relationship is high for the respondents who work in large units (30.91) and low for the respondents who work in small units (22.93). Respondents who are working in large units are found to agree more on employer-employee relationship compared to respondents who are working in small units.

- **Type of Job Activity**

The mean score for opinion towards employer-employee relationship is high for the respondents who are involved in fabrication, compacting and calendaring activities (27.54) and low for the respondents who are involved in cutting, sewing, embroidering and packing activities (25.99). Respondents who are involved in fabrication, compacting and calendaring activities are found to agree more on employer-employee relationship compared to the respondents who are involved in cutting, sewing, embroidering and packing activities.

- **Total Experience in Textile Industry**

The mean score for opinion towards employer-employee relationship is high for the respondents' who have less than 5 years' experience (31.75) and low for the respondents who have experience between 10-15 years (20.95). Hence, the respondents who have less than 5 years' experience are found to agree more on employer-employee relationship compared to the respondents who have experience between 10 and 15 years.

- **Wage**

The mean score for opinion towards employer-employee relationship is high for the respondents who earn below Rs.3000 (28.70) and low for the respondents who earn above Rs.12000 (25.98). Hence, the respondents who earn below Rs.3000 are found to agree more on employer-employee relationship compared to the respondents who earn above Rs.12000.

- **Work Schedule**

The mean score for opinion towards employer-employee relationship is high for the respondents who are working in rotating shift (27.12) and low for the respondents who are working in afternoon shift (25.48). Hence, the respondents who are working in rotating shifts are found to agree more on employer-employee relationship compared to the respondents who are working in afternoon shift.

Factor 2: Incentives

In this section, an attempt has been made to examine the association between the employees opinion towards incentives with their personal and occupational profile. T-test and F-test have been applied to find the association by formulating the null hypothesis.

Ho: There is no significant association between employees' opinion towards incentives and their personal / occupational profile.

1. Personal Profile and Incentives

Table 4.3.5 portrays the mean values of employees' opinion towards incentives for all independent variables that determine the personal profile such as age, gender, marital status, educational qualifications, family size, family income and family debt.

Table 4.3.5: Distribution of Respondents based on the Association between Personal Profile and Their Opinion Towards Incentives

S.No	Variables	Group	Mean	SD	No.	F test	T Test	df.	Table Value	Sig.
1	Age	18 - 25 yrs	12.67	2.81	113	6.114		499	3.357	**
		25 - 35 yrs	13.25	3.27	179					
		35 - 45 yrs	13.62	2.92	95					
		45 - 55 yrs	14.53	4.23	76					
		Above 55 yrs	11.78	2.42	37					
2	Gender	Male	14.09	3.28	289		6.797	498	2.586	**
		Female	12.16	2.95	211					
3	Marital Status	Unmarried	12.32	2.62	124	11.993		499	3.821	**
		Married	14.10	3.46	248					
		Divorced	12.94	3.13	85					
		Widowed	11.95	3.05	43					
4	Educational Qualifications	Illiterate	12.90	3.41	58	3.972		499	3.357	**
		Primary	13.23	3.42	283					
		Higher Secondary	13.11	2.86	137					
		Graduate	16.27	2.81	15					
		Diploma	15.00	2.38	7					
5	Family Members	1 - 3	12.63	3.20	120	14.516		499	4.648	**
		4- 6	13.12	3.22	315					
		Above 6	15.20	3.09	65					
6	Family Income	Rs.5001 - Rs.10000	12.88	3.31	33	2.458		499	2.623	Ns
		Rs.10001 - Rs.15000	12.80	3.19	71					
		Rs.15001 - Rs.20000	13.07	3.22	222					
		Above Rs.20000	13.80	3.36	174					
7	Family Debt	No	12.68	3.41	88		1.873	498	1.968	Ns
		Yes	13.40	3.25	412					

Source: Primary Data

NS-Non Significant,   * - 5 % level of Significance,   ** - 1 % Level of Significance

T-test and F-test results shows that the calculated value is lower than the table value in the case of family income and family debt at 1 percent significance level. The hypothesis is accepted and therefore, there is no association found between these personal variables and the incentives. At the same time, *the calculated value is higher than the table value at 1 percent significance level in the case personal variables such as age, gender, marital status, educational qualifications and family size. Therefore, null hypothesis is rejected* in these cases.

The influence of these variables on employee opinion towards incentives has been discussed as under:

- **Age**

The mean score for opinion towards incentives is high for the respondents who are aged between 45 and 55 years (14.53) and low for the respondents who are aged above 55 years (11.78). That is, the respondents who are between 45 and 55 years of age are found to agree more on incentives compared to the respondents above 55 years.

- **Gender**

The mean score for opinion towards incentives is high for male respondents (14.09) and low for female respondents (12.16). That is, the male respondents are found to agree more on incentives compared to female respondents.

- **Marital Status**

The mean score for opinion towards incentives is high for married respondents (14.10) and low for widowed respondents (11.95). That is, the married respondents are found to agree more on incentives compared to widow respondents.

- **Educational Qualifications**

The mean score for opinion towards incentives is high for graduate respondents (16.27) and low for illiterate respondents (12.90). That is, the respondents who are at graduate level are found to agree more on incentives compared to illiterate groups.

- **Family Size**

The mean score for opinion towards incentives is high for the respondents whose family has above 6 members (15.20) and low for the respondents whose family consists between 1 and 3 members (12.63). That is, respondents whose family has above 6 members are found to agree more on incentives compared to the respondents whose family members are between 1 and 3.

- **Family Income**

The mean score for opinion towards incentives is high for the respondents whose family income is above Rs.20000 (13.80) and low for the respondents whose family income is between Rs.10001 and Rs.15000 (12.80). That is, respondents whose family income is above Rs.20000 are found to agree more on incentives compared to the respondents whose family income is between Rs.10001 and Rs.15000.

- **Family Debt**

The mean score for opinion towards incentives is high for the respondents who have family debt (13.40) and low for the respondents who do not have family debt (12.68). That is, respondents who have family debt are found to agree more on incentives compared to the respondents who do not have family debt.

2. *Occupational Profile and Incentives*

Table 4.3.6 portrays the mean values of employees' opinion towards incentives for all independent variables that determine the occupational profile such as unit size, type of job activity, work experience, wage and work schedule.

Table 4.3.6: Distribution of Respondents based on the Association between Occupational Profile and their Opinion Towards Incentives

S.No	Variables	Group	Mean	SD	No.	F test	T - Test	df.	Table Value	Sig.
1	Size of Unit	Small	12.25	2.69	200	17.311		499	4.648	**
		Medium	13.95	3.56	200					
		Large	13.99	3.30	100					
2	Type of job Activity	Fabrication, Compacting and Calendaring	13.83	3.45	106	7.671		499	3.821	**
		Dyeing, Bleaching and Printing	14.21	3.13	52					
		Cutting, Sewing, Embroidering and packing	12.46	3.06	205					
		Composite unit	13.71	3.31	137					
3	Total Experience in Textile Industry	Less than 5	12.80	2.89	59					
		5 - 10	13.06	3.17	250	8.549		499	3.357	**
		10 - 15	12.80	3.00	122					
		15 - 20	14.53	3.80	15					
		Above 20	15.52	3.80	54					
4	Wage (p.m)	Below Rs.3000	12.70	4.08	10	13.104		499	3.357	**
		Rs.3001 -Rs. 6000	12.37	2.86	49					
		Rs.6001 -Rs. 9000	12.23	2.73	107					
		Rs. 9001 -Rs. 12000	12.78	3.13	155					
		Above Rs.12000	14.61	3.38	179					
5	Work Schedule	Day shift	12.35	3.02	165	7.092		499	3.357	**
		Afternoon shift	12.31	2.92	29					
		Night shift	13.89	3.41	9					
		Irregular shift on cal	13.51	3.12	93					
		Rotating shift	14.03	3.42	204					

Source: Primary Data

NS-Non Significant,   * - 5 % level of Significance,   ** - 1 % Level of Significance

F-test results shows that *the calculated value is higher than the table value at 1 percent significance level in the case of unit size , type of job activity, work experience, wage and work schedule. Null hypothesis is rejected in these cases and therefore, there is a relationship found between these occupational variables and the opinion towards incentives.* The influence of these variables on the employee opinion towards incentives has been discussed as under:

- **Size of Unit**

The mean score for opinion towards incentives is high for the respondents who are working in large units (13.99) and low for the respondents who are working in small units (12.25). That is, respondents who are working in large units are found to agree more on incentives compared to employees working in small units.

- **Type of Job Activity**

The mean score for opinion towards incentives is high for the respondents who are working in dyeing, bleaching and printing sections (14.21) and low for the respondents who are working in cutting, sewing, embroidering and packing sections (12.46). That is, respondents who are working in dyeing, bleaching and printing sections are found to agree more on incentives compared to employee involved in cutting, sewing, embroidering and packing activities.

- **Total Experience in Textile Industry**

The mean score for opinion towards incentives is high for the respondents above 20 years experience (15.52) and low for the respondents less than 5 years experience and between 10 and 15 years experience (12.80). That is, the respondents above 20 years experience are found to agree more on incentives compared to the respondents less than 5 years and between 10 and 15 years of experience.

- **Wage**

The mean score for opinion towards incentives is high for the respondents who earn above Rs.12000 (14.61) and low for the respondents who earn between Rs.6001 and Rs.9000 (12.23). That is, the respondents who earn above Rs.12000 are found to agree more on incentives compared to the respondents who earn between Rs.6001 and Rs.9000.

- **Work Schedule**

The mean score for opinion towards incentives is high for the respondents who are working in rotating shifts (14.03) and low for the respondents who are working in afternoon shift (12.31). That is, the respondents who are working in rotating shift are found to agree more on incentives compared to the respondents working in afternoon shifts.

Factor 3: Development and Encouragement

In this section, an attempt has been made to examine the association between the employees' opinion towards development and encouragement with their personal and occupational profile. T-test and F-test have been applied to find the association by formulating the null hypothesis.

Ho: There is no significant association between employees' opinion towards development and encouragement and their personal / occupational profile.

1. *Personal Profile and Employees Opinion Towards Development and Encouragement*

Table 4.3.7 portrays the mean values of employees' opinion towards development and encouragement for all independent variables that determine the personal profile such as age, gender, marital status, educational qualifications, family size, family income and family debt.

Table 4.3.7: Distribution of Respondents based on the Association between Personal Profile and their Opinion Towards Development and Encouragement

S.No	Variables	Group	Mean	SD	No.	F test	T Test	df.	Table Value	Sig.
1	Age	18 - 25 yrs	22.72	2.52	113	23.252		499	3.357	**
		25 - 35 yrs	21.90	2.60	179					
		35 - 45 yrs	23.08	3.75	95					
		45 - 55 yrs	20.58	1.83	76					
		Above 55 yrs	25.46	2.53	37					
2	Gender	Male	23.44	2.44	289		10.297	498	2.586	**
		Female	20.91	3.03	211					
3	Marital Status	Unmarried	22.51	2.38	124	2.687		499	2.623	*
		Married	22.29	3.05	248					
		Divorced	21.89	3.07	85					
		Widowed	23.42	3.65	43					
4	Educational Qualifications	Illiterate	22.84	3.29	58	.653		499	2.390	Ns
		Primary	22.32	3.08	283					
		Higher Secondary	22.20	2.72	137					
		Graduate	22.87	2.50	15					
		Diploma	22.86	1.35	7					
5	Family Members	1 - 3	22.23	2.99	120	2.810		499	3.014	Ns
		4- 6	22.26	3.01	315					
		Above 6	23.18	2.66	65					
6	Family Income	Rs.5001 - Rs.10000	21.85	3.15	33	1.026		499	2.623	Ns
		Rs.10001 - Rs.15000	22.03	3.08	71					
		Rs.15001 - Rs.20000	22.37	3.01	222					
		Above Rs.20000	22.61	2.85	174					
7	Family Debt	No	21.70	3.01	88		2.329	498	1.968	*
		Yes	22.51	2.95	412					

Source: Primary Data

NS-Non Significant,   * - 5 % level of Significance,   ** - 1 % Level of Significance

T-test and F-test results shows that the calculated value is lower than the table value in the case of educational qualifications, family members and family income at either 5 percent or 1 percent significance level.

The hypothesis is accepted and therefore, there is no association found between these personal variables and opinion towards development and encouragement.

At the same time, *the calculated value is higher than the table value at either 5 percent or 1 percent significance level in the case of personal variables such as age, gender, marital status, and family debt. Therefore, null hypothesis is rejected* in these cases.

The influence of these variables on the employee opinion towards development and encouragement has been discussed as under:

- **Age**

The mean score for opinion towards development and encouragement is high for respondents above 55 years (25.46) and low for respondents between 45 and 55 years (20.58).

That is, respondents who are above 55 years are found to agree more on development and encouragement compared to the respondents between 45-55 years.

- **Gender**

The mean score for opinion towards development and encouragement is high for male respondents (23.44) and low for female respondents (20.91). That is, male respondents are found to agree more on development and encouragement compared to female respondents.

- **Marital Status**

The mean score for opinion towards development and encouragement is high for widow respondents (23.42) and low for divorced respondents (21.89). That is, respondents who are widowed are found to agree more on development and encouragement compared to divorced groups.

- **Educational Qualifications**

The mean score for opinion towards development and encouragement is high for the respondents who are graduated (22.87) and low for the respondents who are qualified up to higher secondary level (22.20).

That is, respondents who are graduates are found to agree more on development and encouragement compared to the respondents who are educated up to higher secondary level.

- **Family Size**

The mean score for opinion towards development and encouragement is high for the respondents whose family has above 6 members (23.18) and low for the respondents whose family has between 1 and 3 members (22.23).

That is, respondents whose family has above 6 members are found to agree more on development and encouragement compared to the respondents whose family has between 1 and 3 members.

- **Family Income**

The mean score for opinion towards development and encouragement is high for the respondents whose family income is above Rs.20000 (22.61) and low for the respondents whose family income is between Rs.5001 and Rs.10000 (21.85).

That is, respondents whose family income is above Rs.20000 are found to agree more on development and encouragement compared to the respondents whose family income is between Rs.5001 and Rs.10000.

- **Family Debt**

The mean score for opinion towards development and encouragement is high for the respondents who have family debt (22.51) and low for the respondents who do not have family debt (21.70).

That is, the respondents who have family debt are found to agree more on development and encouragement compared to the respondents who do not have family debt.

2. *Occupational Profile and Opinion Towards Development and Encouragement*

Table 4.3.8 portrays the mean values of employees' opinion towards development and encouragement for all independent variables that determine the occupational profile such as unit size, type of job activity, work experience, wage and work schedule.

Table 4.3.8: Distribution of Respondents based on the Association between Occupational Profile and their Opinion Towards Development and Encouragement

S.No	Variables	Group	Mean	SD	No.	F test	T Test	df.	Table Value	Sig.
1	Size of Unit	Small	21.52	3.19	200	14.994		499	4.648	**
		Medium	22.82	2.83	200					
		Large	23.19	2.35	100					
2	Type of job Activity	Fabrication, Compacting and Calendaring	22.52	2.82	106	2.701		499	2.623	*
		Dyeing, Bleaching and Printing	22.15	2.72	52					
		Cutting, Sewing, Embroidering and packing	22.00	3.11	205					
		Composite unit	22.90	2.92	137					
3	Total Experience in Textile Industry	Less than 5	22.85	2.82	59	9.088		499	3.357	**
		5 - 10	21.63	2.72	250					
		10 - 15	22.94	3.14	122					
		15 - 20	23.93	2.69	15					
		Above 20	23.56	3.11	54					
4	Wage (p.m)	Below Rs.3000	21.80	2.20	10	18.072		499	3.357	**
		Rs.3001 -Rs. 6000	23.65	3.22	49					
		Rs.6001 -Rs. 9000	20.75	2.84	107					
		Rs. 9001 -Rs. 12000	21.99	2.96	155					
		Above Rs.12000	23.36	2.50	179					
5	Work Schedule	Day shift	21.08	3.08	165	18.177		499	3.357	**
		Afternoon shift	22.79	3.79	29					
		Night shift	22.56	2.19	9					
		Irregular shift on cal	24.11	2.53	93					
		Rotating shift	22.55	2.50	204					

Source: Primary Data

NS-Non Significant,   * - 5 % level of Significance, ** - 1 % Level of Significance

F-test results shows that *the calculated value is higher than the table value at either 5 percent or 1 percent significance level in the case of unit size, type of job activity, experience, wage and work schedule.*

The null hypothesis is rejected in these cases and therefore, there is association between these occupational variables and opinion towards development and encouragement.

The influence of these variables on employee opinion towards development and encouragement has been discussed as under:

- **Size of Unit**

The mean score for opinion towards development and encouragement is high for the respondents who are working in large units (23.19) and low for the respondents who are working in small units (21.52). That is, the respondents who are working in large units are found to agree more on development and encouragement compared to the respondents who are working in small units.

- **Type of Job Activity**

The mean score for opinion towards development and encouragement is high for the respondents who are working in composite units (22.90) and low for the respondents who are working in cutting, sewing, embroidering and packing units (22.00). That is, the respondents who are working in composite units are found to agree more on development and encouragement compared to the respondents who are working in cutting, sewing, embroidering and packing units.

- **Total Experience in Textile Industry**

The mean score for opinion towards development and encouragement is high for the respondents having between 15 and 20 years experience (23.93) and low for the respondents having between 5 and 10 years experience (21.63). That is, the respondents having between 15 and 20 years experience are found to agree more on development and encouragement compared to the respondents having between 5 and 10 years experience.

- **Wage**

The mean score for opinion towards development and encouragement is high for the respondents whose wage is between Rs.3001 and Rs.6000 (23.65) and low for the respondents whose wage is between Rs.6001 and Rs.9000 (20.75). That is, the respondents whose wage lies between Rs.3001 and Rs.6000 are found to agree more on development and encouragement compared to the respondents whose wage lies between Rs.6001 and Rs.9000.

- **Work Schedule**

The mean score for opinion towards development and encouragement is high for the respondents who are working in irregular shifts (24.11) and low for the respondents who are working in day shifts (21.08). That is, the respondents who are working in irregular shifts are found to agree more on development and encouragement compared to the respondents who are working in day shifts.

Factor 4: Grievance Redressal

In this section, an attempt has been made to examine the association between the employees opinion towards grievance redressal with their personal and occupational profile. T-test and F-test have been applied to find the association by formulating the null hypothesis.

Ho: There is no significant association between employees' opinion towards grievance redressal and their personal / occupational profile.

1. *Personal Profile and Grievance Redressal*

Table 4.3.9 portrays the mean values of employees' opinion towards grievance redressal for all independent variables that determine the personal profile such as age, gender, marital status, educational qualifications, family size, family income and family debt.

Table 4.3.9: Distribution of Respondents based on the Association between Personal Profile and their Opinion towards Grievance Redressal

S.No	Variables	Group	Mean	SD	No.	F test	T Test	df.	Table Value	Sig.
1	Age	18 - 25 yrs	14.46	2.00	113	78.115		499	3.357	**
		25 - 35 yrs	14.67	1.64	179					
		35 - 45 yrs	15.81	2.22	95					
		45 - 55 yrs	12.18	3.33	76					
		Above 55 yrs	9.00	2.88	37					
2	Gender	Male	13.62	3.10	289		3.908	498	2.586	**
		Female	14.62	2.41	211					
3	Marital Status	Unmarried	14.44	1.82	124	8.918		499	3.821	**
		Married	14.07	2.91	248					
		Divorced	14.41	3.02	85					
		Widowed	12.00	3.90	43					
4	Educational Qualifications	Illiterate	12.07	4.14	58	8.247		499	3.357	**
		Primary	14.27	2.77	283					
		Higher Secondary	14.37	2.07	137					
		Graduate	14.40	2.16	15					
		Diploma	14.14	3.24	7					
5	Family Members	1 - 3	13.64	3.58	120	2.779		497	3.014	Ns
		4- 6	14.27	2.63	315					
		Above 6	13.66	2.41	65					
6	Family Income	Rs.5001 - Rs.10000	13.97	2.90	33	.171		499	2.623	Ns
		Rs.10001 - Rs.15000	13.94	2.99	71					
		Rs.15001 - Rs.20000	13.99	2.89	222					
		Above Rs.20000	14.17	2.81	174					
7	Family Debt	No	13.58	3.16	88		1.668	498	1.968	Ns
		Yes	14.14	2.80	412					

Source: Primary Data

NS-Non Significant, * - 5 % level of Significance, ** - 1 % Level of Significance

T-test and F-test results shows that the calculated value is lower than the table value in the case of family size, family income and family debt at 1 percent significance level. The hypothesis is accepted and therefore, there is no association found between these personal variables and the grievance redressal. At the same time, *the calculated value is higher than the table value at 1 percent significance level in the case of personal variables such as age, gender, marital status, and educational qualifications. Therefore, null hypothesis is rejected* in these cases.

The influence of these variables on employee opinion towards the grievance redressal has been discussed as under:

- **Age**

The mean score for opinion towards grievance redressal is high for the respondents who are aged between 35 and 45 years (15.81) and low for the respondents who are aged above 55 years (9.00). That is, the respondents who are aged between 35 and 45 years are found to agree more on grievance redressal compared to the respondents who are aged above 55 years.

- **Gender**

The mean score for opinion towards grievance redressal is high for female employees (14.62) and low for male employees (13.62). That is, female respondents are found to agree more on grievance redressal compared to male respondents.

- **Marital Status**

The mean score for opinion towards grievance redressal is high for unmarried respondents (14.44) and low for widow respondents (12.00). That is, respondents who are unmarried are found to agree more on grievance redressal compared to the respondents who are widow.

- **Educational Qualifications**

The mean score for opinion towards grievance redressal is high for graduate employees (14.40) and low for illiterate employees (12.07). That is, the respondents who are graduates are found to agree more on grievance redressal compared to the respondents who are illiterates.

- **Family Members**

The mean score for opinion towards grievance redressal is high for the respondents family consisting between 4 and 6 members (14.27) and low for the respondents family consisting between 1 and 3 members (13.64). That is, the respondents whose family consists between 4 and 6 members are found to agree more on grievance redressal compared to the respondents whose family consists between 1 and 3 members.

- **Family Income**

The mean score for opinion towards grievance redressal is high for the respondents whose family incomes is above Rs.20000 (14.17) and low for the respondents whose family income is between Rs.10001 and Rs.15000 (13.94). That is, the respondents whose family income is above Rs.20000 groups are found to agree more on grievance redressal compared to the respondents whose family income is between Rs.10001 and Rs.15000.

- **Family Debt**

The mean score for opinion towards grievance redressal is high for those who have family debt (14.14) and low for those who do not have family debt (13.58). That is, the respondents who have family debt are found to agree more on grievance redressal compared to who do not have family debt.

2. *Occupational Profile and Grievance Redressal*

Table 4.3.10 portrays the mean values of employees' opinion towards grievance redressal for all independent variables that determine the occupational profile such as unit size, type of job activity, work experience, wage and work schedule.

Table 4.3.10: Distribution of Respondents based on the Association between Occupational Profile and their Opinion Towards Grievance Redressal

S.No	Variables	Group	Mean	SD	No.	F test	T Test	df.	Table Value	Sig.
1	Size of Unit	Small	13.49	3.28	200	6.592		499	4.648	**
		Medium	14.35	2.50	200					
		Large	14.55	2.51	100					
2	Type of Job Activity	Fabrication, Compacting and Calendaring	14.51	2.17	106	8.102		499	3.821	**
		Dyeing, Bleaching and Printing	13.83	2.68	52					
		Cutting, Sewing, Embroidering and packing	14.49	2.70	205					
		Composite unit	13.09	3.40	137					
3	Total Experience in Textile Industry	Less than 5	14.73	2.03	59	38.467		499	3.357	**
		5 - 10	14.62	1.89	250					
		10 - 15	14.44	3.43	122					
		15 - 20	12.13	4.26	15					
		Above 20	10.22	2.51	54					
4	Wage (p.m)	Below Rs.3000	14.10	3.38	10	2.266		499	2.390	Ns
		Rs.3001 -Rs. 6000	13.39	3.28	49					
		Rs.6001 -Rs. 9000	14.69	2.59	107					
		Rs. 9001 -Rs. 12000	13.82	2.94	155					
		Above Rs.12000	14.02	2.77	179					
5	Work Schedule	Day shift	14.61	2.39	165	3.138		499	3.357	*
		Afternoon shift	12.97	3.29	29					
		Night shift	13.56	3.36	9					
		Irregular shift on cal	13.98	3.14	93					
		Rotating shift	13.79	2.95	204					

Source: Primary Data

NS-Non Significant, * - 5 % level of Significance,   ** - 1 % Level of Significance

F-test results shows that the calculated value is lower than the table value in the case of wage at either 5 percent or 1 percent significance level. The hypothesis is accepted and therefore, there is no association found between these occupational variables and the grievance redressal. At the same time, *the calculated value is higher than the table value at either 5 percent or1 percent significance level in the case of occupational variables such as unit size, type of job activity, experience and work schedule. Therefore, null hypothesis is rejected* in these cases.

The influence of these variables on opinion towards grievance redressal has been discussed as under:

- **Size of Unit**

The mean score for opinion towards grievance redressal is high for the respondents who are working in large units (14.55) and low for the respondents who are working in small units (13.49). That is, the respondents who are working in large units are found to agree more on grievance redressal compared to the respondents are working in small units.

- **Type of Job Activity**

The mean score for opinion towards grievance redressal is high for the respondents who are working in fabrication, compacting and calendaring units (14.51) and low for the respondents who are working in composite units (13.09). That is, the respondents who are working in fabrication, compacting and calendaring units are found to agree more on grievance redressal compared to the respondents who are working in composite units.

- **Total experience in Textile Industry**

The mean score for opinion towards grievance redressal is high for the respondents whose experience is less than 5 years (14.73) and low for the respondents whose experience is above 20 years (10.22). That is, the respondents who have less than 5 years experience are found to agree more on grievance redressal compared to the respondents who have above 20 years experience.

- **Wage**

The mean score for opinion towards grievance redressal is high for the respondents whose wage is between Rs.6001 and Rs.9000 (14.69) and low for the respondents whose wage is between Rs.3001 and Rs.6000 (13.39). That is, the respondents who earn between Rs.6001 and Rs.9000 are found to agree more on grievance redressal compared to the respondents who earn between Rs.3001 and Rs.6000.

- ## Work Schedule

The mean score for opinion towards grievance redressal is high for the respondents who are working in day shifts (14.61) and low for the respondents who are working in afternoon shifts (12.97). That is, the respondents who are working in day shifts are found to agree more on grievance redressal compared to the respondents who are working in afternoon shifts.

Factor 5: Stress Management

In this section, an attempt has been made to examine the association between the employees opinion towards stress management with their personal and occupational profile. T-test and F-test have been applied to find the association by formulating the null hypothesis.

Ho: There is no significant association between employees' opinion towards stress management and their personal / occupational profile.

1. *Personal Profile and Stress Management*

Table 4.3.11 portrays the mean values of employees' opinion towards stress management for all independent variables that determine the personal profile such as age, gender, marital status, educational qualifications, family size, family income and family debt

Table 4.3.11: Distribution of Respondents based on the Association between Personal Profile and their Opinion Towards Stress Management

S.No	Variables	Group	Mean	SD	No.	F test	T Test	df.	Table Value	Sig.
1	Age	18 - 25 yrs	11.78	1.78	113	18.941		499	3.357	**
		25 - 35 yrs	11.41	1.27	179					
		35 - 45 yrs	10.85	1.44	95					
		45 - 55 yrs	9.64	4.42	76					
		Above 55 yrs	8.70	3.83	37					
2	Gender	Male	11.50	2.38	289	6.133		498	2.586	**
		Female	10.13	2.58	211					
3	Marital Status	Unmarried	11.42	1.83	124	4.792		499	3.821	**
		Married	10.92	2.67	248					
		Divorced	10.79	2.54	85					
		Widowed	9.74	3.28	43					
4	Educational Qualifications	Illiterate	9.79	3.55	58	5.086		499	3.357	**
		Primary	10.84	2.60	283					
		Higher Secondary	11.40	1.83	137					
		Graduate	11.93	1.49	15					
		Diploma	11.86	2.12	7					
5	Family Members	1 - 3	10.40	2.96	120	7.527		499	4.648	**
		4- 6	10.91	2.42	315					
		Above 6	11.91	2.07	65					
6	Family Income	Rs.5001 - Rs.10000	10.30	2.11	33	6.621		499	3.821	**
		Rs.10001 - Rs.15000	10.51	2.57	71					
		Rs.15001 - Rs.20000	10.61	2.74	222					
		Above Rs.20000	11.60	2.25	174					
7	Family Debt	No	10.80	2.62	88	0.503		498		Ns
		Yes	10.95	2.54	412					

Source: Primary Data

NS-Non Significant, * - 5 % level of Significance, ** - 1 % Level of Significance

T-test and F-test results shows that the calculated value is lower than the table value in the case of family debt at 1 percent significance level. The hypothesis is accepted and therefore, there is no association found between these personal variables and the stress management. At the same time, *the calculated value is higher than the table value at 1 percent significance level in the case of personal variables such as age, gender, marital status, educational qualifications, family size and family income. Therefore, null hypothesis is rejected* in these cases. The influence of these variables on opinion towards the stress management has been discussed as under:

- **Age**

The mean score for opinion towards stress management is high for the respondents whose age groups is between 18 and 25 years (11.78) and low for the respondents whose age group is above 55 years (8.70). That is, the respondents whose age group is between 18 and 25 years are found to agree more on stress management compared to the respondents whose age group is above 55 years.

- **Gender**

The mean score for opinion towards stress management is high for male respondents (11.50) and low for female respondents (10.13). That is, the male respondents are found to agree more on stress management compared to female respondents.

- **Marital Status**

The mean score for opinion towards stress management is high for unmarried respondents (11.42) and low for widow respondents (9.74). That is, the respondents who are unmarried are found to agree more on stress management compared to the respondents who are widows.

- **Educational Qualifications**

The mean score for opinion towards stress management is high for graduate employees (11.93) and low for illiterate employees (9.79). That is, the respondents who are graduates found to agree more on stress management compared to the respondents who are illiterate.

- **Family Size**

The mean score for opinion towards stress management is high for the respondents family having above 6 member (11.91) and low for the respondents family having between 1 and 3 member (10.40). That is, the respondents whose family has above 6 member are found to agree more on stress management compared to the respondents whose family has between 1 and 3 member.

- **Family Income**

The mean score for opinion towards stress management is high for the respondents who earn above Rs.20000 (11.60) and low for respondent who earn between Rs.5001 and Rs.10000 per month (10.30). That is, the respondents who earn above Rs.20000 are found to agree more on stress management compared to the respondents who earn between Rs.5001 and Rs.10000 per month.

- **Family Debt**

The mean score for opinion towards stress management is high for those who have family debt (10.95) and lower for those who do not have family debt (10.80). That is, the respondents who have family debt are found to agree more on stress management compared to who do not have family debt.

2. *Occupational Profile and Stress Management*

Table 4.3.12 portrays the mean values of employees' opinion towards stress management for all independent variables that determine the occupational profile such as unit size, type of job activity, work experience, wage and work schedule.

Table 4.3.12: Distribution of Respondents based on the Association between Occupational Profile and their Opinion Towards Stress Management

S.No	Variables	Group	Mean	SD	No.	F test	T Test	df.	Table Value	Sig.
1	Size of Unit	Small	9.71	3.08	200	45.614		499	4.648	**
		Medium	11.56	1.74	200					
		Large	12.07	1.63	100					
2	Type of job Activity	Fabrication, Compacting and Calendaring	11.04	2.09	106	10.029		499	3.821	**
		Dyeing, Bleaching and Printing	11.44	2.48	52					
		Cutting, Sewing, Embroidering and packing	10.23	2.64	205					
		Composite unit	11.66	2.54	137					
3	Total Experience in Textile Industry	Less than 5	11.95	1.95	59	50.084		499	3.357	**
		5 - 10	11.45	1.46	250					
		10 - 15	8.57	3.11	122					
		15 - 20	11.87	2.42	15					
		Above 20	12.39	2.45	54					
4	Wage (p.m)	Below Rs.3000	10.90	.88	10	7.605		499	3.357	**
		Rs.3001 -Rs. 6000	10.94	1.77	49					
		Rs.6001 -Rs. 9000	10.41	2.52	107					
		Rs. 9001 -Rs. 12000	10.35	3.27	155					
		Above Rs.12000	11.71	1.83	179					
5	Work Schedule	Day shift	10.26	2.65	165	5.055		499	3.357	**
		Afternoon shift	10.45	2.64	29					
		Night shift	11.11	1.76	9					
		Irregular shift on cal	11.38	2.58	93					
		Rotating shift	11.30	2.38	204					

Source: Primary Data

NS-Non Significant, * - 5 % level of Significance, ** - 1 % Level of Significance

F-test results shows that *the calculated value is higher than the table value either at 1 percent significance level in the case of unit size, type of job activity, experience, wage and work schedule. The null hypothesis is rejected in these cases and therefore, there is association found between these occupational variables and stress management.* The influence of these variables on employee opinion towards stress management has been discussed as under:

- **Size of Unit**

The mean score for opinion towards stress management is high for the respondents who are working in large units (12.07) and low for the respondents who are working in small units (9.71). That is, the respondents who are working in large units are found to agree more on stress management compared to those who are working in small units.

- **Type of Job Activity**

The mean score for opinion towards stress management is high for the respondents who are working in composite units (11.66) and low for the respondents who are working in cutting, sewing, embroidering and packing units (10.23). That is, the respondents who are working in composite units are found to agree more on stress management compared to the respondents who are working in cutting, sewing, embroidering and packing units.

- **Total experience in Textile Industry**

The mean score for opinion towards stress management is high for respondents above 20 years experience in Textile Industry (12.39) and low for those between 10 and 15 years experience (8.57). That is, the respondents who are having above 20 years experience in Textile Industry are found to agree more on stress management compared to those between 10 and 15 years experience.

- **Wage**

The mean score for opinion towards stress management is high for the respondents who earn above Rs.12000 (11.71) and low for the respondents who earns between Rs.9001 and Rs.12000 (10.35). That is, the respondents who are earning above Rs.12000 are found to agree more on stress management compared to the respondents who earn between Rs.9001 and Rs.12000.

- **Work Schedule**

The mean score for opinion towards stress management is high for the respondents working in irregular shifts (11.38) and low for the respondents working in day shifts (10.26).

That is, the respondents who are working in irregular shifts are found to agree more on stress management compared to those working in day shifts.

Factor 6: Wage Structure

In this section, an attempt has been made to examine the association between the employees opinion towards wage structure with their personal and occupational profile. T-test and F-test have been applied to find the association by formulating the null hypothesis.

Ho: There is no significant association between employees' opinion towards wage structure and their personal / occupational profile.

1. Personal Profile and Wage Structure

Table 4.3.13 portrays the mean values of employees' opinion towards wage structure for all independent variables that determine the personal profile such as age, gender, marital status, educational qualifications, family size, family income and family debt

Table 4.3.13: Distribution of Respondents based on the Association between Personal Profile and their Opinion Towards Wage Structure

S.No	Variables	Group	Mean	SD	No.	F test	T Test	df.	Table Value	Sig.
1	Age	18 - 25 yrs	12.99	1.79	113	27.647		499	3.357	**
		25 - 35 yrs	12.36	1.79	179					
		35 - 45 yrs	10.79	2.46	95					
		45 - 55 yrs	13.58	1.76	76					
		Above 55 yrs	13.14	1.75	37					
2	Gender	Male	12.33	1.64	289		1.447	498	1.968	Ns
		Female	12.61	2.64	211					
3	Marital Status	Unmarried	12.49	1.89	124	.630		499	2.623	Ns
		Married	12.33	2.25	248					
		Divorced	12.60	2.07	85					
		Widowed	12.70	2.12	43					
4	Educational Qualifications	Illiterate	12.52	2.49	58	.954		499	2.390	Ns
		Primary	12.57	2.02	283					
		Higher Secondary	12.21	2.20	137					
		Graduate	12.47	1.41	15					
		Diploma	11.57	2.70	7					
5	Family Members	1 - 3	12.67	2.28	120	.914		499	3.014	Ns
		4- 6	12.39	2.14	315					
		Above 6	12.29	1.70	65					
6	Family Income	Rs.5001 - Rs.10000	12.85	2.03	33	.989		499	2.623	Ns
		Rs.10001 - Rs.15000	12.63	2.01	71					
		Rs.15001 - Rs.20000	12.29	2.24	222					
		Above Rs.20000	12.49	2.04	174					
7	Family Debt	No	12.91	1.85	88		2.263	498	1.968	*
		Yes	12.35	2.17	412					

Source: Primary Data

NS-Non Significant,   * - 5 % level of Significance,   ** - 1 % Level of Significance

T-test and F-test results shows that the calculated value is lower than the table value in the case of gender, marital status, educational qualifications, family size and family income at either 5 percent or 1 percent significance level. The hypothesis is accepted and therefore, there is no association found between these personal variables and the wage structure. At the same time, *the calculated value is higher than the table value at either 5 percent or 1 percent significance level in the case of personal variables such as age and family debt. Therefore, null hypothesis is rejected* in these cases. The influence of these variables on employee opinion towards the wage structure has been discussed as under:

- **Age**

The mean score for opinion towards wage structure is high for the respondents whose age is between 45 and 55 years (13.58) and low for the respondents whose age is between 35 and 45 years (10.79). That is, the respondents whose age is between 45 and 55 years are found to agree more on wage structure compared to the respondents whose age is between 35 and 45 years.

- **Gender**

The mean score for opinion towards wage structure is high for female employees (12.61) and low for male employees (12.33). That is, the female respondents are found to agree more on wage structure compared to male group.

- **Marital Status**

The mean score for opinion towards wage structure is high for widow groups (12.70) and low for married groups (12.33). That is, the respondents who are widows are found to agree more on wage structure compared to married groups.

- **Educational Qualifications**

The mean score for opinion towards wage structure is high for primary level educated respondents (12.57) and low for diploma level educated respondents (11.57). That is, the respondents who are educated at primary level are found to agree more on wage structure compared to respondents who are educated at diploma level.

- **Family Members**

The mean score for opinion towards wage structure is high for respondents whose family consists between 1 and 3 members (12.67) and low for those having above 6 members (12.29). That is, the respondents who have between 1 and 3 members in their family are found to agree more on wage structure compared to those who have above 6 members.

- **Family Income**

The mean score for opinion towards wage structure is high for respondents between Rs.5001 and Rs.10000 family income (12.85) and low for those between Rs.15001 and

Rs.20000 family income (12.29). That is, the respondents between Rs.5001 and Rs.10000 family income are found to agree more on wage structure compared to those between Rs.15001 and Rs.20000 family income.

- **Family Debt**

The mean score for opinion towards wage structure is high for those who do not have family debt (12.91) and low for those who have family debt (12.35). That is, the respondents who do not have family debt are found to agree more on wage structure compared to those who have family debt.

2. *Occupational Profile and Wage Structure*

Table 4.3.14 portrays the mean values of employees' opinion towards wage structure for all independent variables that determine the occupational profile such as unit size, type of job activity, work experience, wage and work schedule.

Table 4.3.14: Distribution of Respondents based on the Association between Occupational Profile and their Opinion Towards Wage Structure

S.No	Variables	Group	Mean	SD	No.	F test	T Test	df.	Table Value	Sig.
1	Size of Unit	Small	12.39	2.40	200	1.476		499	3.014	Ns
		Medium	12.35	1.98	200					
		Large	12.77	1.77	100					
2	Type of Job Activity	Fabrication, Compacting and Calendaring	12.17	1.79	106	3.841		499	3.821	**
		Dyeing, Bleaching and Printing	12.38	1.99	52					
		Cutting, Sewing, Embroidering and packing	12.82	2.09	205					
		Composite unit	12.12	2.37	137					
3	Total Experience in Textile Industry	Less than 5	12.80	1.88	59	3.409		499	3.357	**
		5 - 10	12.10	2.31	250					
		10 - 15	12.75	1.90	122					
		15 - 20	12.87	2.26	15					
		Above 20	12.85	1.69	54					
4	Wage (p.m)	Below Rs.3000	12.10	2.77	10	4.957		499	3.357	**
		Rs.3001 -Rs. 6000	12.78	1.86	49					
		Rs.6001 -Rs. 9000	13.17	2.09	107					
		Rs. 9001 -Rs. 12000	12.19	2.59	155					
		Above Rs.12000	12.16	1.56	179					
5	Work Schedule	Day shift	12.62	2.56	165	1.431		499	2.390	Ns
		Afternoon shift	11.93	2.15	29					
		Night shift	12.56	2.51	9					
		Irregular shift on cal	12.70	1.71	93					
		Rotating shift	12.26	1.86	204					

Source: Primary Data

NS-Non Significant,   * - 5 % level of Significance, ** - 1 % Level of Significance

F-test results shows that the calculated value is lower than the table value in the case of unit size and work schedule at 1 percent significance level. The hypothesis is accepted and therefore, there is no association found between these occupational variables and the wage structure. At the same time, *the calculated value is higher than the table value at 1 percent significance level in the case of occupational variables such as* type *of job activity, experience and wage. Therefore, null hypothesis is rejected* in these cases. The influence of these variables on employee opinion towards the wage structure has been discussed as under:

- **Size of Unit**

The mean score for opinion towards wage structure is high for the respondents those who are working in large units (12.77) and low for the respondents those who are working in medium units (12.35). That is, the respondents who are working in large units are found to agree more on wage structure compared to the respondents who are working in medium units.

- **Type of Job Activity**

The mean score for opinion towards wage structure is high for the respondents who are working in cutting, sewing, embroidering and packing units (12.82) and low for the respondents who are working in composite units (12.12). That is, the respondents who are working in cutting, sewing, embroidering and packing units are found to agree more on wage structure compared to the respondents who are working in composite units.

- **Total Experience in Textile Industry**

The mean score for opinion towards wage structure is high for the respondents whose experience is between 15 and 20 years in Textile Industry (12.87) and low for the respondents whose experience is between 5 and 10 years in Textile Industry (12.10). That is, the respondents who have experience between 15 and 20 years in Textile Industry are found to agree more on wage structure compared to the respondents who have experience between 5 and 10 years in Textile Industry.

- **Wage**

The mean score for opinion towards wage structure is high for the respondents whose wage is between Rs.6001 and Rs.9000 (13.17) and low for the respondents whose wage is below Rs.3000 (12.10). That is, the respondents who earn between Rs.6001 and Rs.9000 are found to agree more on wage structure compared to the respondents who earn below Rs.3000.

- **Work Schedule**

The mean score for opinion towards wage structure is high for the respondents who are working in irregular shifts (12.70) and low for the respondents who are working in afternoon shifts (11.93). That is, the respondents who are working in irregular shifts are found to agree more on wage structure compared to the respondents who are working in afternoon shifts.

Factor 7: Training

In this section, an attempt has been made to examine the association between the employees opinion towards training with their personal and occupational profile. T-test and F-test have been applied to find the association by formulating the null hypothesis.

Ho: There is no significant association between employees' opinion towards training and their personal / occupational profile.

1. Personal Profile and Training

Table 4.3.15 portrays the mean values of employees' opinion towards training for all independent variables that determine the personal profile such as age, gender, marital status, educational qualifications, family size, family income and family debt.

Table 4.3.15: Distribution of Respondents based on the Association between Personal Profile and their Opinion Towards Training

S.No	Variables	Group	Mean	SD	No.	F test	T Test	df.	Table Value	Sig.
1	Age	18 - 25 yrs	10.71	2.27	113	49.857		499	3.357	**
		25 - 35 yrs	8.95	2.41	179					
		35 - 45 yrs	9.72	2.22	95					
		45 - 55 yrs	10.91	1.86	76					
		Above 55 yrs	5.46	1.64	37					
2	Gender	Male	10.04	1.97	289		5.201	498	2.586	**
		Female	8.84	3.17	211					
3	Marital Status	Unmarried	10.38	2.28	124	29.379		499	3.821	**
		Married	9.93	2.36	248					
		Divorced	8.45	2.63	85					
		Widowed	6.95	2.63	43					
4	Educational Qualifications	Illiterate	7.60	2.92	58	10.454		499	3.357	**
		Primary	9.69	2.56	283					
		Higher Secondary	10.00	2.36	137					
		Graduate	9.13	1.64	15					
		Diploma	10.71	1.60	7					
5	Family Members	1 - 3	8.93	2.72	120	7.878		499	4.648	**
		4- 6	9.88	2.49	315					
		Above 6	8.94	2.70	65					
6	Family Income	Rs.5001 - Rs.10000	9.09	2.94	33	2.650		499	2.623	*
		Rs.10001 - Rs.15000	8.92	2.68	71					
		Rs.15001 - Rs.20000	9.53	2.59	222					
		Above Rs.20000	9.87	2.51	174					
7	Family Debt	No	8.56	2.87	88		3.913	498	2.586	**
		Yes	9.74	2.51	412					

Source: Primary Data

NS-Non Significant,   * - 5 % level of Significance,   ** - 1 % Level of Significance

T-test and F-test results shows that *the calculated value is higher than the table value at either 5 percent or 1 percent significance level in the case of age, gender, marital status, educational qualifications, family size, family income and family debt. The null hypothesis is rejected in these cases and therefore, there is association found between these personal variables and training.* The influence of these variables on employee opinion towards the training has been discussed as under:

- **Age**

The mean score for opinion towards training is high for respondents whose age is between 45 and 55 years (10.91) and low for the respondents whose age is above 55 years (5.46). That is, the respondents whose age is between 45 and 55 years are found to agree more on training compared to the respondents whose age is above 55 years.

- **Gender**

The mean score for opinion towards training is high for male respondents (10.04) and low for female respondents (8.84). That is, the respondents who are male are found to agree more on training compared to the female respondents.

- **Marital Status**

The mean score for opinion towards training is high for respondents who are unmarried (10.38) and lower for respondents who are widows (6.95). That is, the respondents who are unmarried are found to agree more on training compared to the respondents who are widows.

- **Educational Qualifications**

The mean score for opinion towards training is high for diploma holders (10.71) and low for illiterates (7.60). That is, the respondents who are diploma holders are found to agree more on training compared to the respondents who are illiterates.

- **Family Members**

The mean score for opinion towards training is high for the respondents whose family members are between 4 and 6 (9.88) and low for the respondents whose family members are between 1 and 3 (8.93). That is, the respondents whose family members are between 4 and 6 are found to agree more on training compared to the respondents whose family members are between 1 and 3.

- **Family Income**

The mean score for opinion towards training is high for the respondents whose family income is above Rs.20000 (9.87) and low for the respondents whose family income is between Rs.10001 and Rs.15000 (8.92). That is , the respondents whose family income is above

Rs.20000 are found to agree more on training compared to the respondents whose family income are between Rs.10001 and Rs.15000.

- **Family Debt**

The mean score for opinion towards training is high for those who have family debt (9.74) and low for those who do not have family debt (8.56). That is, the respondents who have family debt are found to agree more on training compared to the respondents who do not have family debt.

2. *Occupational Profile and Training*

Table 4.3.16 portrays the mean values of employees' opinion towards training for all independent variables that determine the occupational profile such as unit size, type of job activity, work experience, wage and work schedule

Table 4.3.16: Distribution of respondents based on the association between occupational profile and their opinion towards training

S.No	Variables	Group	Mean	SD	No.	F test	T Test	df.	Table Value	Sig.
1	Size of Unit	Small	8.74	2.82	200	24.208		499	4.648	**
		Medium	9.68	2.38	200					
		Large	10.84	1.98	100					
2	Type of Job Activity	Fabrication, Compacting and Calendaring	9.81	2.14	106	2.534		499	2.623	Ns
		Dyeing, Bleaching and Printing	9.19	2.69	52					
		Cutting, Sewing, Embroidering and packing	9.23	2.80	205					
		Composite unit	9.90	2.58	137					
3	Total Experience in Textile Industry	Less than 5	10.42	2.52	59	3.635		499	3.357	**
		5 - 10	9.38	2.51	250					
		10 - 15	9.80	2.45	122					
		15 - 20	9.33	3.11	15					
		Above 20	8.72	3.09	54					
4	Wage (p.m)	Below Rs.3000	8.50	3.44	10	10.979		499	3.357	**
		Rs.3001 -Rs. 6000	8.59	3.42	49					
		Rs.6001 -Rs. 9000	8.44	3.06	107					
		Rs. 9001 -Rs. 12000	9.91	2.53	155					
		Above Rs.12000	10.17	1.65	179					
5	Work Schedule	Day shift	8.88	3.10	165	9.839		499	3.357	**
		Afternoon shift	8.21	2.73	29					
		Night shift	7.67	3.28	9					
		Irregular shift on cal	9.83	2.32	93					
		Rotating shift	10.20	1.97	204					

Source: Primary Data

NS-Non Significant,   * - 5 % level of Significance,   ** - 1 % Level of Significance

F-test results shows that the calculated value is lower than the table value in the case of type of job activity at 1 percent significance level. The hypothesis is accepted and therefore, there is no association found between this occupational variable and the training. At the same time, *the calculated value is higher than the table value at 1 percent significance level in the case of occupational variables such as unit size, experience, wage and work schedule. Therefore, the null hypothesis is rejected* in these cases. The influence of these variables on employee opinion towards training has been discussed as under:

- **Size of Unit**

The mean score for opinion towards training is high for the respondents who are working in large units (10.84) and low for the respondents who are working in small units (8.74). That is, the respondents who are working in large units are found to agree more on training compared to the respondents who are working in small units.

- **Type of Job Activity**

The mean score for opinion towards training is high for respondents who are working in composite units (9.90) and low for the respondents who are working in dyeing, bleaching and printing units (9.19). That is, the respondents who are working in composite units are found to agree more on training compared to the respondents who are working in dyeing, bleaching and printing units.

- **Total Experience in Textile Industry**

The mean score for opinion towards training is high for the respondents who have an experience less than 5 years (10.42) and low for the respondents who have an experience above 20 years (8.72). That is, the respondents who have less than 5 years experience are found to agree more on training compared to the respondents who have experience above 20 years.

- **Wage**

The mean score for opinion towards training is high for the respondents whose wages are above Rs.12000 (10.17) and low for the respondents whose wages are between Rs.6001 and Rs.9000 (8.44). That is, the respondents whose wages are above Rs.12000 are found to agree more on training compared to the respondents whose wages are between Rs.6001 and Rs.9000.

- **Work Schedule**

The mean score for opinion towards training is high for the respondents who are working in rotating shifts (10.20) and low for the respondents who are working in night shifts (7.67). That is, the respondents who are working in rotating shifts are found to agree more on training compared to the respondents who are working in night shifts.

Factor 8: Working Conditions

In this section, an attempt has been made to examine the association between the employees opinion towards working conditions with their personal and occupational profile. T-test and F-test have been applied to find the association by formulating the null hypothesis.

Ho: There is no significant association between employees' opinion towards working conditions and their personal / occupational profile.

1. Personal Profile and Working Conditions

Table4.3.17 portrays the mean values of employees' opinion towards working conditions for all independent variables that determine the personal profile such as age, gender, marital status, educational qualifications, family size, family income and family debt

Table 4.3.17: Distribution of Respondents based on the Association between Personal Profile and their Opinion Towards Working Conditions

S.No	Variables	Group	Mean	SD	No.	F test	T Test	df.	Table Value	Sig.
1	Age	18 - 25 yrs	16.42	1.44	113	12.608		499	3.357	**
		25 - 35 yrs	15.07	1.71	179					
		35 - 45 yrs	15.44	1.93	95					
		45 - 55 yrs	14.75	2.53	76					
		Above 55 yrs	15.08	1.92	37					
2	Gender	Male	15.12	1.97	289		3.726	498	2.586	**
		Female	15.77	1.85	211					
3	Marital Status	Unmarried	15.67	1.79	124	1.606		499	2.623	Ns
		Married	15.40	2.06	248					
		Divorced	15.09	1.94	85					
		Widowed	15.23	1.63	43					
4	Educational Qualifications	Illiterate	15.16	2.06	58	.931		499	2.390	Ns
		Primary	15.34	1.99	283					
		Higher Secondary	15.64	1.77	137					
		Graduate	15.47	1.64	15					
		Diploma	14.86	2.85	7					
5	Family Members	1 - 3	15.23	1.84	120	.732		499	3.014	Ns
		4- 6	15.48	1.95	315					
		Above 6	15.32	2.11	65					
6	Family Income	Rs.5001 - Rs.10000	15.36	2.09	33	.284		499	2.623	Ns
		Rs.10001 - Rs.15000	15.59	1.75	71					
		Rs.15001 - Rs.20000	15.38	1.97	222					
		Above Rs.20000	15.34	1.98	174					
7	Family Debt	No	15.41	2.02	88		.059	498	1.968	Ns
		Yes	15.40	1.93	412					

Source: Primary Data

NS-Non Significant, * - 5 % level of Significance, ** - 1 % Level of Significance

T-test and F-test results shows that the calculated value is lower than the table value in the case of marital status, educational qualifications, family members, family income and family debt at 1 percent significance level. The hypothesis is accepted and therefore, there is no association found between these personal variables and the working conditions. At the same time, *the calculated value is higher than the table value at 1 percent significance level in the case of personal variables such as age and gender. Therefore, null hypothesis is rejected* in these cases.

The influence of these variables on employee opinion towards working conditions has been discussed as under:

- **Age**

The mean score for opinion towards working conditions is high for the respondents who belong to the age group between 18 and 25 years (16.42) and low for the respondents who belong to the age group between 45 and 55 years (14.75). That is, the respondents who belong to the age group between 18 and 25 years are found to agree more on working conditions compared to the respondents who belong to age group between 45 and 55 years.

- **Gender**

The mean score for opinion towards working conditions is high for female employees (15.77) and low for male employees (15.12). That is, the female respondents are found to agree more on working conditions compared to the male respondents.

- **Marital Status**

The mean score for opinion towards working conditions is high for the respondents who are unmarried (15.67) and low for the respondents who are divorced (15.09). That is, the respondents who are unmarried are found to agree more on working conditions compared to the respondents who are divorced.

- **Educational Qualifications**

The mean score for opinion towards working conditions is high for the respondents who are educated up to higher secondary level (15.64) and low for the respondents who are educated up to diploma (14.86). That is, the respondents who are educated up to higher secondary level are found to agree more on working conditions compared to the respondents who are educated up to diploma.

- **Family size**

The mean score for opinion towards working conditions is high for the respondents who have family members between 4 and 6 (15.48) and low for the respondents who have family members between 1 and 3 (15.23). That is, the respondents who have family members between 4 and 6 are found to agree more on working conditions compared to the respondents who have family members between 1 and 3.

- **Family Income**

The mean score for opinion towards working conditions is high for the respondents whose family income is between Rs.10001 and Rs.15000 (15.59) and low for respondents whose family income is above Rs.20000 (15.34). That is, the respondents whose family income is between Rs.10001 and Rs.15000 are found to agree more on working conditions compared to respondents whose family income is above Rs.20000.

- **Family Debt**

The mean score for opinion towards working conditions is high for those who do not have family debt (15.41) and low for those who have family debt (15.40). That is, the respondents who do not have family debt are found to agree more on working conditions compared to those who have family debt.

2. *Occupational Profile and Working Conditions*

Table 4.3.18 portrays the mean values of employees' opinion towards working conditions for all independent variables that determine the occupational profile such as unit size, type of job activity, work experience, wage and work schedule

Table 4.3.18: Distribution of Respondents based on the Association between Occupational Profile and their Opinion Towards Working Conditions

S.No	Variables	Group	Mean	SD	No.	F test	T Test	df.	Table Value	Sig.
1	Size of Unit	Small	15.03	1.98	200	10.484		499	4.648	**
		Medium	15.42	1.98	200					
		Large	16.10	1.59	100					
2	Type of Job Activity	Fabrication, Compacting and Calendaring	15.32	1.83	106	2.465		499	2.623	Ns
		Dyeing, Bleaching and Printing	15.50	1.69	52					
		Cutting, Sewing, Embroidering and packing	15.63	1.88	205					
		Composite unit	15.07	2.17	137					
3	Total Experience in Textile Industry	Less than 5	16.59	1.37	59	12.676		499	3.357	**
		5 - 10	15.41	1.74	250					
		10 - 15	15.41	2.15	122					
		15 - 20	15.07	1.83	15					
		Above 20	14.11	2.14	54					
4	Wage (p.m)	Below Rs.3000	15.50	1.43	10	8.609		499	3.357	**
		Rs.3001 -Rs. 6000	15.86	1.68	49					
		Rs.6001 -Rs. 9000	15.76	1.93	107					
		Rs. 9001 -Rs. 12000	15.76	1.97	155					
		Above Rs.12000	14.74	1.86	179					
5	Work Schedule	Day shift	15.68	1.91	165	1.621		499	2.390	Ns
		Afternoon shift	15.31	1.81	29					
		Night shift	15.00	1.50	9					
		Irregular shift on cal	15.44	2.19	93					
		Rotating shift	15.18	1.88	204					

Source: Primary Data

NS-Non Significant,   * - 5 % level of Significance,   ** - 1 % Level of Significance

F-test results shows that the calculated value is lower than the table value in the case of type of job activity and work schedule at 1 percent significance level. The hypothesis is accepted and therefore, there is no association found between these occupational variables and the working conditions. At the same time, *the calculated value is higher than the table value at 1 percent significance level in the case of occupational variables such as unit size, experience and wage. Therefore, null hypothesis is rejected* in these cases.

The influence of these variables on employee opinion towards working conditions has been discussed as under:

- **Size of Unit**

The mean score for opinion towards working conditions is high for the respondents who are working in large units (16.10) and low for the respondents who are working in small units (15.03). That is, the respondents who are working in large units are found to agree more on working conditions compared to the respondents who are working in small units.

- **Type of Job Activity**

The mean score for opinion towards working conditions is high for the respondents who are working in cutting, sewing, embroidering and packing units (15.63) and low for the respondents who are working in composite units (15.07). That is, the respondents who are working in cutting, sewing, embroidering and packing units are found to agree more on working conditions compared to the respondents who are working in composite units.

- **Total Experience in Textile Industry**

The mean score for opinion towards working conditions is high for the respondents who are having less than 5 years experience (16.59) and low for the respondents who are having above 20 years experience (14.11). That is, the respondents who are having less than 5 years experience are found to agree more on working conditions compared to the respondents who are having above 20 years experience.

- **Wage**

The mean score for opinion towards working conditions is high for the respondents whose wages are between Rs.3001 and Rs.6000 (15.86) and low for the respondents whose wages are above Rs.12000 (14.74). That is, the respondents whose wages are between Rs.3001 and Rs.6000 are found to agree more on working conditions compared to the respondents whose wages are above Rs.12000.

- **Work Schedule**

The mean score for opinion towards working conditions is high for the respondents who are working in day shifts (15.68) and low for the respondents who are working in night shifts (15.00). That is, the respondents who are working in day shifts are found to agree more on working conditions compared to the respondents who are working in night shifts.

Factor 9: Work Life Balance

In this section, an attempt has been made to examine the association between the employees opinion towards work life balance with their personal and occupational profile. T-test and F-test have been applied to find the association by formulating the null hypothesis.

Ho: There is no significant association between employees' opinion towards work life balance and their personal / occupational profile.

1. Personal Profile and Work Life Balance

Table4.3.19 portrays the mean values of employees' opinion towards work life balance for all independent variables that determine the personal profile such as age, gender, marital status, educational qualifications, family size, family income and family debt.

Table 4.3.19: Distribution of Respondents based on the Association between Personal Profile and their Opinion Towards Work Life Balance

S.No	Variables	Group	Mean	SD	No.	F test	T Test	df.	Table Value	Sig.
1	Age	18 - 25 yrs	8.39	1.42	113	9.976		499	3.357	**
		25 - 35 yrs	8.08	1.23	179					
		35 - 45 yrs	8.27	1.02	95					
		45 - 55 yrs	7.88	1.49	76					
		Above 55 yrs	9.43	1.66	37					
2	Gender	Male	8.20	1.38	289		1.100	498	1.968	Ns
		Female	8.34	1.34	211					
3	Marital Status	Unmarried	8.38	1.36	124	4.604		499	3.821	**
		Married	8.06	1.33	248					
		Divorced	8.39	1.33	85					
		Widowed	8.79	1.49	43					
4	Educational Qualifications	Illiterate	8.47	1.61	58	1.624		499	2.390	Ns
		Primary	8.29	1.34	283					
		Higher Secondary	8.21	1.28	137					
		Graduate	7.53	1.25	15					
		Diploma	7.86	1.46	7					
5	Family Members	1 - 3	8.52	1.36	120	6.475		499	4.648	**
		4- 6	8.26	1.35	315					
		Above 6	7.77	1.32	65					
6	Family Income	Rs.5001 - Rs.10000	8.94	1.46	33	3.833		499	3.821	**
		Rs.10001 - Rs.15000	8.41	1.40	71					
		Rs.15001 - Rs.20000	8.23	1.27	222					
		Above Rs.20000	8.11	1.41	174					
7	Family Debt	No	8.53	1.39	88		2.100	498	1.968	*
		Yes	8.20	1.35	412					

Source: Primary Data
NS-Non Significant, * - 5 % level of Significance, ** - 1 % Level of Significance
T-test and F-test results shows that the calculated value is lower than the table value in the case of gender and educational qualifications at either 5 percent or 1 percent significance level. The

hypothesis is accepted and therefore, there is no association found between these personal variables and the work life balance. At the same time, *the calculated value is higher than the table value at either 5 percent or 1 percent significance level in the case of personal variables such as age, marital status, and family size, family income and family debt. Therefore, null hypothesis is rejected* in these cases. The influence of these variables on employee opinion towards work life balance has been discussed as under:

- **Age**

The mean score for opinion towards work life balance is high for the respondents who belong to the age group above 55 years (9.43) and low for the respondents who belong to the age group between 45 and 55 years (7.88). That is, the respondents who belong to the age group above 55 years are found to agree more on work life balance compared to the respondents who belong to the age group between 45 and 55 years.

- **Gender**

The mean score for opinion towards work life balance is high for female employees (8.34) and low for male employees (8.20). That is, female employees are found to agree more on work life balance compared to male employees.

- **Marital Status**

The mean score for opinion towards work life balance is high for widow employees (8.79) and low for married employees (8.06). That is, the respondents who are widows are found to agree more on work life balance compared to the respondents who are married.

- **Educational Qualifications**

The mean score for opinion towards work life balance is high for the respondents who are illiterate (8.47) and low for the respondents who are educated up to graduate level (7.53). That is, the respondents who are illiterate are found to agree more on work life balance compared to the respondents who are educated up to graduate level.

- **Family Size**

The mean score for opinion towards work life balance is high for the respondents whose family members are between 1 and 3 (8.52) and low for the respondents whose family members are above 6 (7.77). That is, the respondents whose family members are between 1 and 3 are found to agree more on work life balance compared to the respondents whose family members are above 6.

- **Family Income**

The mean score for opinion towards work life balance is high for the respondents whose family income is between Rs.5001 and Rs.10000 (8.94) and low for the respondents whose family income is above Rs.20000 (8.11). That is, the respondents whose family income is between Rs.5001 and Rs.10000 are found to agree more on work life balance compared to the respondents whose family income is above Rs.20000 .

- **Family Debt**

The mean score for opinion towards work life balance is high for those who do not have family debt (8.53) and low for those who have family debt (8.20). That is, the respondents who do not have family debt are found to agree more on work life balance compared to the respondents who do not have family debt.

2. *Occupational Profile and Work Life Balance*

Table 4.3.20 portrays the mean values of employees' opinion towards work life balance for all independent variables that determine the occupational profile such as unit size, job activity, work experience, wage and work schedule

Table 4.3.20: Distribution of respondents based on the association between occupational profile and their opinion towards work life balance

S.No	Variables	Group	Mean	SD	No.	F test	T Test	df.	Table Value	Sig.
1	Size of Unit	Small	8.21	1.42	200	.554		499	3.014	Ns
		Medium	8.25	1.21	200					
		Large	8.38	1.54	100					
2	Type of job activity	Fabrication, Compacting and Calendaring	8.31	1.48	106	.893		499	2.623	Ns
		Dyeing, Bleaching and Printing	7.98	1.32	52					
		Cutting, Sewing, Embroidering and packing	8.25	1.33	205					
		Composite unit	8.33	1.33	137					
3	Total Experience in Textile Industry	Less than 5	8.36	1.34	59	2.988		499	2.390	*
		5 - 10	8.09	1.24	250					
		10 - 15	8.36	1.51	122					
		15 - 20	8.07	1.44	15					
		Above 20	8.74	1.47	54					
4	Wage (p.m)	Below Rs.3000	8.50	1.43	10	3.122		499	2.390	*
		Rs.3001 -Rs. 6000	8.57	1.38	49					
		Rs.6001 -Rs. 9000	8.56	1.40	107					
		Rs. 9001 -Rs. 12000	8.09	1.36	155					
		Above Rs.12000	8.12	1.30	179					
5	Work Schedule	Day shift	8.24	1.30	165	.344		499	2.390	Ns
		Afternoon shift	8.41	1.32	29					
		Night shift	8.33	1.41	9					
		Irregular shift on cal	8.37	1.43	93					
		Rotating shift	8.20	1.40	204					

Source: Primary Data

NS-Non Significant,   * - 5 % level of Significance,   ** - 1 % Level of Significance

F-test results shows that the calculated value is lower than the table value in the case of unit size, type of job activity and work schedule at 5 percent significance level. The hypothesis is accepted and therefore, there is no association found between these occupational variables and the work life balance. At the same time, *the calculated value is higher than the table value at 5 percent significance level in the case of occupational variables such as experience and wage. Therefore, null hypothesis is rejected* in these cases.

The influence of these variables on employee opinion towards work life balance has been discussed as under:

- **Size of Unit**

The mean score for opinion towards work life balance is high for the respondents who are working in large units (8.38) and low for the respondents who are working in small units (8.21). That is, the respondents who are working in large units are found to agree more on work life balance compared to the respondents who are working in small units.

- **Type of Job Activity**

The mean score for opinion towards work life balance is high for respondents who are working in composite units (8.33) and low for respondents who are working in dyeing, bleaching and printing units (7.98). That is, the respondents who are working in composite units are found to agree more on work life balance compared to the respondents who are working in dyeing, bleaching and printing units.

- **Total Experience in Textile Industry**

The mean score for opinion towards work life balance is high for the respondents who are having above 20 years experience (8.74) and low for the respondents who are having between 15 and 20 years experience (8.07). That is, the respondents who are having above 20 years experience are found to agree more on work life balance compared to the respondents who are having between 15 and 20 years experience.

- **Wage**

The mean score for opinion towards work life balance is high for the respondents whose wages are between Rs.3001 and Rs.6000 (8.57) and low for the respondents whose wages are between Rs.9001 and Rs.12000 (8.09). That is, the respondents whose wages are between Rs.3001 and Rs.6000 are found to agree more on work life balance compared to the respondents whose wages are between Rs.9001 and Rs.12000.

- **Work Schedule**

The mean score for opinion towards work life balance is high for the respondents who are working in afternoon shifts (8.41) and low for the respondents who are working in rotating shifts (8.20). That is, the respondents who are working in afternoon shifts are found to agree more on work life balance compared to respondents working in rotating shifts.

Factor 9: Job Satisfaction

In this section, an attempt has been made to examine the association between the employees opinion towards job satisfaction with their personal and occupational profile. T-test and F-test have been applied to find the association by formulating the null hypothesis.

Ho: There is no significant association between employees' opinion towards job satisfaction and their personal / occupational profile.

1. *Personal Profile and Job Satisfaction*

Table4.3.21 portrays the mean values of employees' opinion towards job satisfaction for all independent variables that determine the personal profile such as age, gender, marital status, educational qualifications, family size, family income and family debt

Table 4.3.21: Distribution of Respondents based on the Association between Personal Profile and their Opinion Towards Job Satisfaction

S.No	Variables	Group	Mean	SD	No.	F test	T Test	df.	Table Value	Sig.
1	Age	18 - 25 yrs	8.39	1.00	113	8.485		499	3.357	**
		25 - 35 yrs	7.90	1.16	179					
		35 - 45 yrs	7.71	.91	95					
		45 - 55 yrs	8.25	.94	76					
		Above 55 yrs	7.35	2.32	37					
2	Gender	Male	7.52	1.13	289		11.336	498	2.586	**
		Female	8.63	1.03	211					
3	Marital Status	Unmarried	8.07	1.18	124	1.645		499	2.623	Ns
		Married	8.00	.99	248					
		Divorced	8.00	1.39	85					
		Widowed	7.60	1.93	43					
4	Educational Qualifications	Illiterate	7.74	1.75	58	5.056		499	3.357	**
		Primary	8.04	1.10	283					
		Higher Secondary	8.12	1.07	137					
		Graduate	7.40	1.06	15					
		Diploma	6.43	2.07	7					
5	Family Members	1 - 3	7.99	1.49	120	3.340		499	3.014	*
		4- 6	8.06	1.14	315					
		Above 6	7.63	.96	65					
6	Family Income	Rs.5001 - Rs.10000	8.24	1.71	33	.859		499	2.623	Ns
		Rs.10001 - Rs.15000	7.90	1.42	71					
		Rs.15001 - Rs.20000	8.03	1.20	222					
		Above Rs.20000	7.92	1.03	174					
7	Family Debt	No	8.13	1.57	88		1.181	498	1.968	Ns
		Yes	7.96	1.13	412					

Source: Primary Data

NS-Non Significant,   * - 5 % level of Significance,   ** - 1 % Level of Significance

T-test and F-test results shows that the calculated value is lower than the table value in the case of marital status, family income and family debt at either 5 percent or 1 percent significance level. The hypothesis is accepted and therefore, there is no association found between these personal variables and the job satisfactions. At the same time, *the calculated value is higher than the table value at either 5 percent or 1 percent significance level in the case of personal variables such as age, gender, educational qualifications and family size. Therefore, null hypothesis is rejected* in these cases. The influence of these variables on employee opinion towards the job satisfactions has been discussed as under:

- **Age**

The mean score for opinion towards job satisfaction is high for respondents between 18 and 25 years of age (8.39) and low for respondents above 55 years of age (7.35). That is, the respondents who are between 18 and 25 years of age are found to agree more on job satisfaction compared to respondent above 55 years of age.

- **Gender**

The mean score for opinion towards job satisfaction is high for female employees (8.63) and low for male employees (7.52). That is, the female respondents are found to agree more on job satisfaction compared to male employees.

- **Marital Status**

The mean score for opinion towards job satisfaction is high for unmarried employees (8.07) and low for widow employees (7.60). That is, unmarried employees are found to agree more on job satisfaction compared to widow employees.

- **Educational Qualifications**

The mean score for opinion towards job satisfaction is high for higher secondary level educated respondents (8.12) and low for diploma holders (6.43). That is, the respondents who are at higher secondary level are found to agree more on job satisfaction compared to diploma holders.

- **Family Members**

The mean score for opinion towards job satisfaction is high for the respondents whose family members are between 4 and 6 (8.06) and low for the respondents whose family members are above 6 (7.63). That is, the respondents whose family members are between 4 and 6 are found to agree more on job satisfaction compared to the respondents whose family members are above 6 .

- ## Family Income

The mean score for opinion towards job satisfaction is high for respondents whose family income is between Rs.5001 and Rs.10000 (8.24) and low for the respondents whose family income is between Rs.10001 and Rs.15000 (7.90). That is, the respondents whose family income is between Rs.5001 and Rs.10000 are found to agree more on job satisfaction compared to the respondents whose family income is between Rs.10001 and Rs.15000.

- ## Family Debt

The mean score for opinion towards job satisfaction is high for those who do not have family debt (8.13) and low for those who have family debt (7.96). That is, the respondents who are do not have family debt are found to agree more on job satisfaction compared to those who have family debt .

2. *Occupational Profile and Job Satisfaction*

Table 4.3.22 portrays the mean values of employees' opinion towards job satisfaction for all independent variables that determine the occupational profile such as unit size, type of job activity, work experience, wage and work schedule

Table 4.3.22: Distribution of Respondents based on the Association between Occupational Profile and their Opinion Towards Job Satisfaction

S.No	Variables	Group	Mean	SD	No.	F test	T Test	df.	Table Value	Sig.
1	Size of Unit	Small	7.78	1.45	200	5.655		499	4.648	**
		Medium	8.07	1.04	200					
		Large	8.23	.93	100					
2	Type of Job Activity	Fabrication, Compacting and Calendaring	7.62	1.11	106	11.291		499	3.821	**
		Dyeing, Bleaching and Printing	7.79	1.47	52					
		Cutting, Sewing, Embroidering and packing	8.35	1.20	205					
		Composite unit	7.80	1.08	137					
3	Total Experience in Textile Industry	Less than 5	8.19	1.06	59	3.274		499	2.390	*
		5 - 10	8.06	1.09	250					
		10 - 15	7.66	1.45	122					
		15 - 20	8.00	1.36	15					
		Above 20	8.19	1.21	54					
4	Wage (p.m)	Below Rs.3000	8.50	1.35	10	10.936		499	3.357	**
		Rs.3001 -Rs. 6000	8.31	1.45	49					
		Rs.6001 -Rs. 9000	8.43	1.27	107					
		Rs. 9001 -Rs. 12000	8.03	1.26	155					
		Above Rs.12000	7.57	.90	179					
5	Work Schedule	Day shift	8.35	1.18	165	8.032		499	3.357	**
		Afternoon shift	8.28	1.19	29					
		Night shift	8.33	1.50	9					
		Irregular shift on cal	7.59	1.23	93					
		Rotating shift	7.82	1.15	204					

Source: Primary Data

NS-Non Significant,   * - 5 % level of Significance,   ** - 1 % Level of Significance

F-test results shows that *the calculated value is higher than the table* value *at either 5 percent or 1 percent significance level in the case of unit size, type of job activity, experience, wage and work schedule. The null hypothesis is rejected in these cases and therefore, there is association found between these occupational variables and the job satisfaction.* The influence of these variables on employee opinion towards job satisfaction has been discussed as under:

- **Size of Unit**

The mean score for opinion towards job satisfaction is high for the respondents who are working in large units (8.23) and low for the respondents who are working in small units (7.78). That is, the respondents who are working in large units are found to agree more on job satisfaction compared to small units.

- **Type of Job Activity**

The mean score for opinion towards job satisfaction is high for respondents who are working in cutting, sewing, embroidering and packing units (8.35) and low for the respondents who are working in fabrication, compacting and calendaring units (7.62). That is, the respondents who are working in cutting, sewing, embroidering and packing units are found to agree more on job satisfaction compared to the respondents who are working in fabrication, compacting and calendaring units.

- **Total Experience in Textile Industry**

The mean score for opinion towards job satisfaction is high for respondents who have less than 5 years and above 20 years experience in textile industry (8.19) and low for the respondents who have between 10 and 15 years of experience in textile industry (7.66). That is, the respondents who have less than 5 years and above 20 years experience in textile industry are found to agree more on job satisfaction compared to the respondents who have between 10 and 15 years experience in textile industry.

- **Wage**

The mean score for opinion towards job satisfaction is high for the respondents who earn below Rs.3000 (8.50) and low for the respondents who earn above Rs.12000 (7.57). That is, the respondents who earn below Rs.3000 are found to agree more on job satisfaction compared to the respondents who earn above Rs.12000.

- **Work Schedule**

The mean score for opinion towards job satisfaction is high for respondents working in day shifts (8.35) and low for respondents working in irregular shifts (7.59). That is, the respondents who are working in day shift are found to agree more on job satisfaction compared to those in irregular shifts.

Factor 11: Autonomy

In this section, an attempt has been made to examine the association between the employees opinion towards autonomy with their personal and occupational profile. T-test and F-test have been applied to find the association by formulating the null hypothesis.

Ho: There is no significant association between employees' opinion towards autonomy and their personal / occupational profile.

1. Personal Profile and Autonomy

Table4.3.23 portrays the mean values of employees' opinion towards autonomy for all independent variables that determine the personal profile such as age, gender, marital status, educational qualifications, family size, family income and family debt

Table 4.3.23: Distribution of Respondents based on the Association between Personal Profile and their Opinion Towards Autonomy

S.No	Variables	Group	Mean	SD	No.	F test	T Test	df.	Table Value	Sig.
1	Age	18 - 25 yrs	9.96	1.88	113	9.316		499	3.357	**
		25 - 35 yrs	9.91	1.86	179					
		35 - 45 yrs	10.84	1.56	95					
		45 - 55 yrs	10.08	1.86	76					
		Above 55 yrs	8.81	1.76	37					
2	Gender	Male	10.16	1.90	289		1.726	498	1.968	Ns
		Female	9.87	1.80	211					
3	Marital Status	Unmarried	9.91	1.86	124	3.274		499	2.623	*
		Married	10.08	1.86	248					
		Divorced	10.44	1.74	85					
		Widowed	9.40	2.00	43					
4	Educational Qualifications	Illiterate	9.98	2.01	58	5.286		499	3.357	**
		Primary	10.35	1.88	283					
		Higher Secondary	9.52	1.65	137					
		Graduate	9.40	1.50	15					
		Diploma	9.71	2.43	7					
5	Family Members	1 - 3	10.04	1.87	120	.244		499	3.014	Ns
		4- 6	10.07	1.90	315					
		Above 6	9.89	1.65	65					
6	Family Income	Rs.5001 - Rs.10000	10.15	2.21	33	.556		499	2.623	Ns
		Rs.10001 - Rs.15000	10.07	1.91	71					
		Rs.15001 - Rs.20000	9.92	1.76	222					
		Above Rs.20000	10.16	1.91	174					
7	Family Debt	No	10.33	1.84	88		1.609	498	1.968	Ns
		Yes	9.98	1.86	412					

Source: Primary Data

NS-Non Significant,   * - 5 % level of Significance,   ** - 1 % Level of Significance

T-test and F-test results shows that the calculated value is lower than the table value in the case of gender, family size, family income and family debt at either 5 percent or 1 percent significance level. The hypothesis is accepted and therefore, there is no association found between these personal variables and the autonomy. At the same time, *the calculated value is higher than the table value at either 5 percent or 1 percent significance level in the case of personal variables such as age, marital status and educational qualifications. Therefore, null hypothesis is rejected* in these cases. The influence of these variables on employee opinion towards autonomy has been discussed as under:

- **Age**

The mean score for opinion towards autonomy is high for the respondents who belong to the age group between 35 and 45 years (10.84) and low for the respondents who belong to the age group above 55 years (8.81). That is, the respondents who belong to the age group between 35 and 45 years are found to agree more on autonomy compared to the respondents who belong to the age group above 55 years.

- **Gender**

The mean score for opinion towards autonomy is high for male employees (10.16) and low for female employees (9.87). That is, male employees are found to agree more on autonomy compared to female employees.

- **Marital Status**

The mean score for opinion towards autonomy is high for divorced employees (10.44) and low for widow employees (9.40). That is, the divorced employees are found to agree more on autonomy compared to widow employees.

- **Educational Qualifications**

The mean score for opinion towards autonomy is high for the respondents who have educated up to primary level (10.35) and low for the respondents who have educated up to graduate level (9.40). That is, the respondents who are educated up to primary level are found to agree more on autonomy compared to the respondents who are educated up to graduate level.

- **Family Size**

The mean score for opinion towards autonomy is high for the respondents whose family member are between 4 and 6 (10.07) and low for the respondents whose family member are above 6 (9.89). That is, the respondents whose family members are between 4 and 6 are found to agree more on autonomy compared to the respondents whose family members are above 6.

- ### Family Income

The mean score for opinion towards autonomy is high for the respondents whose family income is above Rs.20000 (10.16) and low for the respondents whose family income is between Rs.15001 and Rs.20000 (9.92). That is, the respondents whose family income is above Rs.20000 are found to agree more on autonomy compared to the respondents whose family income is between Rs.15001 and Rs.20000.

- ### Family Debt

The mean score for opinion towards autonomy is high for the respondents who do not have family debt (10.33) and low for the respondents who have family debt (9.98). That is, the respondents who do not have family debt are found to agree more on autonomy compared to the respondents who have family debt.

2. Occupational Profile and Autonomy

Table 4.3.24 portrays the mean values of employees' opinion towards autonomy for all independent variables that determine the occupational profile such as unit size, type of job activity, work experience, wage and work schedule.

Table 4.3.24: Distribution of Respondents based on the Association between Occupational Profile and their Opinion Towards Autonomy

S.No	Variables	Group	Mean	SD	No.	F test	T Test	df.	Table Value	Sig.
1	Size of Unit	Small	9.72	1.85	200	7.240		499	4.648	**
		Medium	10.11	1.89	200					
		Large	10.56	1.73	100					
2	Type of Job Activity	Fabrication, Compacting and Calendaring	10.09	1.90	106	.544		499	2.623	Ns
		Dyeing, Bleaching and Printing	9.98	1.60	52					
		Cutting, Sewing, Embroidering and packing	9.93	1.93	205					
		Composite unit	10.18	1.82	137					
3	Total Experience in Textile Industry	Less than 5	10.64	1.85	59	5.477		499	3.357	**
		5 - 10	9.83	1.67	250					
		10 - 15	10.46	1.97	122					
		15 - 20	9.87	1.88	15					
		Above 20	9.44	2.16	54					
4	Wage (p.m)	Below Rs.3000	9.70	1.83	10	1.713		499	2.390	Ns
		Rs.3001 -Rs. 6000	9.41	1.94	49					
		Rs.6001 -Rs. 9000	10.16	1.85	107					
		Rs. 9001 -Rs. 12000	10.10	1.67	155					
		Above Rs.12000	10.11	1.99	179					
5	Work Schedule	Day shift	9.95	1.77	165	2.908		499	2.390	*
		Afternoon shift	9.31	1.51	29					
		Night shift	8.89	2.62	9					
		Irregular shift on cal	10.37	1.70	93					
		Rotating shift	10.12	1.98	204					

Source: Primary Data

NS-Non Significant, * - 5 % level of Significance, ** - 1 % Level of Significance.

F-test results shows that the calculated value is lower than the table value in the case of type of job activity and wage at either 5 percent or 1 percent significance level. The hypothesis is accepted and therefore, there is no association found between these occupational variables and autonomy. At the same time, *the calculated value is higher than the table value at either 5 percent or percent significance level in the case of occupational variables such as unit size, experience and work schedule. Therefore, null hypothesis is rejected* in these cases.

The influence of these variables on employee opinion towards the autonomy has been discussed as under:

- **Size of Unit**

The mean score for opinion towards autonomy is high for the respondents who are working in large units (10.56) and low for the respondents who are working in small units (9.72). That is, the respondents who are working in large units are found to agree more on autonomy compared to small units.

- **Type of Job Activity**

The mean score for opinion towards autonomy is high for the respondents who are working in composite units (10.18) and low for the respondents who are working in cutting, sewing, embroidering and packing units (9.93). That is, the respondents who are working in composite unit are found to agree more on autonomy compared to the respondents who are working in cutting, sewing, embroidering and packing units.

- **Total Experience in Textile Industry**

The mean score for opinion towards autonomy is high for the respondents who have less than 5 years experience in textile industry (10.64) and low for the respondents who have above 20 years experience in textile industry (9.44). That is, the respondents who are having less than 5 years experience in textile industry are found to agree more on autonomy compared to the respondents who are having above 20 years experience in textile industry.

- **Wage**

The mean score for opinion towards autonomy is high for the respondents whose wage is between Rs.6001 and Rs.9000 (10.16) and low for the respondents whose wage is between Rs.3001 and Rs.6000 (9.41). That is, the respondents whose wage is between Rs.6001 and Rs.9000 are found to agree more on autonomy compared to the respondents whose wage is between Rs.3001 and Rs.6000.

- **Work Schedule**

The mean score for opinion towards autonomy is high for the respondents who are working in irregular shifts (10.37) and low for the respondents who are working in night shifts (8.89). That is, the respondents who are working in irregular shifts are found to agree more on autonomy compared to the respondents who are working in night shifts.

4.3.6. *Composite Factors of QWL - Factor Analysis*

Factor analysis is used to summarize the information contained in the 44 original variables of QWL in to a smaller set of new composite dimensions (Factors) with minimum loss of information. That is, the factor analysis tries to identify and define the underlying dimensions in the original variables of QWL.

4.3.6.1. *Steps in Factor Analysis*

1. First, the correlation matrix for all variables is computed. Variables that do not appear to be related to other variables can be identified from the matrix. The appropriateness of the factor model can also be calculated.
2. Factor extraction, the number of factors necessary to represent the data and the method of calculating them must be determined. At this step, how well the chosen model fits the data is also ascertained.
3. Rotation focuses on transforming the factors to make them more interpretable.
4. Scores for each factor can be computed for each case. These scores are then used for further analysis.

The set of 44 items included in the Quality of Work Life scale was used to find the underlying factors in it.

Step 1

Correlation matrix for the variables, item1 to item 44, was analyzed initially for possible inclusion in Factor Analysis. (The results of the correlation between items 1 to item 44 are given in Appendix II.

Since one of the goals of the factor analysis is to obtain 'factors' that help explain these correlations, the variables must be related to each other for the factor model to be appropriate. A closer examination of the correlation matrix may reveal what are the variables which do not have any relationship. Usually a correlation value of 0.3 (absolute value) is taken as sufficient to explain the relation between variables. All the variables from 1 to 44 have been retained for further analysis. Further, two tests are applied to the resultant correlation matrix to test whether the relationship among the variables is significant or not.

Table 4.3.25: KMO and Bartlett's Test

Kaiser-Meyer-Olkin Measure of Sampling Adequacy.		0.770
Bartlett's Test of Sphericity	Approx. Chi-Square	8255.091
	df	946
	Sig.	**

Source: Primary Data

One is Bartlett's test of sphericity. This is used to test whether the correlation matrix is an identity matrix. i.e., all the diagonal terms in the matrix are 1 and the off diagonal terms in the matrix are 0. In short, the correlations between all the variables are 0. The test value (8255.091) and the significance level (P<.01) are given above. With the value of test statistic and the associated significance level is so small, it appears that the correlation matrix is not an identity matrix, i.e., there exists correlations between the variables.

Another test is Kaiser-Meyer-Olkin (KMO) measure of sampling adequacy. This test is based on the correlations and partial correlations of the variables. If the test value, or KMO measure is closer to 1, then it is good to use factor analysis. If KMO is closer to 0, then the factor analysis is not a good idea for the variables and data. The value of test statistic is given above as 0.770 which means the factor analysis for the selected variables is found to be appropriate to the data.

Step 2

Next step is to determine the method of factor extraction, number of initial factors and the estimates of factors. Here Principal Components Analysis (PCA) is used to extract factors. PCA is a method used to transform a set of correlated variables into a set of uncorrelated variables (here factors) so that the factors are unrelated and the variables selected for each factor are related. Next PCA is used to extract the no. of factors required to represent the data.

The question then is, how many factors do we want to extract? Note that as we extract consecutive factors, they account for less and less variability. The decision of when to stop extracting factors basically depends on when there is only very little "random" variability left.

The results from principal components analysis are given below.

To start with, in the correlation matrix, where the variances of all variables are equal to 1.0. Therefore, the total variance in that matrix is equal to the number of variables. For our study, we have 44 variables (items) each with a variance of 1 then the total variability that can potentially be extracted is equal to 44 times 1. The variance accounted for by successive factors would be summarized as follows:

Table 4.3.26: Total Variance Explained

S.No	Initial Eigen values			Extraction Sums of Squared Loadings (after rotation)		
Component	Total	% of Variance	Cumulative %	Total	% of Variance	Cumulative %
1	5.806	13.195	13.195	4.527	10.289	10.289
2	3.642	8.277	21.472	2.915	6.625	16.915
3	3.203	7.280	28.752	2.899	6.589	23.504
4	2.780	6.318	35.070	2.633	5.985	29.488
5	2.377	5.402	40.472	2.605	5.921	35.410
6	2.120	4.817	45.289	2.377	5.403	40.813
7	1.840	4.182	49.472	2.205	5.011	45.824
8	1.643	3.735	53.206	2.060	4.682	50.506
9	1.323	3.008	56.214	1.893	4.301	54.808
10	1.206	2.741	58.956	1.471	3.343	58.151
11	1.070	2.431	61.386	1.424	3.236	61.386
12	0.999	2.272	63.658			
13	.991	2.252	65.910			
14	.905	2.057	67.967			
15	.866	1.968	69.935			
16	.808	1.837	71.773			
17	.798	1.813	73.586			
18	.742	1.687	75.273			
19	.732	1.664	76.937			
20	.686	1.560	78.496			
21	.657	1.492	79.988			
22	.615	1.398	81.387			
23	.592	1.346	82.733			
24	.579	1.317	84.049			
25	.569	1.293	85.342			
26	.537	1.220	86.563			
27	.507	1.152	87.715			
28	.461	1.047	88.761			
29	.445	1.010	89.772			
30	.413	.939	90.711			
31	.402	.913	91.624			
32	.377	.857	92.481			
33	.354	.804	93.284			
34	.347	.789	94.073			
35	.324	.735	94.809			
36	.308	.701	95.510			
37	.297	.674	96.184			
38	.280	.637	96.820			
39	.276	.628	97.448			
40	.269	.611	98.059			
41	.237	.540	98.598			
42	.233	.529	99.127			
43	.206	.469	99.596			
44	.178	.404	100.000			

In the second column (Initial *Eigen values*) the column titled 'Variance, we find the variance on the new factors that were successively extracted. In the third column, these values are expressed as a percent of the total variance. As we can see, factor 1 account for about 13 percent of the total variance, factor 2 about 8 percent, and so on. As expected, the sum of the eigen values is equal to the number of variables. The third column contains the cumulative variance extracted. The variances extracted by the factors are called the *eigen values*.

Table 4.3.27: Component Matrix

Items	Component										
	1	**2**	**3**	**4**	**5**	**6**	**7**	**8**	**9**	**10**	**11**
19	0.776	0.049	-0.228	0.044	0.054	0.025	0.186	-0.036	0.045	0.063	-0.084
18	0.767	-0.105	-0.026	0.009	0.146	0.032	0.169	-0.044	-0.11	-0.105	-0.139
30	0.677	0.182	-0.034	0.032	-0.21	-0.096	-0.018	0.016	0.061	0.132	-0.017
31	0.645	0.21	-0.012	0.194	-0.354	-0.03	-0.184	0.12	0.232	0.067	-0.009
41	0.592	0.179	0.253	0.074	-0.211	0.436	0.057	-0.058	0.096	0.057	-0.011
28	-0.581	0.015	-0.425	0.034	0.062	0.254	-0.014	-0.158	0.149	0.136	0.172
17	0.577	-0.299	-0.184	0.174	0.061	-0.065	0.206	-0.332	-0.172	0.089	-0.17
29	0.57	-0.279	0.23	-0.042	0.044	-0.314	-0.155	-0.247	-0.204	0.016	-0.201
27	0.521	0.253	0.229	0.148	-0.035	0.349	0.063	0.372	0.167	-0.091	0.146
22	0.459	0.24	0.145	0.09	0.008	0.141	-0.03	-0.264	0.104	0.013	-0.072
36	0.446	0.256	-0.406	0.225	-0.174	-0.141	-0.026	0.045	-0.138	0.102	0.116
32	0.418	-0.085	0.36	0.293	-0.369	-0.177	0.012	0.242	-0.19	-0.059	-0.031
35	0.395	-0.042	0.077	0.181	0.234	0.008	-0.297	-0.15	0.107	0.022	0.302
14	0.394	-0.299	-0.197	-0.351	0.188	0.204	-0.003	0.289	0.089	-0.162	-0.122
38	-0.303	-0.166	0.224	-0.066	0.263	0.087	0.288	0.121	0.026	0.006	-0.216
43	-0.078	-0.58	0.111	-0.171	0.278	-0.021	-0.111	0.032	0.033	-0.045	0.311
20	0.094	-0.526	0.248	0.177	0.241	-0.048	0.236	-0.346	0.062	-0.067	-0.073
2	0.257	0.437	-0.286	-0.303	0.379	0.031	0.262	0.02	0.039	-0.094	-0.01
1	0.194	0.422	-0.255	-0.117	0.311	-0.119	0.146	-0.321	-0.085	0.032	0.21
13	0.38	-0.388	-0.161	-0.367	0.023	-0.038	0.11	0.244	0.338	-0.233	-0.044
21	-0.223	0.107	0.651	-0.407	-0.014	-0.145	-0.099	-0.031	0.109	-0.188	-0.051
25	0.072	0.418	0.561	-0.265	-0.012	-0.105	0.029	-0.085	-0.139	-0.001	-0.093
26	0.173	0.319	0.496	-0.208	0.334	-0.154	-0.037	0.07	0.084	-0.125	0.021
24	0.166	0.324	0.373	-0.023	0.35	-0.108	0.013	-0.283	0.288	-0.167	-0.052
6	-0.077	-0.274	0.329	0.558	-0.025	0.047	0.103	0.005	0.321	-0.022	-0.037
10	-0.101	0.354	-0.052	0.548	0.266	-0.021	-0.004	0.093	-0.16	0.046	-0.281
7	-0.041	-0.502	0.178	0.516	0.036	-0.048	0.062	0.027	-0.012	0.083	0.173
9	0.429	-0.356	-0.106	-0.462	-0.026	0.182	0.117	0.179	-0.075	0.14	0.193
11	-0.066	0.295	-0.312	0.416	0.184	-0.067	0.129	0.187	0.126	-0.076	-0.067
3	-0.153	0.35	-0.025	0.368	-0.071	-0.122	-0.087	-0.045	0.32	-0.071	0.051
8	-0.172	-0.015	-0.213	0.33	0.496	-0.178	0.287	0.202	0.102	-0.222	-0.11
15	0.201	-0.043	0.195	0.257	0.49	0.47	-0.317	0.084	-0.097	0.086	-0.01
42	-0.223	-0.313	0.275	0.046	-0.388	0.313	0.163	-0.363	0.122	-0.148	-0.041
44	0.149	-0.203	0.085	-0.042	0.366	-0.517	0.134	0.193	-0.197	0.256	0.088
16	0.358	-0.156	0.261	0.084	0.387	0.469	-0.232	0.075	-0.162	0.066	0.116
4	-0.046	-0.006	0.24	0.13	-0.113	-0.437	-0.332	0.356	-0.156	-0.179	0.022
33	-0.125	0.329	0.301	-0.069	-0.196	0.174	0.484	0.279	-0.187	-0.037	-0.027
5	-0.068	-0.311	0.336	0.346	-0.01	-0.01	0.439	0.187	-0.065	0.071	0.228
34	-0.16	0.352	0.139	-0.049	0.03	0.175	0.432	0.101	0.026	0.111	0.175
12	-0.382	0.194	0.101	0.061	0.27	0.36	-0.417	0.111	-0.201	0.056	-0.196
37	-0.189	0.086	0.108	-0.058	-0.123	0.297	0.205	-0.066	-0.383	0.095	-0.096
39	-0.171	-0.031	0.275	-0.093	0.081	-0.105	0.128	-0.041	0.261	0.609	-0.22
40	0.035	0.143	0.22	-0.194	0.087	-0.172	-0.078	0.175	0.275	0.549	0.057
23	0.05	0.406	0.268	0.104	0.068	-0.128	0.135	-0.246	-0.197	-0.132	0.464

Now that we have a measure of how much variance each successive factor extracts and we can decide about the number of factors to retain. We can retain only factors with eigen values greater than 1. In essence, this is like saying that, unless a factor extracts at least as much as the equivalent of one original variable, we drop it. This criterion is probably the one most widely used and is followed in this study also. In our example above, using this criterion, we would retain 11 factors (principal components).

The table shown above gives the Component Matrix or Factor Matrix where PCA extracted 11 factors. These are all coefficients used to express a standardized variable in terms of the factors. These coefficients are called factor loadings, since they indicate how much weight is assigned to each factor. Factors with large coefficients (in absolute value) for a variable are closely related to that variable. For example, Factor 1 is the factor with largest loading (0.776) for the variable, Statement 19 (I trust the management at the place where I work). These are all the correlations between the factors and the variables, Hence the correlation between Statement 19 and Factor 1 is 0.776. Thus the factor matrix is obtained. These are the initially obtained estimates of factors.

Table 4.3.28: Communalities

Items	Initial	Extraction	Items	Initial	Extraction
Quality of work life-1	1.000	.582	Quality of work life-24	1.000	.622
Quality of work life-2	1.000	.654	Quality of work life-25	1.000	.600
Quality of work life-3	1.000	.421	Quality of work life-26	1.000	.612
Quality of work life-4	1.000	.573	Quality of work life-27	1.000	.585
Quality of work life-5	1.000	.623	Quality of work life-28	1.000	.733
Quality of work life-6	1.000	.619	Quality of work life-29	1.000	.683
Quality of work life-7	1.000	.596	Quality of work life-30	1.000	.725
Quality of work life-8	1.000	.656	Quality of work life-31	1.000	.569
Quality of work life-9	1.000	.678	Quality of work life-32	1.000	.731
Quality of work life-10	1.000	.626	Quality of work life-33	1.000	.664
Quality of work life-11	1.000	.478	Quality of work life-34	1.000	.638
Quality of work life-12	1.000	.668	Quality of work life-35	1.000	.443
Quality of work life-13	1.000	.699	Quality of work life-36	1.000	.465
Quality of work life-14	1.000	.616	Quality of work life-37	1.000	.576
Quality of work life-15	1.000	.732	Quality of work life-38	1.000	.373
Quality of work life-16	1.000	.701	Quality of work life-39	1.000	.396
Quality of work life-17	1.000	.712	Quality of work life-40	1.000	.638
Quality of work life-18	1.000	.695	Quality of work life-41	1.000	.561
Quality of work life-19	1.000	.710	Quality of work life-42	1.000	.706
Quality of work life-20	1.000	.628	Quality of work life-43	1.000	.671
Quality of work life-21	1.000	.732	Quality of work life-44	1.000	.574
Quality of work life-22	1.000	.405	Quality of work life-43	1.000	.641

The table titled **Communalities** given above provides communalities for each variable calculated from the factor matrix described above. The proportion of variance explained by the common factors is called Communality of the variable. For example the proportion of variance explained by the 11 factors in the variable, that is the statement, 'Quality of Work Life-1' (The employees are satisfied with the spirit of team work) 0.582. That is 58.2% of the variance in Statement 1 is explained by all the 11 factors. So the communality of the variable Item 1 is 0.582. Further, the table titled **Total Variance Explained** gives the proportion of total variance explained by all the factors. The column '% of Variance' explains how much variance is attributed to each factor and the next column is the cumulative percent of variance. So, Factor 1 is the one which accounts for maximum proportion of total variance. These eigen values are calculated from the factor matrix described above. Thus for any factor, its corresponding highest factor loading will contribute much to that factor. By looking at the last column it is understood that the 11 factor model explains 61.4% of the variance in the selected variables.

Step 3

Although the factor matrix (Table titled **Component Matrix**) obtained in the extraction phase indicates the relationship between the factors and the individual variables it is usually, difficult to identify meaningful factors based on this matrix. Often variables and factors do not appear correlated in any interpretable pattern. Most factors are correlated with many variables.

Since the idea of factor analysis is to identify the factors that meaningfully summarize the sets of closely related variables, the Rotation phase of the factor analysis attempts to transfer initial matrix into one that is easier to interpret. It is called the rotation of the factor matrix.

There are several methods available for rotating factor matrix. The one used in this analysis is Varimax Rotation, the most commonly used method, which attempts to minimize the number of variables that have high loadings on a factor. This should enhance the interpretability of the factors.

Thus Varimax rotation has been used here. The Rotated Factor Matrix (Table titled **Rotated Component Matrix**) using Varimax rotation is given in Table 4.3.29 where each factor identifies itself with a few set of variables.

The variables which identify with each of the factors were sorted in the decreasing order and are highlighted against each column and row.

Table 4.3.29: Rotated Component Matrix

Statements	Component										
	1	2	3	4	5	6	7	8	9	10	11
31	**0.814**	0.012	-0.032	-0.032	-0.025	-0.02	-0.046	-0.185	0.153	-0.06	0.043
41	**0.711**	0.063	0.08	0.131	0.049	-0.2	0.244	0.184	-0.183	-0.027	-0.05
30	**0.682**	0.087	-0.131	-0.01	0.209	-0.031	-0.067	-0.075	0.09	0.074	0.101
27	**0.653**	0.239	0.111	0.161	-0.221	0.124	0.307	0.204	0.07	0.065	-0.049
19	**0.614**	0.282	-0.116	-0.082	0.411	0.184	0.021	-0.055	-0.136	0.094	0.007
36	**0.498**	-0.082	-0.239	-0.357	0.124	0.181	-0.097	-0.092	0.118	0.233	-0.05
22	**0.487**	-0.107	-0.042	0.234	0.18	-0.042	0.137	-0.059	-0.199	0.051	-0.03
38	**-0.373**	0.11	0.204	0.181	0.04	0.147	0.072	0.283	-0.092	-0.191	0.126
13	0.129	**0.759**	0.016	0.052	0.067	0.032	-0.17	-0.189	-0.014	-0.175	-0.044
14	0.098	**0.692**	-0.156	-0.032	0.124	0.055	0.177	-0.068	-0.027	-0.2	-0.083
9	0.138	**0.679**	-0.088	-0.196	0.164	-0.295	0.092	0.079	-0.026	0.104	0.106
43	-0.394	**0.409**	0.289	-0.005	0.033	-0.188	0.187	-0.267	0.063	0.145	0.036
3	0.162	**-0.38**	0.084	0.097	-0.325	0.269	-0.148	-0.178	-0.04	0.027	-0.012
6	0.084	-0.155	**0.72**	0.073	-0.063	0.141	0.048	-0.081	-0.029	-0.173	0.024
7	-0.082	-0.052	**0.685**	-0.22	0.12	0.04	0.127	-0.118	0.136	0.06	0.021
5	-0.057	0.068	**0.667**	-0.07	0.044	0.075	0.003	0.318	0.132	0.18	0.081
20	-0.167	0.098	**0.541**	0.151	0.464	-0.023	0.036	-0.13	-0.198	-0.004	-0.044
2	0.123	0.252	**-0.495**	0.189	0.072	0.377	-0.004	0.131	-0.266	0.244	0.004
42	-0.072	-0.101	**0.45**	0.056	-0.044	-0.44	-0.145	0.131	-0.318	-0.222	-0.256
21	-0.222	-0.003	0.005	**0.7**	-0.157	-0.331	-0.076	0.096	0.175	-0.083	0.082
24	0.127	-0.112	0.001	**0.684**	0.075	0.147	0.06	-0.14	-0.181	0.134	0.05
26	0.071	0.065	-0.101	**0.678**	0.001	0.07	0.156	0.044	0.162	0.166	0.146
25	0.101	-0.185	-0.183	**0.589**	0.066	-0.213	0.011	0.301	0.149	0.089	0.129
17	0.293	0.101	0.113	-0.202	**0.717**	0.037	-0.009	-0.115	-0.162	0.052	-0.074
29	0.221	0.076	0.038	0.183	**0.678**	-0.22	0.045	-0.257	0.24	-0.017	0.023
29	0.472	0.339	-0.02	0.068	**0.549**	0.109	0.137	-0.005	-0.017	0.056	-0.131
8	-0.261	0.056	0.16	0.019	0.049	**0.742**	-0.012	-0.019	-0.018	0.025	-0.072
11	0.094	-0.176	-0.019	-0.128	-0.141	**0.63**	-0.032	-0.008	-0.032	0.024	-0.05
10	0.042	-0.486	-0.018	-0.034	0.069	**0.55**	0.232	0.11	0.083	-0.076	-0.005
15	0.086	-0.011	0.099	0.056	0.046	0.106	**0.83**	-0.081	-0.052	-0.029	0.004
16	0.151	0.188	0.121	0.065	0.125	-0.09	**0.77**	-0.018	-0.017	0.079	-0.021
12	-0.293	-0.312	-0.216	0.039	-0.23	0.03	**0.565**	0.069	0.031	-0.241	-0.013
33	0.077	-0.023	0.031	0.158	-0.167	0.032	-0.092	**0.749**	0.072	0.034	-0.01
37	-0.123	-0.172	-0.055	-0.094	0.068	-0.189	0.109	**0.498**	-0.097	-0.03	-0.079
34	0.019	-0.034	0.018	0.118	-0.239	0.117	-0.042	**0.49**	-0.192	0.239	0.142
35	0.269	0.031	0.11	0.082	0.077	-0.025	0.321	**-0.42**	-0.001	0.294	0.01
4	-0.041	-0.101	0.05	0.118	-0.091	0.022	-0.044	-0.136	**0.716**	-0.037	-0.036
32	0.463	-0.028	0.31	0.021	0.187	-0.11	-0.038	0.142	**0.526**	-0.043	-0.072
28	-0.404	-0.171	-0.063	-0.358	-0.385	0.064	-0.015	-0.08	**-0.445**	0.036	0.006
23	0.093	-0.275	0.023	0.291	-0.031	-0.033	-0.009	0.133	0.04	**0.642**	-0.135
1	0.078	-0.077	-0.389	0.098	0.171	0.2	-0.041	-0.049	-0.275	**0.51**	0.01
39	-0.102	-0.119	0.133	0.124	0.057	-0.066	-0.055	0.086	-0.162	-0.181	**0.709**
40	0.093	0.035	-0.064	0.141	-0.14	-0.062	0.021	-0.043	0.059	0.041	**0.705**
44	-0.188	0.195	0.064	0.013	0.386	0.199	-0.014	-0.047	0.364	0.282	**0.401**

Step 4

Normally, from the factor results arrived above, factor score coefficients can be calculated for all variables (since each factor is a linear combination of all variables) which are then used to calculate the factor scores for each individual. Since PCA was used in extraction of initial factors, all methods will result in estimating same factor score coefficients. However, for the study, original values of the variables were retained for further analysis and factor scores were thus obtained by adding the values (ratings given by the respondents) of the respective variables for that particular factor, for each respondent.

Conclusion

Thus the 44 variables in the data were reduced to 11 factor model and each factor is identified with the corresponding variables as follows:

Table 4.3.30: Factors Identified Against Statements of the Quality of Work Life Scale

Item No.	Statement	Factor Names
31	The Company properly promotes and maintains human relations	1. Employer-Employee relationship
41	There is cordial and close relation between management and employees	
30	The Company promotes mutual trust and community of interests	
27	No discrimination based upon race, color, sex, sexual orientation	
19	I trust the management at the place where I work	
36	I am treated with respect in the work place	
22	The employees have sense of community and inter personal openness	
38	The superior is concerned about the welfare activities of the Employees	
13	The Company provides adequate incentives	2. Incentives
14	The Company provides special incentive for prompt work	
9	The Company provides variety of fringe benefits	
43	The Company provides large amount of part time work	
3	The Company provides attractive bonus	
6	Hard work and achievements are recognized appropriately	3. Development and encouragement
7	The Company encourages the employees for their self development	
5	The Employees are invited and encouraged to offer suggestions	
20	The Employees are listened to and their views are taken into consideration	
2	The job requires me to work very fast and keep learning	
42	Having competency is the basis for promotion	4. Grievance Redressal
21	The management is really keen to redress the grievances	
24	The Employees have a sense of fair chance to ventilate their grievance	
26	The Employees are listened to and their views are taken into consideration	
25	The Company provides scope for appeal against redressal of grievance	
17	The Management attempt to understand stresses, its causes	5. Stress management
29	The Management takes efforts to reduce monotonous and disinteresting job	
18	The Management arrange periodical workshops for control and reduction of stress	
8	The Company provides fair and adequate wage	6. Wage structure
11	The wage plan is consistent with the other Companies	
10	The Company provides equal wage to the same cadre	
15	Regular training and development programmes are conducted	7. Training
16	The training helped in improving the quality of work	
12	The organization is providing enough instruction, high quality tools and techniques	
33	The working conditions provide no risk to the employees	8. Working conditions
37	The physical environment of the Company is comfortable	
34	The Company provides adequate safety measures to the employees	
35	The work schedule and timings are followed as per the Government regulations	
4	Shift mechanism affects the maintenance of family relationship	9. Work life balance
32	Hours of work interferes with family relationships	
28	The work schedule provide leisure time	
23	I feel comfortable, secured and satisfied with my job	10. Job satisfaction
1	The employees are satisfied with the spirit of team work	
39	The Management provides greater autonomy to the subordinates	11. Autonomy
40	On the job, I know exactly what is expected of me	
44	Flexible reporting / leaving schedule and lunch timings are allowed	

Source: Primary Data

4.3.7. *Predominant Factors Influencing the overall QWL –Multiple Regression*

The concept of correlation gives the relationship between the variables. Regression gives the degree of dependence of a variable on others. Regression is a statistical measure that attempts to determine the strength of the relationship between one dependent variable (usually denoted by Y) and a series of other changing variables (known as independent variables). Here the variable on which the overall QWL depends is discussed by applying multiple regressions. This is indicated through the Coefficient of determination (r^2).The predominant influence of various personal and occupational related variables on overall quality of work life of the respondents was studied using multiple regression analysis. Overall QWL score was taken as the dependent variable. Age, gender, education, family size, family income and family debt were taken as independent variables related to personal profile. Employment status (permanent / temporary), unit size (small / medium / large), experience, wage and stress were taken as other independent variables related to occupational profile. The results of the multiple regression analysis are given below.

Table 4.3.31: Dependent Variable: Overall Quality of Work Life Score

Variables	B	Std. Error	t	Sig.
(Constant)	137.069	3.186		
Age	-4.395	.396	-11.109	**
Gender	-.720	.722	-.997	Ns
Educational Qualifications	.166	.396	.420	Ns
Family size	.857	.494	1.736	Ns
Family Income	.825	.340	2.427	*
Family debt	0.07598	.739	.103	Ns
Size of Unit	7.230	.434	16.660	**
Employment Status	4.073	1.382	2.948	**
Experience	1.507	.427	3.530	**
Wage	-.181	.327	-.554	Ns
Stress	-.114	.687	-.166	Ns

Source: Primary Data

R	R Square	F	R²(%)	Sig.
.821	.674	91.638	67.4	**

It is seen from the regression table, that all the independent variables except age and wage have positive effect on overall QWL. That is, those who are educated up to higher secondary level were found to be having high QWL. Similarly, the respondents with maximum family members, high family income and long experience are found to have high QWL. The employees who are working in large units are found to be having high QWL compared to employees working in small units. As far as age, is concerned, employees of old age are found to have low QWL compared to those of young age. Female employees are more agreeable on overall QWL compared to male employees. The recognition of employment status indicates that permanent employees are more comfortable with QWL when compared to temporary employees. The employees who are suffering from stress (coded as 1-yes, 0-no) have less QWL when compared to those who do not suffer from stress. T-test was conducted to find in the significant effect of independent variables on QWL. T-test results shows that family income, size of unit, employment status and experience have significant impact on QWL of employees.

The multiple correlations co-efficient (R) was found out to find the degree of relationship between the set of independent variables and dependent variables. The R value was found to be 0.821 which shows that, there is a high degree of correlation between dependent and independent variables included in the regression model. The F-ratio value (91.638) shows that the correlation is significant at 1% level. The R^2 value (0.674) indicates that 67.4% variation in overall QWL is explained by all the independent variables taken together. The R^2 value further explains the goodness of fit of the model. The R^2 value (0.671) shows that the model fits the data well.

Section IV

Employees's Satisfaction at Work

4.4.1. Introduction

Better quality of work life leads to increased employee morale. It also minimizes attrition, checks labor turnover and absenteeism. There will be better communication and understandings among all employees leading to cordial relations. It enhances the brand image for the company and in turn, encourages entry of new talents into the company.Quality of Work Life is defined as those perceived important personal needs, which an individual tries to satisfy by working in an organization. Quality of Work Life strategists emphasizes more on job re-design, formation of autonomous work groups and worker participation in management; there exist wide differences among the pioneers in these areas so that Quality of Work Life factors should be construed.[5] Proper assessment of employees satisfaction will be helpful to know the Quality of Work Life. Therefore, the objective of this analysis aims to assess the employees level of satisfaction with work related aspects in the textile industry. The personal and occupational profile of the employees and its influence on respondents level of satisfaction has been described with the help of ANOVA and T-test. Descriptive statistics have been applied to assess the level of satisfaction. Correlation between employees satisfaction towards each Quality of Work Life factors has also been found.

To evaluate the level of satisfaction, statistical tools such as mean, standard deviation, ANOVA, T-test and correlation have been used. The level of satisfaction by the respondents depends mainly on the demographical factors and occupational factors such as gender, marital status, educational qualifications, family size, family income, family debt, unit size, type of job activity, experience, wage and work schedule. ANOVA technique is applied when three or more number of groups are to be compared on the basis of their means. It is an extension of "t-test" used to test the homogeneity of several means. In this study the ANOVA is used to know the difference of personal and occupational classifications with respect to the level of employee satisfaction. The results are presented with suitable tests of hypothesis and relevant interpretations. Correlation between different factors of quality of work life and employees level of satisfaction has also been studied.

4.4.2. *Employees Level of Satisfaction at Work- Descriptive Analysis*

Five point Likert's scale has been applied to analyze the level of job satisfaction of textile employees in Tirupur District. The respondents were asked to give their opinion on various statements with respect to job satisfaction on a five point scale. The response of high satisfaction with the statement was given a score of 5, a score of 4 was allotted for response indicating satisfaction against a statement, a score of 3 was allotted for neutral response, a score of 2 was allotted for response indicating dissatisfied employees and a score of 1 was allow for responses conveying high dissatisfied. Descriptive statistics with minimum, maximum, mean and standard deviation of satisfaction were found out for each factor of QWL and the table is given below.

Table 4.4.1: Discrete Factors Contributing to Employees Job Satisfaction

QWL Factors (level of job satisfaction)	N	Minimum	Maximum	Mean	S.D
Wage	500	2.00	5.00	4.1180	.7135
Health care benefits	500	2.00	5.00	3.4820	.6086
Access to recreational facilities	500	1.00	5.00	2.7560	1.2130
Work load	500	1.00	5.00	1.9220	1.1002
Opportunities to develop new skills and work independently	500	1.00	5.00	2.6560	1.1885
Working environment	500	1.00	5.00	3.7060	1.0343
Fair and equitable performance appraisal	500	1.00	5.00	3.3840	1.0839
Flexibility of working hour	500	1.00	5.00	3.5220	1.0468
Job security and job satisfaction	500	1.00	5.00	3.6520	.8001
Relationship with co-workers and supervisor	500	1.00	5.00	3.7320	.8352
Recognition of achievement	500	1.00	5.00	3.8240	.7630

Source: Primary Data

From the above table, it is seen that the level of satisfaction, varied between a minimum of 1 to maximum of 5. The highest mean was found for wage (4.1180) followed by recognition of achievement (3.8240). The lowest mean was found for work load (1.9220). Hence, it can be inferred that among the various factors of QWL, wage and recognition of achievement contributes more towards employees' job satisfaction.

4.4.3. Association of Level of Job Satisfaction with Employee Personal and Occupational Profile

In this section, an attempt has been made to examine the association of job satisfaction with employees' personal and occupational differences. T-test and F-test have been applied to find such association by formulating the following null hypothesis.

Ho: There is no association between employee job satisfaction and personal /occupational profile of the employees

1. Personal Profile and Employee Job Satisfaction

Table 4.4.21 portrays the mean values of opinion on employee job satisfaction for all independent variables that determine the personal profile such as age, gender, marital status, educational qualifications, family size, family income and family debt

Table 4.4.2: Distribution of Respondents based on the Association between Personal Profile and their Opinion on Employee Job Satisfaction

S.No	Variables	Group	Mean	SD	No.	F test	T Test	df.	Table Value	Sig.
1	Age	18 - 25 yrs	39.66	2.65	113	56.885		499	3.357	**
		25 - 35 yrs	37.03	2.37	179					
		35 - 45 yrs	36.25	2.74	95					
		45 - 55 yrs	33.47	3.82	76					
		Above 55 yrs	34.54	4.57	37					
2	Gender	Male	37.32	3.15	289		4.215	498	2.586	**
		Female	35.98	3.94	211					
3	Marital Status	Unmarried	38.31	3.14	124	12.841		499	3.821	**
		Married	36.46	3.59	248					
		Divorced	36.11	3.22	85					
		Widowed	35.26	3.79	43					
4	Educational Qualifications	Illiterate	34.79	4.27	58	8.476		499	3.357	**
		Primary	36.60	3.40	283					
		Higher Secondary	37.71	3.22	137					
		Graduate	38.60	3.42	15					
		Diploma	36.71	2.75	7					
5	Family Members	1 - 3	36.04	3.70	120	4.233		499	3.014	*
		4- 6	36.86	3.59	315					
		Above 6	37.55	2.96	65					
6	Family Income	Rs.5001 - Rs.10000	36.79	3.71	33	2.887		499	2.623	*
		Rs.10001 - Rs.15000	37.03	3.89	71					
		Rs.15001 - Rs.20000	36.25	3.69	222					
		Above Rs.20000	37.28	3.15	174					
7	Family Debt	No	36.11	3.65	88		1.863	498	1.968	Ns
		Yes	36.89	3.53	412					

Source: Primary Data

NS-Non Significant,   * - 5 % level of Significance,   ** - 1 % Level of Significance

T-test and F-test result shows the calculated value is lower than the table value in the case of family debt at either 5 percent or 1 percent significance level. The hypothesis is accepted and therefore, there is no association found between this personal variable and the employee job satisfaction. At the same time, *the calculated value is higher than the table value at either 5 percent or 1 percent significance* level *in the case of personal variables such as age, gender, marital status, educational qualifications, family size and family income. Therefore, null hypothesis is rejected* in these cases.

The influence of these variables on employee job satisfaction has been discussed as under:

- **Age**

The mean score for opinion on job satisfaction is high for the respondents who belong to the age group between 18 and 25 years (39.66) and low for the respondents who belong to the age group between 45 and 55 years (33.47). That is, the respondents who belong to the age group between 18 and 25 years are found to agree more on employee satisfaction compared to the respondents who belong to the age group between 45 and 55 years.

- **Gender**

The mean score for opinion on satisfaction is high for male employees (37.32) and low for female employees (35.98). That is, male respondents are found to agree more on satisfaction compared to female respondents.

- **Marital Status**

The mean score for opinion on satisfaction is high for unmarried employees (38.31) and low for widow employees (35.26). That is, the respondents who are unmarried are found to agree more on satisfaction compared to the respondents who are widows.

- **Educational Qualifications**

The mean score for opinion on satisfaction is high for the respondents who are educated up to graduate level (38.60) and low for the respondents who are illiterate (34.79). That is, the respondents who are educated up to graduate level are found to agree more on satisfaction compared to the respondents who are illiterate.

- **Family Members**

The mean score for opinion on satisfaction is high for respondents whose family members are above 6 (37.55) and low for the respondents whose family members are between 1 and 3 (36.04). That is, the respondents whose family has above 6 members are found to agree more on satisfaction compared to the respondents whose family members are between 1 and 3.

- **Family Income**

The mean score for opinion on satisfaction is high for the respondents whose family income is above Rs.20000 (37.28) and low for the respondents whose family income is between Rs.15001 and Rs.20000 (36.25). That is, the respondents whose family income is above Rs.20000 are found to agree more on satisfaction compared to the respondents who are earning between Rs.15001 and Rs.20000.

- **Family Debt**

The mean score for opinion on satisfaction is high for the respondents who have family debt (36.89) and low for the respondents who do not have family debt (36.11). That is, the respondents who are have family debt are found to agree more on satisfaction compared to the respondents who do not have family debt.

2. *Occupational Profile and Employee Job Satisfaction*

Table 4.4.3 portrays the mean values of opinion on employee job satisfaction for all independent variables that determine the occupational profile such as unit size, type of job activity, work experience, wage and work schedule

Table 4.4.3: Distribution of Respondents based on the Association between Occupational Profile and their Opinion on Employee Job Satisfaction

S.No	Variables	Group	Mean	SD	No.	F test	T Test	df.	Table Value	Sig.
1	Size of Unit	Small	34.74	3.58	200	71.737		499	4.648	**
		Medium	37.74	2.92	200					
		Large	38.79	2.58	100					
2	Type of Job Activity	Fabrication, Compacting and Calendaring	37.81	3.61	106	4.863		499	3.821	**
		Dyeing, Bleaching and Printing	36.90	3.65	52					
		Cutting, Sewing, Embroidering and packing	36.21	3.73	205					
		Composite unit	36.69	3.05	137					
3	Total Experience in Textile Industry	Less than 5	39.61	2.74	59	28.856		499	3.357	**
		5 - 10	37.22	2.74	250					
		10 - 15	34.44	4.35	122					
		15 - 20	37.47	3.83	15					
		Above 20	36.52	2.48	54					
4	Wage (p.m)	Below Rs.3000	36.50	2.55	10	4.773		499	3.357	**
		Rs.3001 -Rs. 6000	37.90	3.64	49					
		Rs.6001 -Rs. 9000	36.51	3.92	107					
		Rs. 9001 -Rs. 12000	35.92	4.04	155					
		Above Rs.12000	37.32	2.66	179					
5	Work Schedule	Day shift	35.88	3.85	165	5.500		499	3.357	**
		Afternoon shift	35.59	3.85	29					
		Night shift	37.56	2.83	9					
		Irregular shift on cal	37.20	3.33	93					
		Rotating shift	37.38	3.24	204					

Source: Primary Data

NS-Non Significant,   * - 5 % level of Significance,   ** - 1 % Level of Significance

F-test results shows that *the calculated value is higher than the table value at 1 percent significance level in the case of unit size, type of job activity, experience, wage and work schedule. The null hypothesis was rejected in these cases and therefore, there is* association *found between these occupational variables and the employee job satisfaction.*

The influence of these variables on employee job satisfaction has been discussed as under:

- **Size of Unit**

The mean score for opinion on satisfaction is high for the respondents who are working in large units (38.79) and low for the respondents who are working in small units (34.74). That is, the respondents who are working in large units are found to agree more on employee job satisfaction compared to the respondents who are working in small units.

- **Type of Job Activity**

The mean score for opinion on satisfaction is high for the respondents who are working in fabrication, compacting and calendaring units (37.81) and low for the respondent who are working in cutting, sewing, embroidering and packing units (36.21).

That is, the respondents who are working in fabrication, compacting and calendaring units are found to agree more on satisfaction compared to the respondents who are working in cutting, sewing, embroidering and packing units.

- **Total Experience in Textile Industry**

The mean score for opinion on employee satisfaction is high for the respondents who have less than 5 years experience in textile industry (39.61) and low for the respondents who have between 10 and 15 years experience in textile industry (34.44).

That is, the respondents who have less than 5 years experience in textile industry are found to agree more on satisfaction compared to respondents who have between 10 and 15 years experience in textile industry.

- **Wage**

The mean score for opinion on satisfaction is high for the respondents who earn between Rs.3001 and Rs.6000 (37.90) and low for the respondents who earn between Rs.9001 and Rs.12000 (35.92).

That is, the respondents who earn between Rs.3001 and Rs.6000 are found to agree more on satisfaction compared to the respondents who earn between Rs.9001 and Rs.12000.

- **Work Schedule**

The mean score for opinion on satisfaction is high for the respondents who are working in night shifts (37.56) and low for the respondents who are working in afternoon shifts (35.59). That is, the respondents who are working in night shifts are found to agree more on satisfaction compared to the respondents who are working afternoon shifts.

4.4.4. Correlation between Satisfaction and Quality of Work Life Factors

Correlation is studied between different factors of quality of work life and employees' satisfaction. The correlation table is given below.

Table 4.4.4: Correlations between Job Satisfaction and Quality of Work Life Factors

QWL Factors	Level of satisfaction
Employer-Employee relationship	.498(**)
Incentives	.190(**)
Development and encouragement	.267(**)
Grievance Redressal	.152(**)
Stress management	.536(**)
Wage structure	-.033
Training	.143(**)
Working conditions	.095(*)
Work life balance	.008
Job satisfaction	.101(*)
Autonomy	.010

** Correlation is significant at 0.01 level (2-tailed). *Source: Primary Data*

* Correlation is significant at 0.05 level (2-tailed).

The above correlation table shows that there is a moderate positive correlation between quality of work life factors such as employer - employee relationship and stress management with satisfaction.

That is, those who have scored high on employee - employer relationship and stress management have expressed a moderately higher level of satisfaction.

Other quality of work life factors such as incentives, development and encouragement, grievance redressal, training, working conditions and job satisfaction have low positive correlation with employee satisfaction.

Work life balance and autonomy are not found to be significant at either 5% or 1% level and hence they have a very low correlation with employee satisfaction.

Wage structure shows a negative correlation with employee satisfaction.

Section V

Discrimination of Employees on Quality of Work Life - Multiple Discriminant Function Analysis

Introduction

Discriminant Function Analysis was used to study how the different items measured in terms of QWL factors discriminate among the employees who work in three types of units namely Small, Medium and Large.

The goals of multiple discriminant analysis are:

- Determine statistically differences between the average discriminant score profiles.
- Establish a model for classifying individuals or objects into groups on the basis of their values on the independent variables
- Determine how much of the difference in the average score profiles is accounted for by each independent variable.
- The objectives of the Discriminant Function Analysis are outlined below
- Development of discriminant functions, or linear combinations of the predictor or independent variables, that will best discriminate between the categories of the criterion or dependent variable (grouping variable).
- Examination of whether significant differences exist among the groups, in terms of the predictor variables.
- Determination of which predictor variables contribute to most of the intergroup differences.
- Classification of cases to one of the groups based on the values of the predictor variables.
- Evaluation of the accuracy of classification.

4.5.1. *Steps in Conducting the Discriminant Function Analysis*

1. Formulating the discriminant problem requires identification of the objectives and the criterion and predictor variables.
2. Estimation, involves developing a linear combination of the predictors, called discriminant functions, so that the groups differ as much as possible on the predictor values.

3. Determination of statistical significance, it involves testing the null hypothesis that, in the population, the means of all discriminant functions in all groups are equal. If the null hypothesis is rejected, it is meaningful to interpret the results.

4. The interpretation of discriminant weights or coefficients is similar to that in multiple regression analysis. Given the multicollinearity in the predictor variables, there is no unambiguous measure of the relative importance of the predictors in discriminating between the groups. However, some idea of the relative importance of the variables may be obtained by examining absolute magnitude of the standardized discriminant function coefficients and by examining the structural correlations or discriminant loading. These simple correlations between each predictor variable and the discriminant function represent the variance that the predictor variable shares with the function.

5. Validation, involves developing the classification matrix. The discriminant weights estimated by using the analysis sample are multiplied by the values of the predictor variables in the sample. The cases are then assigned to groups based on their discriminant scores and an appropriate decision rule. The percentage of cases correctly classified is determined and compared to the rate that would be expected by chance classification.

Step1: Formulating the Problem

The Multiple Discriminant Function has been used to find whether any significant difference exist among the employees of three types of units, Small, Medium and Large. For the purpose of DFA, the variables which were assumed to differentiate between the employees among three types of units were those composite factors of QWL identified in the study. The composite factor of QWL is listed below.

- Employer-employee relationship.
- Incentives.
- Development and encouragement.
- Grievance redressal.
- Stress management.
- Wage structure.
- Training.
- Working conditions.
- Work life balance.

- Job satisfaction.

- Autonomy.

Development of Discriminant Functions

When the dependent variable consists of 3 groups the number of Discriminant Functions generated will be two. The typical Discriminant Analysis Model involves linear combinations of the following form:

$$D_j = b_{0j} + b_{1j} X_{1j} + b_{2j} X_{2j} + b_{3j} X_{3j} + \ldots + b_{kj} X_{kj}$$

where
D_j = discriminant score for i th subject

B = discriminant coefficient or weight of jth function

X = predictor or independent variable of the jth function.

j = Discriminant Function 1, 2.

i = Number of sample respondents (i=1 to 500)

The statiitics associated with Discriminant Analysis are:

- Group means and group stand deviations: These are computed for each predictor variable for each group.

- Canonical correlation: measures the extent of association between the discriminant scores and the groups. It is a measure of association between the single discriminant function and the set of dummy variables that define the group membership.

- Centroid:is the mean value for the discriminant scores for a particular group. There are as many centroids as there are groups, as there is one for each group. The means for a group on all the functions are the group centroids.

- Classification matrix: sometimes also called confusion matrix, the classification matrix contains the number of correctly classified and misclassified cases.

- Discriminant function coefficients (unstandardized): are the multipliers of variables, when the variables are in the original units of measurement.

- Discriminant scores: The unstandardized coefficients are multiplied by the values of the variables. These products are summed and added to the content term to obtain the discriminant scores.

- Eigen values: For each discriminant function, the eigen value is the ratio of between-group to within-group sums of squares.

- Wilks's lambda and F values and their significance: These are calculated from a one-way ANOVA, with the grouping variable serving as the categorical independent variable. Each predictor, in turn, serves as the metric dependent variable in the ANOVA.

- Structural correlations: Also referred to as discriminant loadings, the structural correlations represent the simple correlations between the predictors and the discriminant function.

- Direct Method: An approach to discriminant analysis that involves estimating the discriminant function so that all the predictors are included simultaneously.

Step 2: Estimation: Descriptive Statistics

The means and standard deviations for each employee group are found out for the selected independent variables. The following table gives the details of Means and S.Ds of the selected variables.

Table 4.5.1: Descriptive statistics for selected independent variables

Quality of Work Life Factors	Type of Unit								
	Small			Medium			Large		
	Mean	S.D	No.	Mean	S.D	No.	Mean	S.D	No.
Employer-Employee relationship	22.93	4.45	200	28.00	4.56	200	30.91	3.85	100
Incentives	12.25	2.69	200	13.95	3.56	200	13.99	3.30	100
Development and encouragement	21.52	3.19	200	22.82	2.83	200	23.19	2.35	100
Grievance Redressal	13.49	3.28	200	14.35	2.50	200	14.55	2.51	100
Stress management	9.71	3.08	200	11.56	1.74	200	12.07	1.63	100
Wage structure	12.39	2.40	200	12.35	1.98	200	12.77	1.77	100
Training	8.74	2.82	200	9.68	2.38	200	10.84	1.98	100
Working conditions	15.03	1.98	200	15.42	1.98	200	16.10	1.59	100
Work life balance	8.21	1.42	200	8.25	1.21	200	8.38	1.54	100
Job satisfaction	7.78	1.45	200	8.07	1.04	200	8.23	.93	100
Autonomy	9.72	1.85	200	10.11	1.89	200	10.56	1.73	100

Source: Primary Data

The table gives a generalized view of the variables to be analyzed. The mean values found for the scores of most of the factors namely employer-employee relationship, development and encouragement, stress management, training, working conditions and job satisfaction are found to be marginally high for large size companies compared to medium and small sized companies. The significance of the means of these variables for the three categories are further tested using Wilk's lambda and ANOVA.

In the ANOVA table given below, the smaller the Wilks's lambda, the more important the independent variable to the discriminant function. The F-ratio values give the results of the ANOVA comparing the employee in three types of units for the selected independent variables. It can be seen that except the factors 'Wage Structure' and 'Work Life balance', all the other factors are significant at 1% level.

Table 4.5.2: Tests of Equality of Group Means

Quality of Work Life Factors	Wilks' Lambda	F	df1	df2	Sig.
Employer-Employee relationship	.659	128.669	2	497	**
Incentives	.935	17.311	2	497	**
Development and encouragement	.943	14.994	2	497	**
Grievance Redressal	.974	6.592	2	497	**
Stress management	.845	45.614	2	497	**
Wage structure	.994	1.476	2	497	Ns
Training	.911	24.208	2	497	**
Working conditions	.960	10.484	2	497	**
Work life balance	.998	.554	2	497	Ns
Job satisfaction	.978	5.655	2	497	**
Autonomy	.972	7.240	2	497	**

Source: Primary Data

Summary of Canonical Discriminant Functions

Since the dependent variable, type of unit, has three groups, the number of discriminant functions computed is two. The two discriminant functions arrived at with their discriminant coefficients are given in Table 4.5.3. The discriminant function coefficients are partial coefficients, reflecting the unique contribution of each variable to the classification of the dependent variable. The coefficient values are used to find the discriminant scores of each case for each group (here Type of unit), by substituting the values for each of the variables in the discriminant functions for each case.

Table 4.5.3: Canonical Discriminant Function Coefficients (unstandardised)

Quality of Work Life Factors	Function	
	1	2
Employer-employee relationship	.128	.136
Incentives	.196	-.025
Development and encouragement	.180	.035
Grievance Redressal	.160	-.065
Stress management	.123	-.048
Wage structure	.055	.125
Training	.006	.234
Working conditions	-.022	.242
Work life balance	.143	.171
Job satisfaction	.168	.009
Autonomy	-.004	.268
(Constant)	-16.493	-14.341

Source: Primary Data

Step 3: Determination of Statistical Significance

The Eigen values show how much of the variance in the dependent variable, type of unit, is accounted for by each of the functions. The column, '% variance' in table 4 explains that the first function accounts for 64.4 per cent of variance between groups and the second function account for 35.6% of variance between groups

Wilks's lambda shows that both the discriminant functions are significant at 1% level. A canonical correlation is given in the table measure the extent of association between the discriminant scores and the groups.

It is a measure of association between the single discriminant function and the set of dummy variables that define the group membership. The canonical correlation of first discriminant function is 0.761, which when squared gives a value of 0.579. This explains 57.9 percent of variation in the dependent variables due to first function. Similarly the value 0.160 suggests that nearly 2.56 percent of variation in the dependent variable is explained by the second discriminant function.

Table 4.5.4: Eigen Values and Canonical Correlations

Function	Eigen value	% of Variance	Cumulative %	Canonical Correlation
1	1.380	98.1	98.1	.761
2	.026	1.9	100.0	.160
Wilks' Lambda				
Test of Function(s)	**Wilks' Lambda**	**Chi-square**	**Df**	**Sig.**
1	.409	439.370	22	**
2	.974	12.724	10	Ns

Source: Primary Data

Step 4: The Interpretation of Discriminant Coefficients

The structure matrix given in table 4.5.5 shows the correlations of each variable with each standardized discriminant function. By identifying the largest absolute correlations associated to the variables with each discriminant function the researcher gains insight into how to name each function. The structure coefficient is used to assign meaningful labels to the discriminant functions.

Thus the first function gives more importance to **'Employee Relations'** expressed by the employees in general which consists of employer-employee relationship, incentives, grievance redressal, stress management and job satisfaction. The second function gives importance to **'Work & Work Life balance'** aspects of respondents.

Table 4.5.5: Structure Matrix

	Function	
Quality of Work Life Factors	**1**	**2**
Employer-Employee relationship	.493($)	.364
Incentives	.495($)	-.282
Development and encouragement	.308($)	-.055
Grievance Redressal	.223($)	-.061
Stress management	.546($)	-.110
Wage structure	-.202	.320($)
Training	-.070	.504($)
Working conditions	-.138	.438($)
Work life balance	-.056	.128($)
Job satisfaction	.119($)	.056
Autonomy	-.025	.260($)

Source: Primary Data

$ Largest absolute correlation between each variable and any discriminant function

Step 5: Classification and Validation

Finally, how efficient the discriminant functions are in discriminating between the three types of employees based on the selected independent variables is established by developing the classification matrix. The classification matrix is developed using table 4.5.6 where the group centroids of each function for each category are given and table 4.5.7 which gives prior probabilities of each group. The table 4.5.6 below is used to establish the cutting points for classifying cases. The optimal cutting point is the weighted average of the paired values. The cutting points set ranges of the discriminant score to classify the respondent into the three categories.

Table 4.5.6: Unstandardized Canonical Discriminant Functions Evaluated at Group Means

Type of Unit	**Function**	
	1	**2**
Small	-1.098	-.784
Medium	.531	.187
Large	1.134	1.195

Source: Primary Data

Table 4.5.7: Prior Probabilities for Groups

Type of Unit	**Prior**	**No. of employees**
Small	.400	200
Medium	.400	200
Large	.200	100
Total	**1.000**	500

Source: Primary Data

Based on group centroids and prior probabilities, the classification matrix is arrived and is given in table 5.4.8. The table below is used to assess how well the discriminant functions work, and whether it works equally well for each group of the dependent variable. A look at the classification matrix reveals that, the function has predicted 71.6 % of the cases correctly in to their respective groups, where as considering each category, the function has predicted 83 % of small unit employees into its own group and 72.5 % of the medium unit employees into its own group and 47 % of large unit employees into its own group indicating that on the whole, the classification accuracy of the discriminant functions is 71.6% for the given selected variables.

Table 4.5.8: Classification Results

Size of Unit			Predicted Group Membership			Total
			Small	Medium	Large	
Original	No.	Small	166	34	0	200
		Medium	29	145	26	200
		Large	2	51	47	100
	%	Small	83.0	17.0	.0	100.0
		Medium	14.5	72.5	13.0	100.0
		Large	2.0	51.0	47.0	100.0

Source: Primary Data

71.6% of original grouped cases are correctly classified

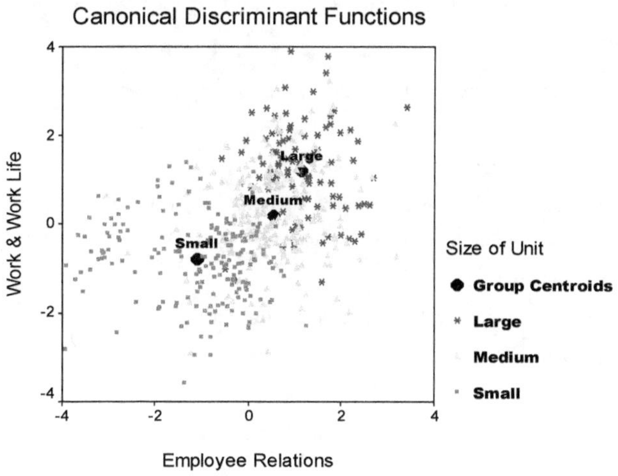

Canonical Discriminant Functions

Exhibit 4.5.1: Exhibit Showing the Canonical Discriminant Functions

Now the question remains to be answered is which variables discriminate more efficiently among the 3 categories of employees as far as 'Employee Relations' and 'Work & Work Life balance' dimensions are considered. A look at the exhibit which gives the cannonical discriminant scores found for each category using the two discriminant functions, which were plotted against each other along with the group centroids, answers this. The scores and the group centroids were plotted with the first discriminant function (Employee Relations) representing horizontal axis and the second function (Work & Work Life balance) representing the Vertical axis. The group centroids suggest that employees of large unit differ from small unit more on both horizontal and vertical axis.

Summary

MDA – Multiple Discriminant Analysis was applied to find how the employees of three types of unit differ in QWL factors. The MDA technique applied resulted in two discriminant functions, of which the factors relating to stress management, incentives, employer-employee relationship contributes to the first function (Employee Relations) and the variables 'training' and 'working conditions' contribute to the second discriminant function (Work and Work Life balance). The efficiency of these functions were tested using classification matrix which predicted 71.6% of the cases correctly, The MDA results further shows that the employees of large units differ more from employees of small units on both 'Employee Relations' and 'work-life balance'.

References

[1] Uma Sekaran(2009) , Organisational Behaviour Text and Cases, 2nd Edition, Tata McGraw Hill Education Pvt Ltd, New Delhi, p.14.

[2] http://www.encyclopedia.com

[3] James W.Walker (1980), Human Resource Planning, Grolier Incorporated, p.18

[4] V.S.PRao (2004), Human Resource Management Text and Cases, 2nd Edition, p.544, Excel Books, New Delhi 028.

[5] Dipak Kumar Bhatacharyya(2009), Human Resource Management, 2th Edition, Excel Books, New Delhi, p.417.

CHAPTER 5

Findings, Suggestions and Conclusions

Findings

The analysis of the primary data collected from the employees of textile firms located in Tirupur district reveal the following facts.

Personal and Occupational Profile of Textile Employees

- Majority of the male employees are aged between 25 and 35 years and are educated up to primary level.
- Majority of the married employees are living in rented house with 4 to 6 members in their family.
- Majority of the employees have family debt and belong to nuclear family with income between Rs.15001 and Rs.20000.
- Majority of the employees are temporary and are working in cutting, sewing, embroidering and packing section of small and medium size units.
- Majority of the employees in stitching section are working in rotating shifts and their average wage is above Rs.12000. They have an experience of 5 to 10 years.

Occupational Stress of Employees in Textile Industry

- Majority of respondents suffer from occupational stress.
- Among the various causes of occupational stress, volume of work and family commitments are found to contribute more towards occupational stress.
- There is no significant relationship between the unit size, job activity, experience and occupational stress of employees. However, relationship strongly exists between wage, work schedule and occupational stress. Occupational factors such as wage and work schedule are found to play an important role in contributing to the occupational stress of employees.

Factors Contributing to Stress Management

- Among the various factors helpful in overcoming the occupational stress of employees, unpaid leave, employees personal health and harmonious family contributes more towards reducing occupational stress.

Factors Determining Quality of Work Life

- Consistent wage plan and attractive bonus contributes more towards the quality of work life. Hence, it is identified that monetary benefits play a major role in deciding the QWL of employees.

- Standard of living (4.36) ranks at the top as the most essential item followed by the state of relationships (4.57). The least important item is found to be the state pursuit (5.65). This strongly expresses the feeling of textile employees that better standard of living leads to better QWL.

Quality of Work life in Association with Personal and Occupational Differences of Employees

Employer-Employee Relationship

- There is no association of employees' opinion on the employer- employee relationships with their gender, family income and debt. However, association of employees' opinion on the employer- employee relationships with age, marital status, educational qualification and family size is found. The respondents in younger age groups are found to agree more on employer-employee relationship compared to older age groups. Unmarried respondent groups are found to agree more on employer-employee relationship compared to widow employees. Higher secondary level respondent groups are found to agree more on employer-employee relationship compared to illiterate groups. Respondents whose family has above 6 members are found to agree more on employer- employee relationship compared to the respondents whose family has members between 1 and 3. Unmarried youth do not have much family responsibility and naturally tend to work hard leading to better relationships.

- There is no association of employees' opinion on the employer- employee relationships with type of job activity and work schedule. However, association of employees' opinion on the employer- employee relationships with unit size, experience and wage is found. Respondents who are working in large units are found to agree more on employer-employee relationship compared to respondents who are working in small units. Respondents who are involved in fabrication, compacting and calendaring activities are found to agree more on employer-employee relationship compared to the respondents who are involved in cutting, sewing, embroidering and packing activities. The respondents who have less than 5 years' experience are found to agree more on employer-employee relationship compared to the respondents who have experience between 10 and 15 years. The respondents who earn below Rs.3000 are found to agree more on employer-employee relationship compared to the respondents who earn above Rs.12000. Hence, employees who are working in large units with less than 5 years experience and who earn below Rs.3000 have a better relationship with the employers.

Incentives

- There is no association of employees' opinion on the incentives with family income and family debt. However, association of employees' opinion on incentives with age, gender, marital status, educational qualification and family size is found. the respondents who are between 45 and 55 years of age are found to agree more on incentives compared to the respondents above 55 years. The male respondents are found to agree more on incentives compared to female respondents. The married respondents are found to agree more on incentives compared to widow respondents. The respondents who are at graduate level are found to agree more on incentives compared to illiterate groups. Respondents whose family has above 6 members are found to agree more on incentives compared to the respondents whose family members are between 1 and 3.

- There is association of employees' opinion on incentives with unit size, type of job activity, experience, wage and work schedule is found. Respondents who are working in large units are found to agree more on incentives compared employees to working in small units. Respondents who are working in dyeing, bleaching and printing sections are found to agree more on incentives compared to employee involved in cutting, sewing, embroidering and packing activities .The respondents above 20 years experience are found to agree more on incentives compared to the respondents less than 5 years and between 10 and 15 years of experience. The respondents who earn above Rs.12000 are found to agree more on incentives compared to respondents who earn between Rs.6001 and Rs.9000. Respondents who are working in rotating shifts are found to agree more on incentives compared to the respondents working in afternoon shifts.

Development and Encouragement

- There is no association of employees' opinion on the development and encouragement with educational qualification, family member and family income. However, association of employees' opinion on the development and encouragement with age, gender, marital status and family debt is found. Respondents who are above 55 years are found to agree more on development and encouragement compared to the respondents between 45-55 years. Male respondents are found to agree more on development and encouragement compared to female respondents. Respondents who are widows are found to agree more on development and encouragement compared to divorced groups. The respondents who have debt in their family are found to agree more on development and encouragement compared to the respondents who do not have family debt.

- There is association of employee opinion on the development and encouragement with unit size, type of job activity, experience, wage and work schedule is found. The respondents who are working in large units are found to agree more on development and encouragement compared to the respondents who are working in small units. The respondents who are working in composite units are found to agree more on development and encouragement compared to the respondents who are working in cutting, sewing, embroidering and packing units. The respondents having between 15 and 20 years experience are found to agree more on development and encouragement compared to the respondents having between 5 and 10 years experience. The respondents whose wage lies between Rs.3001 and Rs.6000 are found to agree more on development and encouragement compared to the respondents whose wage lies between Rs.6001 and Rs.9000.The respondents who are working in irregular shifts are found to agree more on development and encouragement compared to the respondents who are working in day shifts.

Grievance Redressal

- There is no association of employees' opinion on the grievance redressal with family members, family income and family debt. However, association of employees' opinion on the grievance redressal with age, gender, marital status and educational qualification is found. The respondents who are aged are between 35 and 45 years found to agree more on grievance redressal compared to the respondents who are aged above 55 years. Female respondents are found to agree more on grievance redressal compared to male respondents. Respondents who are unmarried are found to agree more on grievance redressal compared to the respondents who are widow. The respondents who are graduates are found to agree more on grievance redressal compared to the respondents who are illiterates.

- There is no association of employee opinion on the grievance redressal with wage. However, association of employee opinion on the grievance redressal with unit size, type of job experience and work schedule is found. The respondents who are working in large units are found to agree more on grievance redressal compared to the respondents are working in small units. The respondents who are working in fabrication, compacting and calendaring units are found to agree more on grievance redressal compared to the respondents who are working in composite units. The respondents who have less than 5 years experience are found to agree more on grievance redressal compared to the respondents who have above 20 years experience. The respondents who are working in day shifts are found to agree more on grievance redressal compared to the respondents who are working in afternoon shifts.

Stress Management

- There is no association of employees' opinion on stress management with family debt. However, there is association of employees' opinion on stress management with age, gender, marital status, educational qualification, family member and family income is found. The respondents whose age group is between 18 and 25 years are found to agree more on stress management compared to the respondents whose age group is above 55 years. The male respondents are found to agree more on stress management compared to female respondents. The respondents who are unmarried are found to agree more on stress management compared to the respondents who are widows. The respondents who are graduates are found to agree more on stress management compared to the respondents who are illiterate. The respondents whose family has above 6 members are found to agree more on stress management compared to the respondents whose family has between 1 and 3 members. The respondents who earn above Rs.20000 are found to agree more on stress management compared to the respondents who earn between Rs.5001 and Rs.10000 per month.

- There is association of employees' opinion on the stress management with unit size, type of job activity, experience, wage and work schedule. The respondents who are working in large units are found to agree more on stress management compared to those who are working in small units. The respondents who are working in composite units are found to agree more on stress management compared to the respondents who are working in cutting, sewing, embroidering and packing units. The respondents who are having above 20 years experience in Textile Industry are found to agree more on stress management compared to those between 10 and 15 years experience. The respondents who are earning above Rs.12000 are found to agree more on stress management compared to the respondents who earn between Rs.9001 and

Rs.12000.The respondents who are working in irregular shifts are found to agree more on stress management compared to those working in day shifts.

Wage Structure

- There is no association of employees' opinion on the wage structure with gender, marital status, educational qualification, family member and family income. However, association of employees' opinion on the wage structure with age and family debt is found. the respondents whose age is between 45 and 55 years are found to agree more on wage structure compared to the respondents whose age is between 35 and 45 years. The respondents who do not have family debt are found to agree more on wage structure compared to those who have family debt.

- There is no association of employees' opinion on the wage structure with unit size and work schedule. However, association of employees' opinion on wage structure with job activity, experience and income is found. Respondents who are working in cutting, sewing, embroidering and packing units are found to agree more on wage structure compared to the respondents who are working in composite units. Respondents who have experience between 15 and 20 years in textile industry are found to agree more on wage structure compared to the respondents who have experience between 5 and 10 years in textile industry. Respondents who earn between Rs.6001 and Rs.9000 are found to agree more on wage structure compared to the respondents who earn below Rs.3000.

Training

- There is association of employees' opinion on the training with age, gender, marital status, educational qualification, family member, family income and family debt is found. The respondents whose age is between 45 and 55 years are found to agree more on training compared to the respondents whose age is above 55 years. The respondents who are male are found to agree more on training compared to the female respondents. The respondents who are unmarried are found to agree more on training compared to the respondents who are widows. The respondents who are diploma holders are found to agree more on training compared to the respondents who are illiterates. The respondents whose family members are between 4 and 6 are found to agree more on training compared to the respondents whose family members are between 1 and 3.The respondents whose family income is above Rs.20000 are found to agree more on training compared to the respondents whose family income are between Rs.10001 and Rs.15000.The respondents who have family debt are found to agree more on training compared to the respondents who do not have family debt.

- There is no association of employees' opinion on the training with type of job activity. However, association of employee opinion on the training with unit size, experience, wage and work schedule is found. The respondents who are working in large units are found to agree more on training compared to the respondents who are working in small units. The respondents who have less than 5 years experience are found to agree more on training compared to the respondents who have experience above 20 years. The respondents whose wages are above Rs.12000 are found to agree more on training compared to the respondents whose wages are between Rs.6001 and Rs.9000.The respondents who are working in rotating shifts are found to agree more on training compared to the respondents who are working in night shifts.

Working Conditions

- There is no association of employees' opinion on the working conditions with marital status, educational qualification, family member, family income and family debt. However, association of employees' opinion on the working conditions with age and gender is found. The respondents who belong age group between 18 and 25 years are found to agree more on working conditions compared to the respondents who belong to age group between 45 and 55 years. The female respondents are found to agree more on working conditions compared to the male respondents.

- There is no association of employees' opinion on the working conditions with type of job activity and work schedule. However, association of employees' opinion on the working conditions with unit size, experience and wage is found. The respondents who are working in large units are found to agree more on working conditions compared to the respondents who are working in small units. The respondents who are having less than 5 years experience are found to agree more on working conditions compared to the respondents who are having above 20 years experience. The respondents whose wages are between Rs.3001 and Rs.6000 are found to agree more on working conditions compared to the respondents whose wages are above Rs.12000.

Work-Life Balance

- There is no association of employees' opinion on work-life balance with gender and educational qualification. However, association of employees' opinion on the work life balance with age, marital status, family member, family income and family debt is found. The respondents who belong to the age group above 55 years are found to agree more on work life balance compared to the respondents who belong to the age group between 45 and 55 years. The respondents who are widows are found to agree more on work life balance compared to the respondents who are married. The respondents whose family members are between 1 and 3 are found to agree more on work life balance compared to the respondents whose family members are above 6.The respondents are whose family income are between Rs.5001 and Rs.10000 are found to agree more on work life balance compared to the respondents whose family income is above Rs.20000 .The respondents who do not have family debt are found to agree more on work life balance compared to the respondents who do not have family debt.

- There is no association of employees' opinion on the work life balance with unit size, type of job activity and work schedule. However, association of employees' opinion on the work life balance with experience and wage is found. The respondents who are having above 20 years experience are found to agree more on work life balance compared to the respondents who are having between 15 and 20 years experience. The respondents whose wages are betweenRs.3001 and Rs.6000 are found to agree more on work life balance compared to the respondents whose wages are betweenRs.9001 and Rs.12000.

Job Satisfaction

- There is no association of employees' opinion on the job satisfaction with marital status, family income and family debt. However, association of employees' opinion on the job satisfaction with age, gender, educational qualification and family member is found. The respondents who are between 18 and 25 years of age are found to agree more on job satisfaction compared to respondent above 55 years of age. The female respondents are found to agree more on job satisfaction compared to male employees. The respondents who are at higher secondary level are found to agree more on job satisfaction compared to diploma holders. The respondents whose family members are between 4 and 6 are found to agree more on job satisfaction compared to the respondents whose family members are above 6 .

- There is association of employees' opinion on the job satisfaction with unit size, type of job activity, experience, wage and work schedule is found. The respondents who are working in large units are found to agree more on job satisfaction compared to small units. The respondents who are working in cutting, sewing, embroidering and packing units are found to agree more on job satisfaction compared to the respondents who are working in fabrication, compacting and calendaring units. The respondents who have less than 5 years and above 20 years experience in textile industry are found to agree more on job satisfaction compared to the respondents who have between 10 and 15 years experience in textile industry. The respondents who earn below Rs.3000 are found to agree more on job satisfaction compared to the respondents who earn above Rs.12000.The respondents who are working in day shift are found to agree more on job satisfaction compared to those in irregular shifts.

Autonomy

- There is no association of employees' opinion on the autonomy with gender, family member, family income and family debt .However, association of employees' opinion on the autonomy with age, marital status and educational qualification is found. The respondents who belong to the age group between 35 and 45 years are found to agree more on autonomy compared to the respondents who belong to the age group above 55 years. The divorced employees are found to agree more on autonomy compared to widow employees. The respondents who are educated up to primary level are found to agree more on autonomy compared to the respondents who are educated up to graduate level.

- There is no association of employees' opinion on the autonomy with type of job activity and wage. However, association of employees' opinion on the autonomy with unit size, experience and work schedule is found. The respondents who are working in large units are found to agree more on autonomy compared to small units. The respondents who are having less than 5 years experience in textile industry are found to agree more on autonomy compared to the respondents who are having above 20 years experience in textile industry. The respondents who are working in irregular shifts are found to agree more on autonomy compared to the respondents who are working in night shifts.

Hence, irregular shift respondents who are working in large units with less than 5 years experience are found to agree more on work schedule.

Predominant Factors Influencing the Overall QWL

- Those who are educated up to higher secondary level were found to be having high QWL. Similarly, the respondents with maximum family members, high family income and long experience are found to have high QWL. The employees who are working in large units are found to be having high QWL compared to employees working in small units. Female employees are more agreeable on overall QWL compared to male employees. The recognition of employment status indicates that permanent employees are more comfortable with QWL when compared to temporary employees. The employees who are suffering from stress have less QWL when compared to those who do not suffer from stress. T-test results shows that family income, size of unit, employment status and experience have significant impact on the QWL of employees.

Employees' Satisfaction at Work

- Wage and recognition for achievement contributes more towards employees' job satisfaction.
- There is no association of employee opinion on job satisfaction with family debt. However, association of employee opinion on job satisfaction with age, gender, marital status, educational qualification, family member and family income is found. The respondents who belong to the age group between 18 and 25 years are found to agree more on employee satisfaction compared to the respondents who belong to the age group between 45 and 55 years. Male respondents are found to agree more on satisfaction compared to female respondents. The respondents who are unmarried are found to agree more on satisfaction compared to the respondents who are widows. The respondents who are educated up to graduate level are found to agree more on satisfaction compared to the respondents who are illiterate. The respondents whose family has above 6 members are found to agree more on satisfaction compared to the respondents whose family members are between 1 and 3.The respondents whose family income is above Rs.20000 are found to agree more on satisfaction compared to the respondents who are earning between Rs.15001 and Rs.20000.
- There is association of employees' opinion on job satisfaction with unit size, type of job activities, experience, wage and work schedule. The respondents who are working in large units are found to agree more on job satisfaction compared to the respondents who are working in small units. The respondents who are working in fabrication, compacting and calendaring units are found to agree more on satisfaction compared to the respondents who are working in cutting, sewing, embroidering and packing units. The respondents who have less than 5 years experience in textile industry are found to agree more on satisfaction compared to respondents who have between 10 and 15 years experience in textile industry. The respondents who earn between Rs.3001 and Rs.6000 are found to agree more on satisfaction compared to the respondents who earn between Rs.9001 and Rs.12000.The respondents who are working in night shifts

are found to agree more on satisfaction compared to the respondents who are working afternoon shifts.

Correlation between Satisfaction and Quality of Work Life Factors

- There is a moderate positive correlation between quality of work life factors such as employer - employee relationship and stress management with satisfaction. That is, those who have scored high on employee - employer relationship and stress management have expressed a moderately higher level of satisfaction.

Discrimination of Employees on Quality of Work Life

- The employees of large units differ more from employees of small units on both 'Employee Relations' and work-life balance.'

Suggestions

The following suggestions are made based on the above findings through the various forms of analysis done on the collected and tabulated data.

- Most of the married employees are living in rented houses and a major portion of the employees' wages are used for paying rent. Hence, employers should provide quarters facilities to employees with subsidised rent. This will help the employers to gain loyalty among the employees and increase job satisfaction.
- Most of the respondents have debt in their family. Employers can create awareness on various loan facilities provided by banks at low interest. Employers can also arrange for loans creating tie-ups with nearby banks. This will make employees happy about the employers and will serve their financial needs during emergency. This will also lead to better employer –employee relationship.
- Wage and work schedule play an important role in overcoming the occupational stress of the employees. So employers should give reasonable wages and offer flexible working schedules. This will create a happy work environment and a peaceful family. Fair wages leads to decent standard of living and retention of efficient and trusted employees.
- Employees are suffering from occupational stress. To overcome occupational stress, employees are expecting unpaid leave, improvement in employees' personal health and family. Hence, employers should consider these points and grant leave at the time of emergency needs and create family welfare awareness among the employees.

Employers can provide hygienic food to employees at reasonable cost, well ventilated rooms, adequate rest rooms and rest time to all employees.

- Among the various factors of quality of work life, consistent wage plan and attractive bonus contributes more towards quality of work life. Hence, variety of monetary and non monetary benefits to employee will increase the Quality of Work Life.

- Standard of living and the state of relationships are ranked high by the employees as the most essential items for a quality life. This articulates the wish of textile employees to live a modern trendy life. So employers should provide adequate wages, bonus, insurance schemes, etc. to improve the standard of living of employees. This will have a huge impact on quality of work life.

- Employer-employee relationship is found poor among married employees and among employees working in small and medium sized units. Hence, employers should concentrate on building better relationships with dissatisfied married employees. Married employees tend to work permanently while the stability of unmarried are uncertain. The topographical life of married employees is much stable and they prefer improvement in the jobs they hold for career growth and upliftment of family. In Tirupur, small and medium type of units are found more compared to large units. So employers of these units should find ways to establish cordial relationships with their employees. Concentration of employers on these aspects shall certainly be a key asset for this type of industry.

- Female employees are found dissatisfied towards the incentives. So the employers should concentrate on dissatisfied female employees and provide appropriate incentives based on their age, marital status, educational qualifications, job activity, experience, work schedule in addition to the normal bases of pay. Incentives provided at the right time will also reckon the employees output.

- Employers should take necessary steps to attract dissatisfied female and young employees by offering benefits such as study allowance, medical allowance and other monetary support at the right time and encourage the employees at their work place. Motivational measures such as rewards for cost cutting and time management may also be given to the employees for a better Quality of Work Life.

- Married, male, and experienced employees of small and medium units are dissatisfied with the grievance redressal mechanisms and hence employers should concentrate on handling the grievances of these employees with great care. Adequate opportunities to ventilate their grievances should be given. Any compliant received from the employees should be treated with more respect and appropriate and quick actions should be taken. The employers may adopt a regular system to assess the grievances and problems of the employees. Every textile unit should form a Grievance Redressal committee to redress the grievance of the employees. The committee should take specified short periods to redress the grievances. The committee will have to work loyally and honestly in redressing the grievances.

- Employers should focus more on building relationships and reducing the stress of employees because there is a high correlation between these two factors - QWL and employee satisfaction. Employers should pay attention to quick redressal of grievances, minimized work load and attractive incentives to improve employees satisfaction on QWL.

- The employees who are unmarried, male, working in large and composite units are satisfied with stress management measures in their firms. So, employers should concentrate on dissatisfied employees who are married, female and work in small and medium units. The employer should provide proper transport facilities, help to solve the employees' personal problems through counseling and provide better working environment.

- Employees who are unmarried, educated up to diploma, male, and working in large units are satisfied with the training given by their firms. So employers should provide proper training to dissatisfied female, small and medium unit employees. Because training is one of the important factors of QWL. It is associated with the performance appraisal and career development of the employees. Before placing female employees, training should be given to them based on their nature of work. This helps the employees to get accommodated easily in the new job and offer better productivity.

- The respondents who are unmarried, female with less than 5 years experience and working in large unit are satisfied with the working conditions of their textile industry. The employer should give more attention on unsatisfied employees by providing better working environment to male and experience workers. Every employee is spending his/her two third of time in the job. Hence, safety and healthy work environment is imperative for employees good health, work-life balance, stress reduction, etc.

- The respondents who are educated up to higher secondary level, young female with less than 5 years experience and working in large units are satisfied in their job. Employers should therefore concentrate on dissatisfied male, experienced, small and medium unit employees in improving their job satisfaction. Job satisfaction can be improved through fair pay, superiors support, co-workers support, better work environment and developmental opportunities.

- The respondents who are educated up to primary level with less than 5 years experience and working in large units are satisfied with autonomy given. The employers should therefore give autonomy in the work place to the rest of the categories. It will make the employees to work sincerely and use their innovative ideas to complete their tasks. It will also create a fear free environment and lead to job enrichment. Employees can be given freedom in deciding about work methods, approval of materials, inviting participation of subordinates, interacting with workers, giving feedback and changing the work environment.

- Wage and recognition of achievements contributes more towards employee job satisfaction. The employees feel that only these two factors will increase their job satisfaction. So employers should concentrate on these two aspects more. Wage plays a pivotal role in deciding the QWL among all units in the textile industry. The employers should provide fair and adequate wages to their employees based on their performance, experience and cost of living.

- The employees of large units differ more from employees of small units on both 'Employee Relations' and 'work-life balance'. The employees of large units feel better about the QWL when compared to small and medium unit employees. So small and medium unit employers should take care of their employees QWL. Employers should develop compassion towards work. This will create positive wave length and will pass positive energy to their peers, subordinates and supervisors. The employers should also recognize those who get rid by themselves from personal and work related problems in passionate ways.

- Employers can create flexible personal vision for their employees. The employees shall review their vision atleast twice in a year for better results. If any deviation is found in their vision, the employees can rearrange the goal to have a better QWL and better employer-employee relationship. The employers shall monitor their employees goal by implementing the 3C model (Manager, Department head and employee) which will improve coordination to achieve the employees goal. Happy employee will work efficiently.

- Employers have to take necessary steps to reduce the stress of their employees who are working in their firms. Stress reduces productivity, low quality product produce, increases absenteeism and increases labour turnover. So the employers have to find ways to reduce stress by sharing their work load with other department and create cordial relationships among employees and with employers. Team work can be encouraged as this will help tackle new challenging situations efficiently and effectively.

- Employers and employees establish relationships to identify the causes of conflicts by themselves. The conflicts should be discussed in an open forum with co-workers, supervisors and manages to get better solutions. The employers can use techniques like Quality Circle and Works Committee to discuss the problems affecting their performance of the units and work environment. This will lead to peaceful and stress free work environment establishing a bonded relationship among the employees and employers.

- Employers should create ample opportunities for fun at work. This is the best medicine to get rid of employees stress easily. Employees should use such opportunities to enjoy themselves without thinking anything else. Surprise birthday gifts, parties, display of achievers name in notice board, etc can be used to have fun among employees. Such situations will excite employees and make them feel that their employers respect and recognize them.

- Employers can arrange seminars focusing employees sound mental and physical health. This will make employees live a happy life and have a better quality of work life. Seminars should emphasize employees on taking right food at right time, taking enough rest, deep sleep and exercise.

- Good quality of work life provides a balance between work and life. That is, family life and work will never disturb each other. So the employers should not force the employees to work overtime and continuously without break. The employers should use contingency work force technique including part time employees, free lancers, subcontractors to cope with unexpected and temporary challenges. The employers utilizing this technique should see to that regular employees are not affected by any means.

- Collective bargaining should be administrated and encouraged by the employers for any demand relating to the factors of QWL. This will increase the faith of employees on QWL.

Conclusion

In the competitive era, employees are the asset of any industry, so every firm should take care of their employees. Better Quality of Work Life increases productivity. The purpose of this study was conducted to understand the Quality of Work Life in Textile Industry of Tirupur District in Tamil Nadu. From the study it is evident that Textile Industry in Tirupur are not exempted to occupational stress and poor Quality of Work Life. Among the eleven factors of QWL, the employees are found comfortable with only two factors of QWL namely employee - employer relationship and stress management. Employees long for job satisfaction through fair wage and recognition of their achievements.

The study clearly articulates that only employees who do not have much commitment and expectation due to their personal or occupational profile feel better on a very few Quality of Work Life aspects. Most of the personal and occupational variables identified are found to influence the Quality of Work Life and hence employers of Textile Industry in Tirupur should focus more on improving each factor of QWL identified in the study.

Quality of Work Life not only retains the existing employees but also attracts the potential talented employees. The employers should strongly bear in their minds that the benefit of QWL is all-pervasive and the employers' duty to provide it not only as businessmen but also as responsible citizen of India.

BIBLIOGRAPHY

I. Text Books

1. F.M. Khri, Indian Textile-ethnic and beyond, Super book house, Mumbai-5, 2009.

2. Meenakshi Rastogi, Textile Forming, Sonoli publications, New Delhi-2, 2009.

3. Uma Sekaran, Organisational Behaviour Text and Cases, 2nd Edition, Tata McGraw Hill Education Pvt Ltd, New Delhi, 2009.

4. James W.Walker, Human Resource Planning, Grolier Incorporated, 1980.

5. John M.Ivancevich, Ronert Konopaske and Michael T.Matteson, Organizational Behavior and Management, 7th edition, Tata McGraw Hill Education Pvt Ltd, New Delhi, 2006.

6. Mirza S Saiyadain, Human Resource Management, 3rd Edition, Tata McGraw Hill Publishing Co., Ltd, New Delhi,2005.

7. T.V. Rav, Readings in Human Resource Development, Oxford and IBH Publishing Co., Pvt Ltd- New Delhi, 2001.

8. Fred Luthans, Organisational Behavior,10th edition, McGraw Hills International Edition , New York, 2005.

9. K. Aswathappa, Human Resource Management Text and Caess,6th Edition, Tata McGraw Hill Education Pvt Ltd, New Delhi1, 2010

10. V.S.P. Rao, Human Resource Management Text and Cases- 2nd Edition, 2004, Excel Books, New Delhi 028.

11. Dipak Kumar Bhatacharyya, Human Resource Management, 2th Edition, Excel Books, New Delhi, 2009

12. O.R. Krishna Swami and M. Ranganatham, Methodology of Research in Social Sciences, Himalaya Publishing House, New Delhi, 2006.

13. C.R. Kothari, Research Methodology: Methods and Techniques, Second Edition, New Age International (P) Ltd., New Delhi, 2000.

14. K. Alagar, Business Statistics, Tata McGraw-Hill Education (P) Ltd, New Delhi, 2009.

II. Journals and Magazines

1. Social Indicators Research, 2001, Vol.55 (Sept).

2. Organizational Development Journal, Vol.19 (3), 2001.

3. ICFAI University Press, Hyderabad, 2001

4. Human Capital, Vol.2(1), 2001

5.   Economic Review, March-2002

6.   Indian Council for research on International Economic Relations (ICRIER), New Delhi, No.94, 2002

7.   Journal of the Indian Academy of Applied Psychology, Jan-July 28(1-2), (2002)

8.   International Journal of Human Resources Development and Management, Vol. 3, No.4, 2003.

9.   Oxford Journal, Vol.19, 2003.

10. Clothesline, Sep-2003

11. Samskriti Publications, First Edition, 2004

12. Business line, May 21,2006

13. The ICFAI Journal of Organizational Behavior, Vol.1,2006

15. Journal of Social Sciences, 2006

16. Child and Youth Services Review, Vol.29,2007

17. Indian Journal of Industrial Relations, January 1, 2007

21. International Journal of Management and Enterprise Development, Vol. 6, No.4, 2009.

22. International Journal of Indian Culture and Business Management, Vol.2, No.6, 2009.

23. International Journal of Quality and Innovation ,Vol.1, No.2 , 2010

24. Journal of Managerial Psychology, Vol.25,Iss.1. 2010

25. International Journal of Green Economics, Vol. 4, No.1, 2010

26. Journal of Managerial Psychology, Vol. 26,Iss. 1. 2011

27. Employee Relations, Vol. 34, Iss. 1. 2011

28. The TQM Journal, Vo. 23, Iss. 2. 2011

29.   International Journal of Health Care Quality Assurance, Vol. 24 Iss, 2. 2011

30. Quarterly journal of Research and Planning in Higher Education, Vol. 17 (1), 2011

31. Nursing and Health Sciences, Vol.13 Iss.1, 2011

32. fibre2fashion. 2011-09-06.

III. News Papers

1.   The Hindu04/04/2012

2.   The Hindu. 2008-12-01

3.   The Hindu. 22013-02-07

4.   The Hindu. 2011-10-15.

5.   The Hindu. 2011-10-15.

IV. Websites

1. www.ibef.org
2. encyclopedia.thefreedictionary.com
3. www.teonline.com
4. www.Dynamiccity-doc-casestudytirupur-rangarajan.pdf
5. tiruppurinfo.blogspot.in
6. en.wikipedia.org
7. www.iosrjournals.org
8. ejournal.srmuniv.ac.in
9. ww.articlesbase.com
10. www.ehow.com
11. www.scribd.com
12. en.wikipedia.org
13. www.china-qualityinspection.coma
14. www.screenprinttekpa.com
15. indiatirupurnew-developmentsfwfcountrystudy.pff
16. http://jobwork.net
17. www.indiantextilejournal.com
18. www.kadavapatidar.com
19. www.indiaknitfair.com
20. pib.nic.in
21. www.tiruppur.com
22. www.thehindu.com
23. mytirupur.biz
24. xklsv.org
25. http://pd.cpim.org/2010/1003_pd/10032010_12.
26. http://www.hindu.com/2010/09/25/ 2013-02-07.
27. hindu.com/2010/09/2013-02-07.

Appendix

Correlation Matrix

Items	1	2	3	4	5	6	7	8	9	10	11	12	13	14	15	16	17	18	19	20	21	22
1	1.000	0.544	0.088	-0.160	-0.197	-0.158	-0.205	0.064	0.020	0.095	0.053	-0.046	-0.073	0.007	-0.007	-0.046	0.113	0.093	0.198	-0.095	-0.117	0.193
2	0.544	1.000	-0.022	-0.161	-0.215	-0.320	-0.354	0.186	0.153	0.068	0.153	-0.049	0.107	0.222	0.012	0.015	0.040	0.249	0.271	-0.162	-0.065	0.127
3	0.088	-0.022	1.000	0.098	-0.064	0.196	-0.033	0.074	-0.311	0.249	0.196	0.023	-0.193	-0.245	-0.033	-0.135	-0.157	-0.178	-0.073	-0.144	-0.063	0.088
4	-0.160	-0.161	0.098	1.000	0.020	0.103	0.083	-0.003	-0.092	0.042	-0.021	0.047	-0.057	-0.121	-0.011	-0.051	-0.127	-0.101	-0.159	-0.047	0.189	-0.067
5	-0.197	-0.215	-0.064	0.020	1.000	0.398	0.381	0.133	0.036	0.078	-0.026	-0.102	-0.031	-0.098	0.020	0.037	0.010	0.042	-0.082	0.257	-0.014	-0.125
6	-0.158	-0.320	0.196	0.103	0.398	1.000	0.445	0.143	-0.160	0.107	0.028	0.008	-0.064	-0.112	0.150	0.059	0.053	-0.078	-0.074	0.299	-0.011	0.017
7	-0.205	-0.354	-0.033	0.083	0.381	0.445	1.000	0.128	-0.045	0.081	0.022	-0.083	-0.047	-0.043	0.116	0.147	0.099	0.019	-0.084	0.347	-0.100	-0.048
8	0.064	0.186	0.074	-0.003	0.133	0.143	0.128	1.000	-0.232	0.278	0.359	-0.019	0.023	-0.035	0.101	-0.053	0.026	-0.004	-0.071	0.094	-0.175	-0.158
9	0.020	0.153	-0.311	-0.092	0.036	-0.160	-0.045	-0.232	1.000	-0.431	-0.303	-0.223	0.399	0.481	0.046	0.208	0.235	0.336	0.284	0.032	-0.133	0.048
10	0.095	0.068	0.249	0.042	0.078	0.107	0.081	0.278	-0.431	1.000	0.262	0.329	-0.326	-0.111	0.168	-0.052	-0.033	-0.024	-0.032	-0.043	-0.200	0.036
11	0.053	0.153	0.196	-0.021	-0.026	0.028	0.022	0.359	-0.303	0.262	1.000	0.008	-0.147	-0.162	0.017	-0.045	-0.051	0.013	0.114	-0.127	-0.245	-0.016
12	-0.046	-0.049	0.023	0.047	-0.102	0.008	-0.083	-0.019	-0.223	0.329	0.008	1.000	-0.328	-0.010	0.299	0.141	-0.308	-0.269	-0.353	-0.121	0.119	-0.102
13	-0.073	0.107	-0.193	-0.057	-0.031	-0.064	-0.047	0.023	0.399	-0.326	-0.147	-0.328	1.000	0.517	-0.082	0.057	0.148	0.298	0.273	0.150	-0.037	0.011
14	0.007	0.222	-0.245	-0.121	-0.098	-0.112	-0.043	-0.035	0.481	-0.111	-0.162	-0.010	0.517	1.000	0.090	0.160	0.164	0.353	0.301	0.070	-0.087	0.045
15	-0.007	0.012	-0.033	-0.011	0.020	0.150	0.116	0.101	0.046	0.168	0.017	0.299	-0.082	0.090	1.000	0.622	0.072	0.145	0.100	0.108	-0.094	0.175
16	-0.046	0.015	-0.135	-0.051	0.037	0.059	0.147	-0.053	0.208	-0.052	-0.045	0.141	0.057	0.160	0.622	1.000	0.164	0.306	0.206	0.149	-0.047	0.168
17	0.113	0.040	-0.157	-0.127	0.010	0.053	0.099	0.026	0.235	-0.033	-0.051	-0.308	0.148	0.164	0.072	0.164	1.000	0.546	0.552	0.328	-0.366	0.197
18	0.093	0.249	-0.178	-0.101	0.042	-0.078	0.019	-0.004	0.336	-0.024	0.013	-0.269	0.298	0.353	0.145	0.306	0.546	1.000	0.667	0.175	-0.179	0.252
19	0.198	0.271	-0.073	-0.159	-0.082	-0.074	-0.084	-0.071	0.284	-0.032	0.114	-0.353	0.273	0.301	0.100	0.206	0.552	0.667	1.000	0.060	-0.308	0.309
20	-0.095	-0.162	-0.144	-0.047	0.257	0.299	0.347	0.094	0.032	-0.043	-0.127	-0.121	0.150	0.070	0.108	0.149	0.328	0.175	0.060	1.000	0.032	0.053
21	-0.117	-0.065	-0.063	0.189	-0.014	-0.011	-0.100	-0.175	-0.133	-0.200	-0.245	0.119	-0.037	-0.087	-0.094	-0.047	-0.366	-0.179	-0.308	0.032	1.000	-0.052
22	0.193	0.127	0.088	-0.067	-0.125	0.017	-0.048	-0.158	0.048	0.036	-0.016	-0.102	0.011	0.045	0.175	0.168	0.197	0.252	0.309	0.053	-0.052	1.000
23	0.211	0.129	0.113	0.056	0.066	-0.102	-0.051	-0.021	-0.176	0.115	0.047	-0.030	-0.274	-0.232	-0.009	0.022	-0.041	0.043	-0.002	-0.003	0.168	0.115
24	0.179	0.148	0.110	-0.040	-0.049	0.068	-0.126	0.038	-0.142	0.100	-0.017	0.024	-0.031	-0.059	0.122	0.086	0.009	0.106	0.090	0.145	0.259	0.224
25	0.109	0.073	0.027	0.095	-0.028	-0.061	-0.240	-0.198	-0.099	0.003	-0.157	0.072	-0.108	-0.188	-0.024	0.059	-0.143	0.062	-0.057	-0.091	0.464	0.155

26	0.127	0.185	-0.008	0.066	0.004	0.001	-0.152	0.007	-0.005	0.034	-0.044	0.031	-0.031	0.039	0.138	0.154	-0.157	0.100	0.056	-0.055	0.367	0.125
27	-0.006	0.174	0.043	0.036	0.083	0.089	-0.059	-0.056	0.133	0.043	0.057	-0.037	0.156	0.175	0.284	0.333	0.074	0.310	0.348	-0.066	-0.028	0.315
28	0.023	-0.047	0.127	-0.240	-0.089	-0.006	-0.008	0.082	-0.173	0.059	0.115	0.240	-0.172	-0.156	-0.069	-0.182	-0.243	-0.418	-0.267	-0.099	-0.175	-0.270
29	0.036	-0.050	-0.156	0.099	-0.005	0.013	0.127	-0.168	0.197	-0.119	-0.181	-0.252	0.199	0.156	0.090	0.222	0.419	0.470	0.358	0.262	0.058	0.226
30	0.108	0.160	-0.017	0.024	-0.103	-0.097	-0.055	-0.168	0.196	-0.003	-0.034	-0.248	0.163	0.139	0.020	0.073	0.336	0.430	0.501	-0.059	-0.115	0.252
31	0.043	0.050	0.098	0.054	-0.119	0.040	-0.045	-0.244	0.090	0.040	0.036	-0.223	0.154	0.114	0.014	0.069	0.189	0.324	0.459	-0.141	-0.150	0.312
32	-0.165	-0.197	0.000	0.235	0.215	0.190	0.210	-0.138	0.066	0.025	-0.092	-0.192	0.023	0.020	0.001	0.080	0.188	0.254	0.175	0.064	0.004	0.119
33	-0.015	0.066	0.020	-0.032	0.149	0.006	-0.096	-0.024	-0.069	0.038	0.027	-0.012	-0.153	-0.113	-0.105	-0.056	-0.197	-0.067	-0.055	-0.151	0.170	0.014
34	0.074	0.114	0.069	-0.073	0.082	-0.037	-0.104	0.015	-0.049	0.136	0.083	0.082	-0.136	-0.113	-0.065	-0.085	-0.149	-0.125	-0.048	-0.065	0.096	0.035
35	0.103	0.013	-0.005	-0.022	-0.017	0.046	0.132	-0.016	0.049	0.028	-0.010	-0.042	0.048	0.079	0.233	0.252	0.182	0.284	0.222	0.074	-0.075	0.182
36	0.256	0.150	0.064	0.008	-0.102	-0.114	-0.079	-0.016	0.077	0.166	0.162	-0.189	0.060	0.058	-0.046	-0.030	0.222	0.219	0.412	-0.179	-0.430	0.144
37	-0.017	-0.039	-0.005	-0.134	0.056	-0.027	-0.034	-0.080	-0.029	0.026	-0.059	0.107	-0.142	-0.068	-0.007	0.018	-0.108	-0.127	-0.134	-0.024	0.047	-0.028
38	-0.132	-0.015	-0.028	-0.045	0.157	0.088	0.109	0.132	0.004	0.041	-0.041	0.100	-0.004	-0.024	0.040	0.049	-0.131	-0.145	-0.167	0.126	0.168	-0.142
39	-0.081	-0.030	-0.034	-0.017	0.078	0.092	0.024	-0.008	-0.044	-0.022	-0.078	0.014	-0.086	-0.112	0.006	-0.051	-0.074	-0.138	-0.157	0.093	0.181	-0.041
40	0.013	0.058	0.028	0.013	-0.005	-0.034	-0.057	-0.073	0.035	-0.040	-0.018	0.011	-0.004	-0.019	-0.022	0.028	-0.138	-0.050	0.030	-0.076	0.181	0.003
41	0.035	0.091	-0.071	-0.172	0.035	0.052	-0.083	-0.247	0.195	-0.028	-0.064	-0.121	0.083	0.097	0.235	0.310	0.225	0.387	0.377	-0.022	-0.038	0.376
42	-0.239	-0.277	-0.027	-0.123	0.196	0.264	0.149	-0.164	-0.031	-0.172	-0.224	-0.035	-0.062	-0.099	-0.093	-0.057	0.007	-0.145	-0.249	0.250	0.158	-0.044
43	-0.160	-0.192	-0.167	0.013	0.111	0.058	0.212	0.030	0.166	-0.215	-0.190	-0.020	0.231	0.220	0.101	0.201	0.029	-0.019	-0.124	0.302	0.082	-0.172
44	0.102	0.012	-0.085	0.158	0.166	-0.022	0.105	0.158	0.152	0.032	-0.040	-0.145	0.133	0.071	0.001	0.014	0.197	0.089	0.080	0.181	-0.006	-0.015

Items	23	24	25	26	27	28	29	30	31	32	33	34	35	36	37	38	39	40	41	42	43	44
1	0.211	0.179	0.109	0.127	-0.006	0.023	0.036	0.108	0.043	-0.165	-0.015	0.074	0.103	0.256	-0.017	-0.132	-0.081	0.013	0.035	-0.239	-0.160	0.102
2	0.129	0.148	0.073	0.185	0.174	-0.047	-0.050	0.160	0.050	-0.197	0.066	0.114	0.013	0.150	-0.039	-0.015	-0.030	0.058	0.091	-0.277	-0.192	0.012
3	0.113	0.110	0.027	-0.008	0.043	0.127	-0.156	-0.017	0.098	0.000	0.020	0.069	-0.005	0.064	-0.005	-0.028	-0.034	0.028	-0.071	-0.027	-0.167	-0.085
4	0.056	-0.040	0.095	0.066	0.036	-0.240	0.099	0.024	0.054	0.235	-0.032	-0.073	-0.022	0.008	-0.134	-0.045	-0.017	0.013	-0.172	-0.123	0.013	0.158
5	0.066	-0.049	-0.028	0.004	0.083	-0.089	-0.005	-0.103	-0.119	0.215	0.149	0.082	-0.017	-0.102	0.056	0.157	0.078	-0.005	0.035	0.196	0.111	0.166
6	-0.102	0.068	-0.061	0.001	0.089	-0.006	0.013	-0.097	0.040	0.190	0.006	-0.037	0.046	-0.114	-0.027	0.088	0.092	-0.034	0.052	0.264	0.058	-0.022
7	-0.051	-0.126	-0.240	-0.152	-0.059	-0.008	0.127	-0.055	-0.045	0.210	-0.096	-0.104	0.132	-0.079	-0.034	0.109	0.024	-0.057	-0.083	0.149	0.212	0.105
8	-0.021	0.038	-0.198	0.007	-0.056	0.082	-0.168	-0.168	-0.244	-0.138	-0.024	0.015	-0.016	-0.016	-0.080	0.132	-0.008	-0.073	-0.247	-0.164	0.030	0.158
9	-0.176	-0.142	-0.099	-0.005	0.133	-0.173	0.197	0.196	0.090	0.066	-0.069	-0.049	0.049	0.077	-0.029	0.004	-0.044	0.035	0.195	-0.031	0.166	0.152
10	0.115	0.100	0.003	0.034	0.043	0.059	-0.119	-0.003	0.040	0.025	0.038	0.136	0.028	0.166	0.026	0.041	-0.022	-0.040	-0.028	-0.172	-0.215	0.032
11	0.047	-0.017	-0.157	-0.044	0.057	0.115	-0.181	-0.034	0.036	-0.092	0.027	0.083	-0.010	0.162	-0.059	-0.041	-0.078	-0.018	-0.064	-0.224	-0.190	-0.040
12	-0.030	0.024	0.072	0.031	-0.037	0.240	-0.252	-0.248	-0.223	-0.192	-0.012	0.082	-0.042	-0.189	0.107	0.100	0.014	0.011	-0.121	-0.035	-0.020	-0.145
13	-0.274	-0.031	-0.108	-0.031	0.156	-0.172	0.199	0.163	0.154	0.023	-0.153	-0.136	0.048	0.060	-0.142	-0.004	-0.086	-0.004	0.083	-0.062	0.231	0.133
14	-0.232	-0.059	-0.188	0.039	0.175	-0.156	0.156	0.139	0.114	0.020	-0.113	-0.113	0.079	0.058	-0.068	-0.024	-0.112	-0.019	0.097	-0.099	0.220	0.071
15	-0.009	0.122	-0.024	0.138	0.284	-0.069	0.090	0.020	0.014	0.001	-0.105	-0.065	0.233	-0.046	-0.007	0.040	0.006	-0.022	0.235	-0.093	0.101	0.001
16	0.022	0.086	0.059	0.154	0.333	-0.182	0.222	0.073	0.069	0.080	-0.056	-0.085	0.252	-0.030	0.018	0.049	-0.051	0.028	0.310	-0.057	0.201	0.014
17	-0.041	0.009	-0.143	-0.157	0.074	-0.243	0.419	0.336	0.189	0.188	-0.197	-0.149	0.182	0.222	-0.108	-0.131	-0.074	-0.138	0.225	0.007	0.029	0.197
18	0.043	0.106	0.062	0.100	0.310	-0.418	0.470	0.430	0.324	0.254	-0.067	-0.125	0.284	0.219	-0.127	-0.145	-0.138	-0.050	0.387	-0.145	-0.019	0.089
19	-0.002	0.090	-0.057	0.056	0.348	-0.267	0.358	0.501	0.459	0.175	-0.055	-0.048	0.222	0.412	-0.134	-0.167	-0.157	0.030	0.377	-0.249	-0.124	0.080
20	-0.003	0.145	-0.091	-0.055	-0.066	-0.099	0.262	-0.059	-0.141	0.064	-0.151	-0.065	0.074	-0.179	-0.024	0.126	0.093	-0.076	-0.022	0.250	0.302	0.181
21	0.168	0.259	0.464	0.367	-0.028	-0.175	0.058	-0.115	-0.150	0.004	0.170	0.096	-0.075	-0.430	0.047	0.168	0.181	0.181	-0.038	0.158	0.082	-0.006
22	0.115	0.224	0.155	0.125	0.315	-0.270	0.226	0.252	0.312	0.119	0.014	0.035	0.182	0.144	-0.028	-0.142	-0.041	0.003	0.376	-0.044	-0.172	-0.015
23	1.000	0.259	0.238	0.229	0.139	-0.064	-0.004	0.070	0.038	0.114	0.128	0.170	0.078	0.107	0.021	-0.019	-0.002	0.003	0.082	-0.016	-0.103	-0.012
24	0.259	1.000	0.283	0.463	0.154	-0.163	0.093	0.087	0.095	-0.032	-0.001	0.076	0.140	-0.037	-0.037	0.020	0.070	0.101	0.141	-0.091	-0.085	0.069
25	0.238	0.283	1.000	0.395	0.140	-0.261	0.149	0.129	-0.010	0.099	0.256	0.227	-0.038	-0.101	0.094	0.004	0.112	0.159	0.196	-0.045	-0.140	0.042
26	0.229	0.463	0.395	1.000	0.144	-0.299	0.156	0.084	0.024	0.096	0.157	0.041	0.127	-0.059	-0.041	0.065	0.055	0.242	0.135	-0.148	-0.008	0.125

27	0.139	0.154	0.140	0.144	1.000	-0.318	-0.028	0.348	0.454	0.306	0.200	0.120	0.167	0.184	-0.036	-0.113	-0.096	0.058	0.546	-0.102	-0.118	-0.046
28	-0.064	-0.163	-0.261	-0.299	-0.318	1.000	-0.522	-0.329	-0.370	-0.479	-0.082	0.056	-0.187	-0.111	0.070	0.086	0.022	-0.084	-0.305	0.054	0.026	-0.213
29	-0.004	0.093	0.149	0.156	-0.028	-0.522	1.000	0.321	0.214	0.318	-0.201	-0.300	0.274	0.114	-0.109	-0.113	-0.023	0.054	0.190	-0.045	0.122	0.221
30	0.070	0.087	0.129	0.084	0.348	-0.329	0.321	1.000	0.592	0.261	-0.075	0.031	0.165	0.397	-0.149	-0.281	-0.059	0.040	0.422	-0.168	-0.169	0.048
31	0.038	0.095	-0.010	0.024	0.454	-0.370	0.214	0.592	1.000	0.436	-0.087	-0.103	0.272	0.387	-0.127	-0.289	-0.084	0.065	0.451	-0.144	-0.238	-0.067
32	0.114	-0.032	0.099	0.096	0.306	-0.479	0.318	0.261	0.436	1.000	0.149	-0.149	0.103	0.183	-0.046	-0.077	-0.049	-0.012	0.316	0.051	-0.078	0.120
33	0.128	-0.001	0.256	0.157	0.200	-0.082	-0.201	-0.075	-0.087	0.149	1.000	0.347	-0.236	-0.122	0.254	0.105	0.027	0.071	0.111	0.062	-0.213	-0.086
34	0.170	0.076	0.227	0.041	0.120	0.056	-0.300	0.031	-0.103	-0.149	0.347	1.000	-0.082	-0.099	0.086	0.118	0.106	0.007	0.049	-0.012	-0.100	-0.043
35	0.078	0.140	-0.038	0.127	0.167	-0.187	0.274	0.165	0.272	0.103	-0.236	-0.082	1.000	0.065	-0.153	-0.139	-0.090	0.040	0.226	-0.129	0.061	0.077
36	0.107	-0.037	-0.101	-0.059	0.184	-0.111	0.114	0.397	0.387	0.183	-0.122	-0.099	0.065	1.000	-0.049	-0.321	-0.200	-0.010	0.182	-0.239	-0.259	0.006
37	0.021	-0.037	0.094	-0.041	-0.036	0.070	-0.109	-0.149	-0.127	-0.046	0.254	0.086	-0.153	-0.049	1.000	0.067	-0.011	-0.020	0.027	0.148	-0.062	-0.072
38	-0.019	0.020	0.004	0.065	-0.113	0.086	-0.113	-0.281	-0.289	-0.077	0.105	0.118	-0.139	-0.321	0.067	1.000	0.182	-0.021	-0.162	0.109	0.098	0.087
39	-0.002	0.070	0.112	0.055	-0.096	0.022	-0.023	-0.059	-0.084	-0.049	0.027	0.106	-0.090	-0.200	-0.011	0.182	1.000	0.237	-0.028	0.058	0.019	0.117
40	0.003	0.101	0.159	0.242	0.058	-0.084	0.054	0.040	0.065	-0.012	0.071	0.007	0.040	-0.010	-0.020	-0.021	0.237	1.000	0.019	-0.112	0.021	0.123
41	0.082	0.141	0.196	0.135	0.546	-0.305	0.190	0.422	0.451	0.316	0.111	0.049	0.226	0.182	0.027	-0.162	-0.028	0.019	1.000	0.147	-0.192	-0.183
42	-0.016	-0.091	-0.045	-0.148	-0.102	0.054	-0.045	-0.168	-0.144	0.051	0.062	-0.012	-0.129	-0.239	0.148	0.109	0.058	-0.112	0.147	1.000	0.103	-0.326
43	-0.103	-0.085	-0.140	-0.008	-0.118	0.026	0.122	-0.169	-0.238	-0.078	-0.213	-0.100	0.061	-0.259	-0.062	0.098	0.019	0.021	-0.192	0.103	1.000	0.227
44	-0.012	0.069	0.042	0.125	-0.046	-0.213	0.221	0.048	-0.067	0.120	-0.086	-0.043	0.077	0.006	-0.072	0.087	0.117	0.123	-0.183	-0.326	0.227	1.000

Interview Scheduled Questionnaire

A Study on the Quality of Work Life of Textile Employees with Special Reference to Tirupur District, Tamil Nadu

Personal Profile

1 Name   :

2 Age   :

a) 18 – 25 years   b) 25 – 35 years

c) 35 – 45 years   d) 45 – 55 years   e) Above 55 years

3 Gender   :

a) Male   b) Female

4 Marital Status   :

a) Unmarried   b) Married

c) Divorced   d) Widowed

5 Educational Qualifications :

a) Illiterate   b) Primary

c) Higher Secondary   d) Graduate   e) Diploma

6. Status of Residence   :

a) Own house   b) Rented

c) Accommodation provided by employer

7. Family Members   :

a) 1 - 3   b) 4- 6   c) Above 6

8. Nature of Family

a) Nuclear   b) Joint

9. Family Income (p.m)   :

a)   Below Rs.5000   b) Rs.5001 - Rs.10000

c)   Rs.10001 – Rs.15000   d) Rs.15001 – Rs.20000

e)   Above Rs.20000

10.Have you incurred any debt in your family?   Yes/No

Organizational Profile

11. Size of Unit   :

a) Small   b) Medium   c) Large

12.Type of Job Activity:

a) Fabrication, Compacting and Calendaring

b) Dyeing, Bleaching and Printing

c) Cutting, Sewing, Embroidering and packing

d) Composite unit

13. Specify the section in which you are working:

a) Fabrication   b) Dyeing   c) Cutting

d) Stitching   e) Checking   f) Ironing

g) Packing

14. Employment Status :

 a) Temporary   b) Permanent

15.Total Experience in Textile Industry:

a) Less than 5 years   b) 5 – 10 years   c) 10 – 15 years

d) 15 – 20 years   e) Above 20 years

16.Wage (p.m) :

a) Below Rs.3000   b) Rs.3001 –Rs. 6000

c) Rs.6001 –Rs. 9000   d) Rs. 9001 –Rs. 12000   e) Above Rs.12000

17. Work Schedule :

a) Day shift   b) Afternoon shift   c) Night shift

d) Irregular shift on cal   e) Rotating shift

18. Do you suffer from stress?

a) Yes   b) No

i). If yes, specify the cause and frequency of stress:

Sl.No	Reasons	Often	Some times	Not sure	Never
1	Volume of work				
2	New duties				
3	Complexities of work				
4	Documentation				
5	Covering for others work				
6	Changes in policy				
7	Job Demands				
8	Family Demands				

19. Factors in overcome stress

Sl.No	Factors	Very Important	Somewhat Important	Not very Important	Not Important
1	Flexible hours				
2	Unpaid leave (at least)				
3	Supportive Supervisor/ Manager				
4	Personal calls at work (if emergency)				
5	promotional opportunities				
6	Relationship with other department and superiors				
7	No Discrimination				
8	Employee's personal health and family peace				

Parameters of the Quality of Work Life

20. Give your opinion regarding the following factors relating to the employment in the Company (Please tick in the relevant boxes to indicate your level of acceptance)

Strongly Agree-5, Agree-4,Neutral-3, Disagree-2 Strongly Disagree-1

Sl.No	PARAMATERS OF QUALITY OF WORK LIFE	5	4	3	2	1
1	The employees are satisfied with the spirit of team work					
2	The job requires me to work very fast and keep learning					
3	The Company provides attractive bonus					
4	Shift mechanism affects the maintenance of family relationship					
5	The Employees are invited and encouraged to offer suggestions					
6	Hard work and achievements are recognized appropriately					
7	The Company encourages the employees for their self development					
8	The Company provides fair and adequate wage					
9	The Company provides variety of fringe benefits					
10	The Company provides equal wage to the same cadre					
11	The wage plan is consistent with the other Companies					
12	The organization is providing enough instruction, high quality tools and techniques					
13	The Company provides adequate incentives					
14	The Company provides special incentive for prompt work					
15	Regular training and development programmes are conducted					
16	The training helped in improving the quality of work					
17	The Management attempt to understand stresses, its causes					
18	The Management arrange periodical workshops for control and reduction of stress					
19	I trust the management at the place where I work					
20	The Employees are listened to and their views are taken into consideration					
21	The management is really keen to redress the grievances					
22	The employees have sense of community and inter personal openness					

23	I feel comfortable, secured and satisfied with my job					
24	The Employees have a sense of fair chance to ventilate their grievance					
25	The Company provides scope for appeal against redressal of grievance					
26	The Employees are listened to and their views are taken into consideration					
27	No discrimination based upon race, color, sex, sexual orientation					
28	The work schedule provide leisure time					
29	The Management takes efforts to reduce monotonous and disinteresting job					
30	The Company promotes mutual trust and community of interests					
31	The Company properly promotes and maintains human relations					
32	Hours of work interferes with family relationships					
33	The working conditions provide no risk to the employees					
34	The Company provides adequate safety measures to the employees					
35	The work schedule and timings are followed as per the Government regulations					
36	I am treated with respect in the work place					
37	The physical environment of the Company is comfortable					
38	The superior is concerned about the welfare activities of the Employees					
39	The Management provides greater autonomy to the subordinates					
40	On the job, I know exactly what is expected of me					
41	There is cordial and close relation between management and employees					
42	Having competency is the basis for promotion					
43	The Company provides large amount of part time work					
44	Flexible reporting / leaving schedule and lunch timings are allowed					

Rank the Factors

21. Rank the following factors from most essential to the level of satisfaction, according to your order of the performance existing Quality of Work Life **(Rank range from 1 to 9).**

S.No	Quality of Work Life	Rank
1	State of physical health	
2	State of pursuits	
3	State of fulfillment	
4	Standard of living	
5	State of relationships	
6	State of mental outlook	
7	Capacity to give.	
8	State of job security	
9	State of job satisfaction	

List of Statements about the Level of Satisfaction

22.Give your opinion regarding the following factors relation to the level of satisfaction, with job related aspects

Highly satisfied-5, Satisfied-4, Neutral –3, Dissatisfied-2, Highly dissatisfied-1

Sl.No	Level of Satisfaction	5	4	3	2	1
1	Wage					
2	Health care benefits					
3	Access to recreational facilities					
4	Work load					
5	Opportunities to develop new skills and work independently					
6	Working environment					
7	Fair and equitable performance appraisal					
8	Flexibility of working hour					
9	Job security and job satisfaction					
10	Relationship with co-workers and supervisor					
11	Recognition of achievement					

Suggestion

23. Offer your suggestion to improve the Quality of Work Life in the Company.

Thanking you.

www.ingramcontent.com/pod-product-compliance
Lightning Source LLC
LaVergne TN
LVHW050602200726
843508LV00010B/1732